Carpenter

Complete Guide

to the

SAS® Macro

Language

Art Carpenter

SAS Publishing

The correct bibliographic citation for this manual is as follows: Carpenter, Art. 1998. *Carpenter's Complete Guide to the SAS® Macro Language*. Cary, NC: SAS Institute Inc.

Carpenter's Complete Guide to the SAS® Macro Language

Carpenter's Complete Guide to the
SAS® System Macro Language

Table of Contents

Acknowledgments

Helen Carey, co-author of *SAS® Today! A Year of Terrific Tips,* made the initial suggestions to take on this project, and she also provided numerous examples and leads to many others.

Mr. Kirk P. Lafler of Software Intelligence Corporation provided his permission to revise the 1991 course book *SAS® System Macro Language,* which had been written by Art Carpenter and produced jointly between California Occidental Consultants and Software Intelligence Corporation.

This book incorporates the efforts of many reviewers of the various draft manuscripts. These include

> Don Stanley, author of *Beyond the Obvious with SAS® Screen Control Language,* reviewed Chapter 8 and offered a number of comments.

> A number of (mostly anonymous) macro language developers and technical consultants at SAS Institute Inc. took time from their busy schedules to provide many carefully thought-out and helpful comments.

> Richard O. Smith of Science Explorations assisted with technical review of both text and code.

Several of the examples in Part III were contributed by other SAS programmers. A special thank you goes to

Justina Flavin STATPROBE, Inc.	Paul Kairis NIKH Corporation
Diane Goldschmidt	Kim Kubasec Consultant
Susan Haviar	Jørn Lodahl
Clarence Jackson CJAC	David Shannon
Jerry Kagan Kagan Associates, Inc.	Richard O. Smith Science Explorations

Preface

This book is designed to both introduce the SAS System Macro Facility and to provide a reference tool for experienced macro programmers. Because of the complexity of the macro language, this book is intended for SAS programmers with a good general grounding in base SAS software. Regardless of how you are planning to use this book, in order to get the maximum benefit, you should be well versed in the use of the DATA step and fairly comfortable in the use of basic procedures.

The macro language has a number of similarities to the language that is used in SAS DATA steps. In order to maximize the usefulness of the examples in the book, you need to be able to build on these similarities. Students unfamiliar with the DATA step should first take a basic programming course in SAS such as *SAS® Fundamentals: A Programming Approach* (offered by SAS Institute Inc.) or an equivalent course.

It is the intent of this book to provide the reader with both a guide and a reference to the SAS macro language. Through its use, the reader will be able to write SAS macros, convert SAS code to macros, and use macros to generalize SAS programs to maximize their usefulness. The book assists the reader so that he or she will

- understand the general make up and operation of the macro facility and the macro language

- know the syntax that is used in the macro language

- be able to define macro variables and pass macro parameters

- understand and be able to utilize the different macro referencing environments or scopes

- know about the phases of execution when macro statements are present

- be able to develop and call SAS macros

- know how to reference SAS macro functions and automatic macro variables

- be able to use macro statements within SAS macros.

About the Author

Art Carpenter's publications list includes the book *Quick Results with SAS/GRAPH® Software*, two chapters in *Reporting from the Field*, and over two dozen papers and posters presented at SUGI, WUSS, and PharmaSUG. Art has served as a steering committee chairperson of both the Southern California SAS User's Group, SoCalSUG, and the San Diego SAS Users Group, SANDS; a conference cochair of the Western Users of SAS Software regional conference, WUSS; and Section Chair at the SAS User's Group International conference, SUGI.

Art has been actively using SAS software since 1976 and each year teaches numerous SAS and statistics courses to companies and institutions nationwide. This book is adapted from his course on the SAS Macro Language.

You may contact the author at

Art Carpenter
California Occidental Consultants
P.O. Box 6199
Oceanside, CA 92058-6199

(760) 945-0613

art@caloxy.com
www.caloxy.com

About This Book

General Organization

This book has been divided into three distinct parts. In addition to changes in subject matter and orientation as to the presentation of the material, these parts nominally represent an increasing level of complexity.

Although primarily designed as a reference to the macro language, this book was also written to provide first-time users to the macro language a step-by-step learning tool. The structure is such that the first two parts of the book can be used as a guide for self-instruction or as the text for a three-day, instructor-led introductory course on SAS macros.

Part I - Macro Basics

These four chapters serve as an introduction to the SAS Macro Facility. The chapters are arranged in a step-by-step fashion and are primarily geared to those with little or no macro experience. These chapters should be read sequentially and are not intended to serve as primary reference material.

Part II - Using Macros

Although the chapters in this part of the book continue to build on each other, it is not as critical (as it is in Part I) to read them in the order that they are presented. The presentation style is topical in nature and can more easily be used as a reference guide for individual topics. The examples in this part of the book highlight specific statements or techniques and tend to build on statements that are covered earlier in the book.

Part III - Advanced Macro Topics, Utilities, and Examples

These examples are presented as complete macros that accomplish specific tasks rather than as examples of the use of certain macro statements. As a general rule, all of the specific statements that are used in these macros have been discussed in the first two parts of the book. The discussion associated with the macro will highlight techniques and relationships among statements.

Headings and Organization

The chapters of the book are numbered sequentually and span the three parts described in the section titled **General Organization**. The chapters are divided into sections and subsections that are all numbered for ease of reference. For example, the second section in Chapter 1 is numbered as 1.2, and the third subsection in Section 1.2 will be numbered 1.2.3. These numbers are used in the **Table of Contents** and in various references within the book whenever the reader's attention is to be directed to another section, for example (see Section 3.3.1).

References

Throughout the book, other sources of information on various macro language topics are pointed out to the reader. The complete references and bibliographic information can be found in the **References** section at the back of the book. In the text, the reference will include at the least the author's last name and year of publication and occasionally the page. An example of a reference might be (Fehd, 1997a), which points to the following reference:

Fehd, Ronald, 1997a, "%ARRAY: construction and usage of arrays of macro variables," *Proceedings of the Twenty-Second Annual SAS Users Group International Conference,* Cary, NC: SAS Institute Inc., pp. 447–450.

Very often, these references are provided under the heading **SEE ALSO** at the end of the section.

Fonts and Text Styles

The main body of text is printed in 10.5-point Century Old Style font. SAS code uses a monospaced font with serifs (`proc contents data=temp;`). Words that have specific meaning in the SAS language and a different usage in English are capitalized when the usage is meant to convey the SAS meaning (for example, DATA, SET, LENGTH). Italics are used most commonly in code to indicate some portion of code that is not literal, but where some option will be supplied by the user (`proc contents data=data-set-name;`).

Exercise Solutions

Several of the chapters contain a section of chapter exercises that you can use to test your understanding of the material. The solutions to these exercise problems are in the section titled (oddly enough) **Exercise Solutions**.

Example and Utilities Appendices

Although the index provides the location of key words and phrases, very often the entries cannot be used to find examples of types of utilities. The **Example Locator** and **Utilities Locator** appendices are designed to aid you in finding these example macros.

The **Example Locator** appendix lists the sections that contain examples that utilize certain macro language statements and functions. The section that contains the primary discussion of the statement is listed separately from the other examples that use, but may not emphasize, that particular statement in the discussion of the example.

The **Utilities Locator** appendix lists those examples that you might find to be directly useful. The appendix, which is ordered by the kinds of tasks that the utility performs, notes the sections that contain the example macros.

Course Notes (Parts I & II)

Although written to be a reference guide to the macro language, the first two parts of this book can also be used as the text for either a self-taught or an instructor-led course on the macro language. For an instructor-led course, the recommended length of the course is three days or about 21 hours of instruction and exercises. In order to facilitate the use of this book as an instructional aid, it is arranged so that it can be used sequentially.

There are a number of topics associated with the macro language that are usually not considered appropriate for an introductory course. However, for completeness, these topics have been added to the first two parts of this book. Depending on the expertise of the students and the time available, some of these topics can be presented briefly or skipped altogether. These topics include the following:

Section 2.6	Automatic Macro Variables
Section 2.7	Using Macro Variables in a PROC SQL Step
Section 3.3.3	Autocall Facility Options
Section 3.3.4	Compiled Stored Macros
Section 3.4	Display Manager Command-Line Macros
Section 3.5	Statement- and Command-Style Macros
Section 5.4.3	%GOTO and %label
Section 5.4.4	Using %SYSEXEC
Section 6.5.2	Using the SYMGET function
Section 6.5.3	Using the RESOLVE function
Section 7.1	Quoting Functions
Section 7.4	Using DATA Step Functions and Routines
Chapter 8	Using Macro References with Screen Control Language (SCL)

A brief introduction to quoting functions (Section 7.1) is often valuable, even when the bulk of the section is skipped. If desired, Sections 7.1.1 and 7.1.2 should provide you sufficient information for a brief overview of this topic.

Chapter 8 assumes a working knowledge of SCL and would not be appropriate for students without this background.

Part 1 **Macro Basics**

Chapter 1 # Introduction

This chapter introduces you to the fundamentals of the SAS macro language, and it includes an overview and some of the terminology of the language. Because the behavior of macros is different from that of code that is written for base SAS, sections are also included on macro execution and how the SAS System sees and uses macros.

1.1 Macro Facility Overview

The *SAS Macro Facility* is a tool within base SAS software that contains the essential elements that enable you to use macros. The macro facility contains a *macro processor* that translates macro code into statements that can be used by the SAS System, and the macro language. The *macro language* provides the means to communicate with the macro processor.

The macro language consists of its own set of commands, options, syntax, and compiler. While macro statements have similarities to the statements in the DATA step, you must understand the differences in behavior in order to effectively write and use macros.

The macro language provides tools that

- pass information between SAS steps

- dynamically create code at execution time

- conditionally execute DATA or PROC steps

- create generalizable and flexible code.

The tools made available through the macro facility include macro (or symbolic) variables, macro statements, and macro functions. These tools are included as part of the SAS code, or program, where they are detected when the code is sent to the SAS Supervisor for execution.

1.2 Terminology

The statement and syntax structure that is used by the macro facility is known as the *macro language* and like any language it has its own terminology. The SAS user familiar with the programming language used in base SAS, however, will discover quickly that much of the syntax and content of the macro language is familiar.

The following terms will be used throughout this book.

text
a collection of characters and symbols that can contain variable names, data set names, SAS statement fragments, complete SAS statements, or even complete DATA and PROC steps.

macro variable
the names of macro variables are almost always preceded by an ampersand (&) in SAS code. Macro variables often are used to store text.

macro
stored text that contains SAS statements and macro language statements.

macro program statement
controls what actions take place during the macro execution. They are always preceded by a percent sign (%) and are often syntactically similar to statements used in the DATA step.

macro expression
one or more macro variable names, text, and/or macro functions combined together by one or more operators and/or parentheses. Macro expressions are very analogous to the expressions used in standard SAS programming.

macro function
predefined routines for processing text in macros and macro variables. Many macro functions are similar to functions used in the DATA step.

operators
symbols that are used for comparisons, logical operation, or arithmetic calculations. The operators are the same ones used in the DATA step.

automatic macro variable
special-purpose macro variables. These are automatically defined and provided by the SAS System. These variable names should be considered as reserved.

open code
SAS program statements that exist outside of any macro definition.

resolving macro references
during the resolution process, elements of the macro language (or references) are replaced with text.

You can find additional terminology in the glossary.

1.3 Macro Execution Phases

When you run a SAS program, it is executed in a series of DATA and PROC steps, one step at a time. GLOBAL statements (for example, TITLE, FOOTNOTE, %LET), which can exist outside of these steps, are executed immediately when they are encountered. For each step, the SAS System first checks to see if macro references exist. *Macro references* may be macro variables, macro statements, macro definitions, or macro calls. If the program does not contain any macro references, then processing continues with the DATA or PROC step processor. If the program does contain macro references, then the macro processor intercepts and resolves them prior to execution. The resolved macro references then become part of the SAS code that is passed to the DATA or PROC step processor.

When code is passed to the SAS supervisor, the following takes place for each step:

- Global statements are executed.

- Macro definitions are compiled and stored until they are called.

- A check is made to see if there are any macro statements, macro variables, or macro calls. If there are, then

  □ macro variables are resolved

  □ called macros are executed (resolved)

  □ macro statements are executed.

- The DATA or PROC step that contains resolved macro references (if there were any) is compiled and executed.

SEE ALSO
SAS® Macro Language Reference, First Edition contains a detailed discussion of how SAS processes statements with macro activity on pp.14–19 and 33–41.

1.4 Referencing Environments

Unlike the values of data set variables, the values of macro variables are stored in memory in a *symbol table*. Each macro variable's definition in the symbol table is also associated with a *referencing environment* or *scope*, which is determined by where and how the macro variable is defined. There are two environments for macro variables: global and local.

A *global* macro variable has a single value available to all macros within the program. Macro variables that are defined outside of any macro will be global.

Local macro variables have values that are available only within the macro in which they are defined.

Because each macro creates its own local referencing environment, macro variable values that are defined in one macro may be undefined within another. Indeed, macro variable names need not be unique even among nested macros. This means that the specific value associated with a given macro variable may depend on how the macro variable is used in the program.

In the following schematic, the macro variable DSN is defined globally and is, therefore, also known inside of the shaded macro. The macro variable COLOR, however, is only defined inside of the shaded macro and is not known outside of the macro.

```
Outside of all macros
Global values

DSN ---> clinics

Inside a macro
Local values

DSN ----> clinics
COLOR ---> blue

DSN ---> clinics
COLOR ---> undefined
```

You can control the referencing environment for a macro variable through the use of the %GLOBAL and %LOCAL statements, which are described in Section 5.4.2.

SEE ALSO

Extensive examples can be found in *SAS® Guide to Macro Processing, Version 6, Second Edition* (pp. 37–54) and the newer *SAS® Macro Language: Reference, First Edition* (pp. 50–66).

SUGI presentations that specifically cover referencing environments include Bercov (1993) and Hubbell (1990).

An example of a macro variable that takes on more than one value at the same time is given in Carpenter (1996, p. 1637).

1.5 Chapter Summary

You can think of the macro facility as a part of the SAS System that passively waits to be evoked. If your SAS code contains no macros and no references to macro variables or macro statements, the macro facility is not used. When the code does contain macro language references, the macro facility wakes up, intercepts the job stream, interprets or executes the macro references, and then releases its control.

The macro facility is made up of two primary components. The *macro processor* provides the ability to compile and execute the *macro language* statements that you use to write macros.

Chapter 2 # Defining and Using Macro Variables

For most SAS programmers, their first encounter with the macro language is through the use of macro variables. Indeed, macro variables are very powerful all by themselves. Even if you know nothing else about macros other than the information contained in this chapter, you will be able to accomplish a great deal.

This chapter introduces macro variables by showing you how they are named, defined, and used in SAS programs. These symbolic variables can be used as a part of any SAS program. Macros and other macro statements need not be present for you to take advantage of their power. An introductory tutorial to various aspects of the macro language can be found in Leighton (1997).

2.1 Naming Macro Variables

Macro variables, which are also known as symbolic variables, are not data set variables. Instead, macro variables belong to the SAS macro language, and once they are defined, they can take on many different values during the execution of a SAS program.

You can use the same basic rules to name macro variables as are used to name data set variables:

- A name can be between one and eight characters in length.

- A name must begin with a letter or underscore (_).

- Any combination of letters, numbers, and underscores can follow the first character.

The following are basic rules that apply to the use of macro variables:

- Text that is stored in macro variables can range in length from 0 to 32K bytes.

- You can reference, or call, macro variables inside or outside of a macro by immediately prefixing an ampersand (&) before its name.

- The macro processor replaces, or substitutes, the name of the symbolic variable with its value.

Another important difference between DATA step variables and macro variables is that there **are** reserved names for macro variables, macro names, and macro labels. No macro name can begin with 'sys' or the name of a SAS supplied macro statement or macro function.

SEE ALSO

Appendix 2, "Reserved Words in the Macro Facility," (p. 285) in *SAS® Guide to Macro Processing, Second Edition* and Appendix 1, "Reserved Words in the Macro Facility," in *SAS® Macro Language: Reference, First Edition* (p. 273) both provide a full list of reserved names.

2.2 Defining Macro Variables

One of the easiest ways to define a macro variable is through the %LET statement. (Macro language statements always start with a %). This statement works much like an assignment statement in the DATA step.

The %LET statement is followed by the macro variable name, an equal sign (=), and then the text value to be assigned to the macro variable. Notice that quotation marks are not used. Unlike data set variables, macro variables are neither character nor numeric (although it is usually easier to think of them as character). Because SAS knows that whatever is to the right of the equal sign is to be assigned to the macro variable, quotes are not needed. Indeed, when they are used they become part of the value that is stored.

The **syntax** of the %LET statement is

```
%LET macro-variable-name = value;
```

The following statement assigns the text string `clinics` to the macro variable DSN:

```
%LET dsn = clinics;
```

If the %LET statement is outside of any macro, its value will be available throughout the entire program, and it is said to be a global macro variable. On the other hand, if the macro variable is defined inside of a macro it may be local, and its value will only be available within that macro. Sections 1.3 and 5.4.2 discuss these issues in more detail.

2.3 Using Macro Variables

You could use the following SAS program to determine the contents and general form of the data set WORK.CLINICS. It uses PROC CONTENTS and PROC PRINT (limiting the print to the first ten observations).

```
PROC CONTENTS DATA=CLINICS;
     TITLE 'DATA SET CLINICS';
RUN;

PROC PRINT DATA=CLINICS (OBS=10);
RUN;
```

Macro variables are especially useful when you generalize programs. The previous program works for only one data set. If you want to apply it to a different data set, you will need to edit it in three different places. This is trivial in this situation but edits of existing production programs can be a serious problem in actual applications.

The program can be rewritten and generalized. ❶ The %LET statement defines the macro variable. ❷ A macro variable call (&dsn) replaces the data set name. The program becomes

```
%LET DSN = CLINICS;❶

PROC CONTENTS DATA=&dsn;❷
     TITLE "DATA SET &dsn";❷
RUN;

PROC PRINT DATA=&dsn ❷(OBS=10);
RUN;
```

To change the data set name, you still need to edit the %LET statement. At least it is now a simpler task. Examples later in the book (see Chapter 4, "Macro Parameters") show easier and even more general ways of accomplishing this same sort of thing.

Notice that in the rewritten code, quotes in the TITLE statement were changed from single to double quotes. Macro variables that appear inside of a quoted string will not be resolved unless you use double quotes (").

You can change the value of a macro variable simply by issuing a new %LET statement. The most recent definition will be used at any given time.

The code in the previous example might be useful during the debugging phase of program development. It would be best if you set up the code so that it can be turned on or off at the flip of a debugging switch. The following code will execute exactly as it did in the previous example. The macro variable &DEBUG ❶ has been assigned a null value (null values are less than blank values; they truly are nothing).

```
%LET DSN = CLINICS;
%LET DEBUG =;❶
&DEBUG PROC CONTENTS DATA=&dsn;
&DEBUG     TITLE "DATA SET &dsn";
&DEBUG RUN;

&DEBUG PROC PRINT DATA=&dsn (OBS=10);
&DEBUG RUN;
```

In each of these statements &DEBUG is resolved to a null value and the statements are executed just as they were in the previous example. It is as if &DEBUG were not even there. However, when you redefine &DEBUG as it is in the following code ❷, each of the statements becomes an asterisk-style comment:

```
%LET DSN = CLINICS;
%LET DEBUG = *;❷
&DEBUG PROC CONTENTS DATA=&dsn;
&DEBUG     TITLE "DATA SET &dsn";
&DEBUG RUN;

&DEBUG PROC PRINT DATA=&dsn (OBS=10);
&DEBUG RUN;
```

The resolved code becomes

```
*  PROC CONTENTS DATA=clinics;
*     TITLE "DATA SET clinics";
*  RUN;

*  PROC PRINT DATA=clinics (OBS=10);
*  RUN;
```

For other ways to use macros to comment-out blocks of code, see Section 3.1.2.

2.4 Displaying Macro Variables

The %PUT statement, which is analogous to the DATA step PUT statement, writes text and the current values of macro variables to the SAS System LOG. As a macro statement the %PUT statement (unlike the PUT statement) does not need to be inside of a DATA step. The following two SAS statements comprise a complete (albeit silly) program:

```
%LET dsn = clinics;

%PUT ***** selected data set is &dsn;
```

Notice that unlike the PUT statement the text string is not enclosed in quotes. The quotes are not needed because the macro facility does not need to distinguish between variables and strings. (Everything is a text string except macro variables, which are preceded by an ampersand).

Because macro statements are executed before the DATA step statements are even compiled, you may need to get used to their execution order. The following DATA step contains both a %PUT and a PUT statement, and both are inside of a DO loop. The associated LOG illustrates the differences between these two statements. The distinction is an important one.

```
data _null_;
    do j = 1 to 5;
        put j ' Placed by PUT';
        %put j ' Placed by macro PUT';
    end;
run;
```

The LOG reads as shown:

```
1        data _null_;
2          do j = 1 to 5;
3              put j ' Placed by PUT';
4              %put j ' Placed by macro PUT';
j ' Placed by macro PUT' ❶
5          end;
6        run;

1 Placed by PUT
2 Placed by PUT
3 Placed by PUT
4 Placed by PUT
5 Placed by PUT
NOTE: The DATA statement used 1.26 seconds.
```

❶ Notice that %PUT is executed (writes to the LOG) as soon as it is encountered, and because there are quotes in the statement they are also displayed. Also, %PUT does not recognize the j as a variable name so it just includes it as part of the string to be displayed.

The following additional options are available for the %PUT statement starting with Release 6.11:

all
> lists all macro variables in all referencing environments.

automatic
> lists all of the macro variables that are automatically defined at your site. The variables may vary from site to site. Automatic macro variables are described further in Section 2.6, "Automatic Macro Variables."

global
> user-created macro variables that will be available in all of the referencing environments.

local
> list of user-defined macro variables that are available only in the current or local referencing environment.

user
> creates a list of all of the user-created macro variables in each of the referencing environments. This option can be especially useful during the debugging process for complicated macros.

The next two statements create the LOG that follows:

```
%LET dsn = clinics;
%PUT _all_;
```

```
1      %let dsn = clinics;
2      %put _all_;
GLOBAL DSN clinics
AUTOMATIC AFDSID 0
AUTOMATIC AFDSNAME
AUTOMATIC AFLIB
AUTOMATIC AFSTR1
AUTOMATIC AFSTR2
AUTOMATIC FSPBDV
AUTOMATIC SYSBUFFR
AUTOMATIC SYSCMD
AUTOMATIC SYSDATE 16JAN97
AUTOMATIC SYSDAY Thursday
AUTOMATIC SYSDEVIC
AUTOMATIC SYSDSN            _NULL_
AUTOMATIC SYSENV FORE
AUTOMATIC SYSERR 0
AUTOMATIC SYSFILRC 0
AUTOMATIC SYSINDEX 0
AUTOMATIC SYSINFO 0
AUTOMATIC SYSJOBID 0000008671
AUTOMATIC SYSLAST _NULL_
AUTOMATIC SYSLCKRC 0
AUTOMATIC SYSLIBRC 0
AUTOMATIC SYSMENV S
AUTOMATIC SYSMSG
AUTOMATIC SYSPARM
AUTOMATIC SYSPBUFF
AUTOMATIC SYSRC 0
AUTOMATIC SYSSCP WIN
AUTOMATIC SYSSCPL WIN_32S
AUTOMATIC SYSSITE 0028569001
AUTOMATIC SYSTIME 19:07
AUTOMATIC SYSVER 6.11
AUTOMATIC SYSVLONG 6.11.0020P092795
```

SEE ALSO
The additional options for %PUT are described fully in Chapter 4, "SAS Macro Language," (pp. 95–98) in *SAS® Software Changes and Enhancements, Release 6.11*, and in *SAS® Macro Language Reference, First Edition*, p. 204.

2.5 Resolving Macro Variables

Prior to the execution of the SAS code, macro variables are resolved. The resolved values are then substituted back into the code. It is, therefore, important to understand the rules associated with how macro variables are resolved.

The use of single macro variables, as shown in the following example, is fairly straightforward:

```
%LET SEX=MALE;
DATA &SEX;
SET CLINICS;
WHERE SEX="&SEX";
RUN;
```

This code will resolve to

```
DATA MALE;
SET CLINICS;
WHERE SEX="MALE";
RUN;
```

It is when you start combining macro variables with text and other macro variables that the fun begins. Macro variables can be concatenated to text or even to other macro variables.

2.5.1 Using the macro variable as a suffix

You can append a macro variable to SAS code that includes variables, text strings, and data set names. When resolved, the value of the macro variable is concatenated to the string that precedes it.

The following code contains the macro variable &SEX. In the second line, `&SEX` is appended to `ONLY` when resolved; `ONLY&SEX` becomes `ONLYMALE`.

```
%LET SEX=MALE;
DATA ONLY&SEX;
      SET CLASS.&SEX;
      WHERE SEX="&SEX";
RUN;
```

This code resolves to

```
DATA ONLYMALE;
      SET CLASS.MALE;
      WHERE SEX="MALE";
RUN;
```

Notice that no special character is required to cause the concatenation. None is required because when the macro variable is used as a suffix the macro facility can easily determine by the & where the macro variable name starts. This is not always true when using the macro variable as a prefix.

2.5.2 Using the macro variable as a prefix

A macro variable may also precede portions of SAS code. When necessary to avoid confusion, a macro variable can be followed by a period to designate the end of the variable name. In this example the period in the SET statement is necessary to avoid ambiguity:

```
%LET DSN=CLINICS;
%LET DSN1=OLDDATA;
DATA &DSN;
      SET &DSN.1  &DSN1;
RUN;
```

This resolves to:

```
DATA CLINICS;
      SET CLINICS1  OLDDATA;
RUN;
```

It is important to note the difference between the &DSN.1 and &DSN1 macro variables. Any macro variable can be followed by a period and when present it can act as a delimiter. The period in &DSN.1 causes &DSN to be resolved to CLINICS with a 1 appended to the end. The period is seen as a delimiter that separates the variable name from the text that is to be appended to the resolved value of the macro variable. Without the period the 1 is seen as part of the macro variable name and &DSN1 is resolved to OLDDATA.

Sometimes the first character of the string that is to be appended to the macro variable is a period. As is shown in the previous code,the period will be used to concatenate the string and will not appear in the resolved text. To get around this you can use a double period (..) when a single period (.) is desired in the text, as shown:

```
%LET LIBREF=CLASS;
DATA &LIBREF..CLINICS;
      ... code not shown ...
RUN;
```

This code resolves to

```
DATA CLASS.CLINICS;
      ... code not shown ...
RUN;
```

The first period is seen as part of the macro variable name (&LIBREF.), and the second is just a character in the string (.CLINICS) that is appended to the macro variable result.

2.5.3   Appending two macro variables to each other

You can join more than one macro variable to form a single result. Consider, for example, the following three macro variable definitions:

```
%LET DSN=CLINICS;
%LET N=5;
%LET DSN5=FRED;
```

Using the rules that are discussed in the previous section, various combinations of these macro variables will resolve as follows:

Combination	Resolves to
&DSN&N	CLINICS5
&DSN.&N	CLINICS5
&DSN..&N	CLINICS.5

The macro processor scans for macro variables and resolves them as encountered. In each of the previous macro variable combinations the resolution is possible in a single pass. When two or more ampersands (&) appear next to each other, successive passes or scans are required to make the final resolution. You can think of the double ampersand (&&) as a special reference that resolves to a single ampersand. This is demonstrated in the following combinations:

Combination	First Scan Resolves to	Second Scan Resolves to
&&DSN&N	&DSN5	FRED
&&&DSN&N	&CLINICS5	&CLINICS5

The macro variable reference &CLINICS5 does not exist and the following message is written to the LOG:

```
WARNING: Apparent symbolic reference CLINICS5 not resolved.
```

A common mistake is to assume that the resolution process proceeds as

&&DSN&N ➡ &CLINICS5

This is incorrect because the && must be resolved to a single & before the &DSN is resolved.

For the same reasons, &&&DSN&N is taken as <u>&& &DSN &N</u>, which resolves to &CLINICS5. This macro variable does not exist on the symbol table and therefore remains unresolved. A warning is written to the LOG.

Using multiple ampersands establishes the ability to create a type of vector or array of macro variables. Examples of the use of this notation are shown in Section 5.3 and various other sections in this book.

2.6 Automatic Macro Variables

Several macro variables are automatically created for you by the macro processor. You can use these variables as you would any other macro variable. Some of the more commonly used automatic variables are shown in the next sections.

SEE ALSO

SAS® Guide to Macro Processing provides the complete list of automatic variables provided with Release 6.06. Depending on your operating environment, others may be available for later releases.

The more recent *SAS® Macro Language: Reference, First Edition* (pp. 22–23 and 156–157) has two tables listing the automatic variables.

2.6.1   **&sysdate, &sysday, &systime**

At the start of a SAS job (or SAS session from within the display manager), three automatic macro variables are loaded; they note the day, date, and time of the job start:

SYSDATE   date that the job began executing.

SYSDAY   day of the week that the job began executing.

SYSTIME   time of the day that the SAS job began executing.

The following program converts the date (DATADATE) and time (DATATIME) for the second observation (BATCH=2) in the data set OLD to new values based on the &SYSDATE and &SYSTIME macro variables.

```
data old;
do batch=1 to 3;
  conc=2;
  datadate='02jan97'd;
  datatime = '09:00't;
  output;
end;
format datadate mmddyy10. datatime time5.;
run;

data new;
set old;
if batch = 2 then do;
  conc=2.5;
  datadate="&sysdate"d;
  datatime="&systime"t;
end;
run;

proc print data=new;
title1 'Drug concentration';
title2 "Mod date &sysdate";
run;
```

Notice that the &SYSDATE and &SYSTIME values are converted from text values to SAS date and time values by treating them as date/time constants. The resulting output is shown:

```
                     Drug concentration
                     Mod date 05FEB97


    OBS      BATCH      CONC      DATADATE      DATATIME

     1         1        2.0      01/02/1997        9:00

     2         2        2.5      02/05/1997       15:30

     3         3        2.0      01/02/1997        9:00
```

2.6.2   &syslast

&syslast stores the name of the last data set that was modified. You can use this variable as you would use any data set name. This variable is useful when you are generating dynamic code, and you don't necessarily know the name of the data set that was just created.

SYSLAST   name of the last SAS data set created.

Assuming that the following PROC PRINT follows the code used in the previous example, it will produce the listing shown:

```
proc print data=&syslast;
title1 'Drug concentration';
title2 "Listing of &syslast";
run;
```

Notice that the name of the data set stored in &SYSLAST includes the associated *libref.*

```
                       Drug concentration
                       Listing of WORK.NEW


      OBS      BATCH      CONC      DATADATE      DATATIME

       1         1         2.0      01/02/1997       9:00

       2         2         2.5      02/05/1997      15:30

       3         3         2.0      01/02/1997       9:00
```

2.6.3   &syserr

It is sometimes handy to be able to determine if a particular PROC or DATA step executed successfully. Each step has a return code that measures the existence and severity of any errors. The return code is stored in &SYSERR, where it can be checked during the execution of the job.

SYSERR   stores the return codes of PROC and DATA steps.

The following program fragment copies the data sets in one library (COMBINE) to another (COMBTEMP). It uses &SYSERR to detect if another user currently has write access to a data set in the library COMBINE (&SYSERR will take on a value of 5 or greater).

```
* Copy the current version of the COMBINE files
* to COMBTEMP;
proc datasets memtype=data;
   copy in=combine out=combtemp;
quit;
%put SYSERR is   &syserr;
```

Section 10.1.4 shows a more sophisticated version of this example.

2.6.4   &sysparm

Usually used in the batch environment, this macro variable accesses the same value as is stored in the SYSPARM= system option and can also be retrieved using the SYSPARM( ) DATA step function. This option is most useful when its value is loaded when SAS is initially executed. You may use it to pass a value into a program through the JCL or batch calling routines.

SYSPARM   specifies up to a 200-character string that can be passed into SAS programs.

In the following example, your programs will automatically direct your data to either a test or production library. To do this assign &SYSPARM the value TST or PROD when you start the SAS session. A typical LIBNAME statement on VAX might be

```
libname projdat "usernode:[study03.gx&sysparm]";
```

Assume that SAS is initiated with

```
$ sas/sysparm=tst
```

The LIBNAME statement becomes

```
libname projdat "usernode:[study03.gxtst]";
```

The method you use to load a value into &SYSPARM depends on the operating environment that you are using. See the SAS Companion for your operating environment for more information. On Windows, -sysparm tst appears on the COMMAND LINE in the Properties Window. In JCL, the option is used on the SYSIN card.

2.6.5   &sysrc

The SYSRC macro variable captures the last return code from system operations that are executed following an X command, X statement, or the %SYSEXEC macro statement.

SYSRC   indicates the last return code from your operating environment.

The value will be an integer, but it will vary according to the operating environment. Successful operations will not always return a value of 0.

2.6.6   &syssite, &sysscp, and &sysscpl

These macro variables contain information about your site and operating system. Primarily you can use them when a particular SAS job or application may be executed in multiple environments and its behavior needs to be altered accordingly.

SYSSITE   new in Release 6.10, it contains the current site number.

SYSSCP   gives the name of the host operating environment.

SYSSCPL   new in Release 6.10, on some operating environments it will be more specific than &SYSSCP.

The following %PUT statement

```
%put &syssite &sysscp &sysscpl;
```

produces the following statement in the LOG when executed in the Windows 3.11 operating environment.

```
13   %put &syssite &sysscp &sysscpl;
0053893001 WIN WIN_32S
```

SEE ALSO
&SYSSITE and &SYSSCPL are documented in *SAS® Software: Changes and Enhancements, Release 6.10* (p. 36) and in *SAS® Macro Language: Reference, First Edition* (pp. 257–260).

Davis (1997) includes an example that uses &SYSSCP.

2.7 Using Macro Variables in a PROC SQL Step

You can use macros and macro variables within a PROC SQL step in much the same way as in other PROC steps. The exception is the syntax related to creating macro variables within SQL.

Unlike most other procedures, statements within an SQL step are processed sequentially and are applied immediately. Furthermore, SQL statements are handled differently and are expected to conform to specific syntax standards.

SEE ALSO
Tassoni (1997) uses a macro to write SQL statements and Palmer (1997) uses macro variables in a PROC SQL step.

2.7.1 Counting observations in a data set
The following example uses SQL to count the number of observations that contain a specified string in the table column CLINNAME. The string is placed in a macro variable (&CLN) and the SQL COUNT function is used to count the observations that match the WHERE clause.

```
%let cln = Beth;
proc sql noprint;
select count(*)
      into :nobs ❶
      from clinics(where=(clinname=:"&cln")); ❸
quit;

%put number of clinics for &cln is &nobs; ❷
```

❶ The INTO clause is used to create the new macro variable NOBS. The colon informs the SELECT statement that the result of the COUNT function is to be written into a macro variable.

❷ Once created, the new macro variable is used in the same way as any other macro variable. Both macro variables are preceded by an ampersand in the %PUT statement.

❸ Notice that the colon in the FROM clause is used as a character comparison operator as in the DATA step.

The example in Section 13.1.1 places this SQL step inside of a macro. A more complex example of a SQL step can be found in Section 13.1.2.

2.7.2   Building a list of values

It is often useful to be able to build a macro variable that contains a list of values. The examples in Section 13.1 create a list of variable names. You may also wish to build a list that can be used with the IN operator, perhaps in a WHERE statement.

In the following example we want to create a subset of the student body (SCHOOL) based on the names in a particular class (CLASS):

```
data class;
input name $ 8. grade $1.;
cards;
Billy    B
Jon      C
Sally    A
run;

data school;
input name $ 8. gradcode $1.;
cards;
Billy    Y
Frank    Y
Jon      N
Laura    Y
Sally    Y
run;

proc sql noprint;
select quote(name)
    into :clnames separated by ' ' ❶
  from class;
quit;

data clasgrad;
set school (where=(name in(&clnames)));  ❷
run;

proc print data=clasgrad;
title 'Class Graduate Status';
run;
```

❶ The macro variable &CLNAMES contains the quoted list of names found in the CLASS data set.

❷ The list of variable names stored in &CLNAMES is used with the IN operator.

The PROC PRINT creates the following output:

```
                      Class Graduate Status

               OBS      NAME      GRADCODE

                1       Billy        Y
                2       Jon          N
                3       Sally        Y
```

SEE ALSO
A similar example can be found in *SAS Communications*, 1Qtr., 1997, page 48. Widawski (1997a) creates a list of file names and places the list in a macro variable.

2.8 Chapter Summary

Macro or symbolic variables are very different from SAS data set variables that reside as part of the Program Data Vector associated with a given DATA or PROC step. Macro variables are stored in a symbol table, are independent of all data sets, and do not depend on either the data set or the observation being processed.

You can use the %LET statement to define a macro variable.

Macro variables that appear inside of a quoted string will not be resolved unless you use double quotes (").

Within a referencing environment, you can change the value of a macro variable at any time by issuing a new %LET statement. The most recent definition will be used at any given time.

You can use the %PUT statement to write text and macro variable values to the SAS System LOG.

The SAS System defines several macro variables automatically for the user. You can access these macro variables and use them in the same way that you can use any other macro variable.

2.9 Chapter Exercises

```
****************************************************;
* The data set, CLASS.CLINICS, contains 80      *;
* observations and 20 variables.  The following *;
* program will be used to complete the exercises*;
* in this chapter.                              *;
****************************************************;

PROC PLOT DATA=CLASS.CLINICS;
      PLOT EDU * DOB;
      TITLE1 'YEARS OF EDUCATION COMPARED TO BIRTH DATE';
RUN;

PROC CHART DATA=CLASS.CLINICS;
      VBAR WT / SUMVAR=HT TYPE=MEAN;
      TITLE1 'AVERAGE HEIGHT FOR WEIGHT GROUPS';
RUN;
```

1. Rewrite the sample program that is presented above by adding at least one macro variable (%LET).

2. (True/False) Macro variables will not be resolved unless you use single quotes (').

3. Given the following macro variable definitions, how will the macro variable combinations be resolved? Take a guess first, and then use %PUT to check your answer.

   %let dsn=clinic;   %let I = 3;   %let b = dsn;
   %let lib = sasuser;   %let dsn3 = studydrg;

   &lib&dsn —> _____   &dsn&I   —> _____

   &lib.&dsn —> _____   &&dsn&I —> _____

   &lib..&dsn —> _____   &dsn.&I —> _____

   &&bb   —> _____   &&&b   —> _____

   Extra Credit: Using the above macro variable definitions, what combination of &dsn and &I resolves to CLINIC.STUDYDRG? Use a %PUT statement to show your answers in the LOG.

4. What are automatic macro variables?

5. What is the purpose of &SYSPARM?

Chapter 3   # Defining and Using Macros

This chapter introduces several of the simplest methods that you can use to create and use macros. Three types of macros are discussed as are several system options that can be used with macros. Several advantages and disadvantages of these types of macros are included.

3.1 Defining a Macro

All macros are created using the two macro language statements; %MACRO and %MEND. Like the DO and END statements in the DATA step, these two macro statements always come in pairs.

Syntax

%**MACRO** *macro-name*;
       . . . *macro text* . . .
%**MEND** *<macro-name>*;

Every macro definition begins with a macro statement (%MACRO), which must contain a name for the macro. The %MEND statement closes the macro definition. This statement can optionally also include the name of the macro (optional but a very good idea) for documentation reasons.

The macro text can include the following:

- constant text
- macro variables
- macro program statements
- macro expressions
- macro functions.

Constant text

The macro language treats constant text in much the same way as character strings are treated in the DATA step. Constant text is not evaluated, resolved, or even examined by the macro processor. It is just passed along. Constant text can include

- SAS data set names

- SAS variable names

- SAS statements.

Macro variables

Macro variables are preceded in the macro text by an ampersand. Chapter 2, "Defining and Using Macro Variables," includes a more complete discussion of the definition and use of macro variables.

Macro program statements

These statements are evaluated and executed when the macro is called. Most macro program statements must be contained inside of a macro and cannot exist in open code. Macro program statements, like DATA step statements start with a keyword. Unlike other SAS statements, however, macro program statements are preceded with a percent sign (%). Sample macro program statements include

```
%let dsn = clinics;

%do i = 1 %to &yr;
```

Chapter 5, "Program Control through Macros," introduces a number of these statements.

Macro expressions

Macro expressions perform the same tasks in the macro language as DATA step expressions do in base SAS. They can be used to determine conditional branches in logic and to create new value assignments. Macro expressions involve the evaluation and assignment of macro variables rather than DATA step variables. The use of macro expressions in conditional processing is described in Section 5.2. Two example %IF statements are shown here:

```
%if &nobs = 0 %then %do;

%if &cond = bad %then %goto badobs;
```

Macro functions

Macro functions operate on macro variables and constant text. Some of the more useful character functions available in the DATA step have analogous macro functions. There are also a number of macro functions that are unique to the macro language. Macro functions are described in Chapter 7, "Using Macro Functions." The %UPCASE function shown here is an example of a macro function:

```
%let upper = %upcase(&name);
```

Most DATA step functions can double as macro functions through the use of the %SYSFUNC macro function that is described in Section 7.4.2.

3.1.1 Creating a macro

The easiest way to create a macro is to surround existing code with the %MACRO and %MEND statements. Remember *every* macro definition must begin and end with these two statements; they come in pairs.

The following code creates a macro that looks at a data set. An existing program that contains a PROC CONTENTS and a PROC PRINT has been enclosed by the %MACRO and %MEND statements.

```
%LET DSN = CLINICS;

%MACRO LOOK;


PROC CONTENTS DATA=&dsn;
TITLE "DATA SET &dsn";
RUN;

PROC PRINT DATA=&dsn (OBS=10);
RUN;

%MEND LOOK;
```

Code that is enclosed in these two statements will not be executed until the macro is called (see Section 3.2). Although the macro is compiled when it is defined, syntax errors and any other problems with the non-macro code inside of the macro will not be detected until the macro is actually executed.

3.1.2 Using a macro to comment a block of code

When evaluating SAS programs you may occasionally find blocks of code that have been effectively commented out by enclosing them with %MACRO and %MEND statements. In effect, a macro is defined, but it is never called. While this certainly works and can be used as a temporary measure, the technique is not generally recommended. This section will help you recognize the problem and understand the issues associated with it.

Although the contents of a macro are compiled when the definition of the macro is encountered, the macro is not executed until the macro is actually called. This means that you can comment out blocks of code by creating macros that you purposely do not call. This style of comment can even contain embedded comments that are defined by /* .... */.

The macro %COMMENT in the following code causes the second DATA step to be ignored:

```
DATA invert.SPECIE;
    INFILE 'SPECIES.mas';
    LENGTH  SPCODE $ 5 SPNAME $ 40;
    INPUT   SPCODE 21-25 SPNAME;
run;

%macro comment;
* Create the POSITION data set;
DATA DBMASTER.POSITION;
    INFILE POS;
    LENGTH POS $ 2;
    INPUT POS 1-2 /*COORD 4-8*/;
```

```
      FILE ERRS;
      IF _ERROR_ THEN PUT '-1';
   run;
   %mend comment;
```

Following is a more common application of this type of macro. Here, the macro is used to comment out debugging steps:

```
   data new;
   set big;
   run;

   %macro debugnew;
   proc print data=new (obs=5);
   title 'listing for NEW';
   run;
   %mend debugnew;
```

During the debugging process, %DEBUGNEW can be executed to view the contents of the data set NEW.

This technique is not without its downside. The macros %COMMENT and %DEBUGNEW will be read, compiled, and stored in the SASMACR catalog for every run of the job that contains them. If %COMMENT appears in multiple places within the program, it will be recompiled each time it is encountered and additional computer resources will be expended. This can be very inefficient. As a general rule this is not a good use of macros.

SEE ALSO
Using macros to comment out sections of code has also been discussed by Grant (1994) and Stuelpner (1997).

3.2 Invoking a Macro

Macros are invoked, or called, by placing a (%) in front of the macro name. Unlike SAS statements, the macro call does not need to be followed by a semicolon. The macro LOOK in Section 3.1.1 is called by

```
   %LOOK
```

When the SAS Supervisor encounters a macro call, in this case %LOOK, the contents of the macro are substituted for the macro name in the program. Because this happens before other program statements in this step are evaluated, you can use the macro to contain statement fragments or complete steps.

In the following example, the macro %DEBUGNEW defines a PROC PRINT that you would want executed when you debug a program. (Section 3.1.2 contains additional discussion of %DEBUGNEW). As long as the macro call remains commented out, ❶ the macro is not executed. Notice that an asterisk-style comment ❷ is used to provide the semicolon for the commented macro.

```
data new;
set big;
run;

%macro debugnew;
proc print data=new (obs=5);
title 'listing for NEW';
run;
%mend debugnew;
```

❶ *%debugnew   ❷* uncomment to use debugnew;

You can also use a macro variable to control all debugging macros. In the following example, the macro variable DEBUG takes on the value of * when the debugging macros are to be turned off. The previous macro call becomes

```
%let debug = *;

... code not shown ...

&debug %debugnew     * uncomment to use debugnew;
```

To execute the macro %DEBUGNEW, the macro variable &DEBUG is cleared or assigned a null text string:

```
%LET DEBUG =;
```

3.3 System Options Used with the Macro Facility

A number of SAS system options apply directly to the use of macros. They determine whether or not the macro facility is available, how it is implemented, what debugging messages are to be printed, and if the macro autocall facility will be available.

3.3.1   General macro options

These system options control the overall use of the macro facility.

IMPLMAC

Statement style macros allow the use of macro names that do not start with the % sign. Although not without value, this style macro is a carry-over from earlier releases of SAS and is rarely used. System resource requirements are greatly increased through the use of these macros, and code can become more difficult to read and debug. By default, the option is usually turned off (NOIMPLMAC). Section 3.5 discusses this style of macro in more detail.

MACRO

The MACRO system option determines if the macro facility is to be available and you must specify at the invocation of SAS (or in a configuration file). When you specify NOMACRO, you remove the ability to use the macro facility capabilities.

MERROR and SERROR

When using and writing macros, the debugging process is often difficult, even when these two options are turned on. Consequently, they will generally be left on whenever working with macros. MERROR allows the macro facility to display a warning in the LOG when a macro call is not resolved, and SERROR displays a warning in the LOG when a macro variable reference is not resolved.

3.3.2 Debugging options

Debugging a macro can be, under the best of conditions, difficult. The LOG is often very cryptic when it presents error messages that deal with macros, macro code, or macro variables. You can use several options that are specifically designed to use for debugging during the writing and processing of macros.

You can include the following two statements near the start of your programs. You can then turn these options on or off at any point in the debugging process:

```
OPTIONS NOMPRINT NOMLOGIC NOSYMBOLGEN;
*OPTIONS MPRINT MLOGIC SYMBOLGEN;
```

When you program in the interactive mode or from the display manager, both statements are needed. This is because any option that you set (or turn on) remains in effect until you turn it off for the duration of that SAS session. Simply deleting the OPTIONS statement will not turn off the options. This is, of course, not an issue if you are debugging in batch mode.

MPRINT

SAS code that is generated by a macro is generally not displayed in the LOG. The MPRINT option displays the text or SAS statements that are generated by macro execution, one statement per line, with macro variable references resolved.

MLOGIC (This option was called MTRACE in Release 6.03 and in earlier releases)

Macros often are designed with logical branches based on %IF-%THEN/%ELSE statements and %DO loop executions. MLOGIC traces the macro logic and follows the pattern of execution. The resolved result of an %IF statement is displayed in the LOG as true or false. Macro invocation, start and finish, and %DO loop evaluations are noted. This option is especially useful for nested macros.

SYMBOLGEN

When you use this option, a message is printed in the LOG whenever a macro variable is resolved. This option is very useful when you trace macro variable references with multiple ampersands, for example, &&DAT&I.

SEE ALSO

A more flexible version of the OPTIONS statements shown in this section can be found in Section 4.4.

A number of SUGI papers address various aspects of the debugging process. Although some are based on Version 5 options, these papers can provide good insight: Frankel (1991), Gilmore (1990), O'Connor (1991), Phillips (1993).

Chapter 10, "Macro Facility Error Messages and Debugging," (pp. 111–130) in *SAS® Macro Language: Reference, First Edition* discusses a variety of topics that relate to the debugging and troubleshooting of macros.

3.3.3 Autocall facility options

The autocall facility enables you to call macros that have been stored as SAS programs. Using this facility enables you to create libraries of macros that you define once. The macros are available to all of your programs or even to other programmers.

The autocall macro facility stores the source for SAS macros in external files that together form an autocall library. The library is an aggregate storage location such as a directory that contains files (or members). The macro definition and the file must have the same name. Generally, an autocall library contains individual files or members, each of which contains one macro definition.

When a macro is called the macro facility searches for the macro definition. It first checks the catalogs that contain compiled macros and then the autocall macros that have not yet been compiled. The search order for a called macro is

1. **work.sasmacr catalog**
   This catalog contains macros that are compiled during the current SAS session.

2. *libref*.**sasmacr catalog**
   This catalog contains stored compiled macros (see Section 3.3.4). The MSTORED and SASMSTORE= options must be in effect to use stored compiled macros.

3. **autocall library**
   When the MAUTOSOURCE option is in effect, each library of source programs listed in the SASAUTOS= option is searched.

Macros in the autocall libraries are never inspected by the SAS macro facility until the macro is called. The macro is then compiled (and its compiled version is loaded into WORK.SASMACR) and executed.

It is important to remember the order in which macros are stored, compiled, and re-executed. If you use the display manager during the debugging process, a change to a macro definition in the program stored in the autocall library (SASAUTOS=) will not change the compiled version in WORK.SASMACR. Re-execution of the macro will not implement changes unless the compiled version of the macro has been eliminated from the WORK.SASMACR catalog or you recompile the macro so that the WORK.SASMACR catalog is updated.

Options that are associated with the autocall facility include

MAUTOSOURCE
controls the availability of the autocall facility. When in effect, autocall libraries (specified with SASAUTOS=) are included in the search for the macro definition.

MRECALL
used to control whether or not the autocall libraries will be searched again when a macro is not found. Typically this option is turned off (the default) and is only really needed when using multiple shared autocall libraries and one or more may be occasionally unavailable.

SASAUTOS=
used to specify the libraries or locations for collections of macros that will be searched when a macro is called. The following OPTIONS statement defines a location for the AUTOCALL library in the Windows operating environment in Release 6.12 of SAS.

```
options SASAUTOS="d:\caltasks\macros";
```

You can specify more than one library in the SASAUTOS= option, and you can use filerefs instead of the actual specification of the library location. The following example specifies three macro libraries:

```
filename grp5mac 'c:\group5\macros';
filename prj5Amac 'c:\group5\prjA\macros';
options mautosource sasautos=(prj5amac, grp5mac, sasautos);
```

In addition to any autocall libraries that you might create, a number of macros have been included in the autocall library supplied with SAS software. Some of these macros have been described in Chapter 12, "SAS System Autocall Macros."

SEE ALSO

Further discussion of the autocall facility can be found in Tindall (1991), O'Connor (1992), and Carey (1996, p.142).

The management of large macro libraries can be problematic and Bryant (1997) includes a macro that will identify and list the macros in a system.

Chapter 9, "Storing and Reusing Macros," (pp. 105–110) in *SAS® Macro Language: Reference, First Edition* provides additional information on autocall macros.

3.3.4   Compiled stored macros

The compiled stored macro facility takes the concepts that were discussed in the previous section regarding the autocall macro facility one further step. Autocall libraries store text or source code that defines macros. This text can be called (by calling the macro) and at that point it is compiled and executed. Using the autocall library for macros that are called over and over in different sessions means that the macro is compiled each time it is called.

The compiled macro facility allows you to compile the macro one time and then store the compiled version. When called, it is already compiled so you save time and resources.

The MSTORED and SASMSTORE system options that are analogous to the ones used with the autocall facility must be turned on so that you can use compiled macros.

MSTORED
> turns on the ability to use the facility. Most sites have this turned off (NOMSTORED) by default.

SASMSTORE=
> specifies the libref (not a path like in SASAUTOS=) that contains a SAS catalog named SASMACR. This catalog is analogous to WORK.SASMACR, which temporarily stores macros compiled in the current session.

During normal macro operations, you may notice that SAS temporarily compiles macros (known as *session compiled macros*) and places them in WORK.SASMACR. This means that the libref that you use with SASMSTORE= cannot be WORK.

To compile and store a macro, use the STORE option on the %MACRO statement:

```
options mstored sasmstore=mydir;

%macro doit(dsn,var1) / store;
... macro code not shown ...
```

The macro %DOIT will be compiled and stored as the entry DOIT in the catalog MYDIR.SASMACR.

SEE ALSO

You can find an easy to read and thorough description of compiled stored macros in O'Connor (1992).

A brief introduction to compiled stored macros is in *SAS® Macro Language: Reference, First Edition* (pp. 108–109) and in Carey (1996, p. 223).

Davis (1997) includes a description and example of the use of compiled stored macros.

3.4 Display Manager Command-Line Macros

Usually macros are executed from within programs, but they can also be written to help us do our work in the display manager. Command-line macros can contain any statement that you enter on a command line, and they can then be called from the command line or assigned to a specific key.

The following string of commands can be assigned to a key in the KEYS window. When executed together, they will switch to the program editor, recall the last submitted code, and maximize the window:

```
pgm; recall; zoom on;
```

These same commands can be placed in a macro:

```
%macro pgm;
   pgm;
   recall;
   zoom on;
%mend pgm;
```

Notice that the semicolons are included to chain the commands together. Entering the macro call %PGM on the command line will execute the macro and the display manager will see a series of commands. The call to the macro can also be assigned to a hot key, as is shown in the following portion of the KEYS window:

```
F9          :ts
F11         command bar
F12         zoom
SHF F1      subtop
SHF F2      %pgm
SHF F3
SHF F6
```

Before the macro can be executed, you must have defined it. If you are going to add the macro call to the KEYS definitions, consider adding the macro definition to the autocall library (see Section 3.3.3 for more information on using the Autocall Facility).

The command-line macro can include other macro statements, macro parameters, and macro logic. If you find yourself doing a series of command-line commands over and over again try putting them in a macro.

SEE ALSO

Additional information on command-line macros can be found in Carey (1996, pp. 69, 296) and in *SAS® Screen Control Language: Reference, Version 6, Second Edition* (p. 160).

The *Observations* article by Johnson (1993, pp. 50–54) provides detailed information on command-line macros and the use of macros in PMENUs.

3.5 Statement- and Command-Style Macros

All of the macros used in this book (exclusive of this section) are what is known as named-style macros. When using named-style macros, the macro is always called by preceding its name by a percent sign (%) and parameters are passed within parentheses (see Chapter 4 for more on using macro parameters). Statement-style and command-style macros do not require the use of the preceding %.

Statement-style macros allow you to create macro calls that *look* like SAS statements. Command-style macros are used to mimic Display Manager command line commands.

As a general rule, few programmers use either of these macro styles. There are two very good reasons why they are not often used:

- The lack of the % in the macro call, makes the code more difficult to read and recognize as a macro call because it is not what programmers are used to seeing.

- Substantial additional system resources are needed to scan for the macro names. This can slow the execution of all jobs, even those that do not contain statement-style macro references.

SEE ALSO

Additional information statement-style macros can be found in *SAS® Guide to Macro Processing, Version 6, Second Edition* (pp. 91–100) and in *SAS® Macro Language: Reference, First Edition* (p. 133).

Command-style macros were not available in Version 6 until Release 6.07. Additional examples and syntax can be found in SAS Technical Report P-222, *Changes and Enhancements to Base SAS® Software, Release 6.07* (pp. 309–310) and in *SAS® Macro Language: Reference, First Edition* (p. 133).

The general inefficiency of statement- and command-style macros is briefly mentioned in *SAS® Macro Language: Reference, First Edition* (p. 133).

3.5.1   Turning on system options

Normally the system options that are required to use these macro styles are turned off. You can turn them on by using the IMPLMAC and CMDMAC system options (the default is NOIM-PLMAC and NOCMDMAC). The following OPTION statement turns on statement-style macros:

```
options implmac;
```

You can initiate the ability to use command-style macros if you use

```
options cmdmac;
```

3.5.2   Defining statement- and command-style macros

Macros for both of these macro styles are defined in the usual way using the %MACRO statement. Defined macros will be named-style unless the CMD ❶ or STMT option is used on the %MACRO statement. The macro described in Section 3.4 could be redefined as this command-style macro:

```
option cmdmac;

%macro zpgm / cmd; ❶
   pgm;
   recall;
   zoom on;
%mend zpgm;
```

After the macro is created, you can enter ZPGM (not %ZPGM) on the command line to execute the macro.

```
Command ===> zpgm
```

Most users are accustomed to using the % sign with macro calls and as was mentioned earlier statement-style macros often cause additional confusion. Command-style macros can make more sense in developer controlled applications.

3.6 Chapter Summary

Macros are defined using two macro language statements: %MACRO *macro-name* and %MEND *<macro-name>*. Text is then enclosed between these two statements. Macros are invoked or called by placing a % in front of the macro name.

Debugging a macro can be, under the best of conditions, difficult. The LOG is often very cryptic with its isolation of error messages. Several options that are specifically designed for use with macros may be useful during the writing and processing of macros. These include MPRINT, MLOGIC, and SYMBOLGEN.

The autocall facility enables you to define and store macros for later use, including use in programs in different SAS sessions. SAS software is shipped with some predefined macros in the autocall library.

You can increase efficiency by storing compiled macros in compiled stored libraries. Macros stored here will not be recompiled when called.

Macros can also be defined for use on the display manager command line.

Command-style and statement-style macros are available with the macro facility, but their use is not recommended.

3.7 Chapter Exercises

Sample Program:

```
*******************************************************;
**** The class data set, CLINICS,  contains 80     ****;
**** observations and 20 variables.  The following ****;
**** program will be used to complete the exercises ****;
**** in this chapter.                               ****;
*******************************************************;

PROC PLOT DATA=CLASS.CLINICS;
     PLOT EDU * DOB;
     TITLE1 'YEARS OF EDUCATION COMPARED TO BIRTH DATE';
RUN;

PROC CHART DATA=CLASS.CLINICS;
     VBAR WT / SUMVAR=HT TYPE=MEAN;
     TITLE1 'AVERAGE HEIGHT FOR WEIGHT GROUPS';
RUN;
```

1. Convert the sample program into a macro and execute it. Then examine the SAS LOG.

2. In the macro program you wrote in the previous exercise, use the following options separately and in combination to see how the SAS LOG changes.

   OPTIONS: MLOGIC, MPRINT, AND SYMBOLGEN.

3. (True/False) To invoke a macro, a percent sign (%) is placed before the macro name.

Chapter 4 **Macro Parameters**

4.1 Introducing Macro Parameters

4.2 Positional Parameters

4.3 Keyword Parameters

4.4 Using Positional and Keyword Parameters Together

4.5 Chapter Summary

4.6 Chapter Exercises

Macros are made more powerful and flexible when information can be transferred to them through the macro call. This chapter expands the use of macro variables by detailing their use as parameters that can be passed into and between macros. The chapter introduces two types of macro parameters, and their relative merits are discussed.

4.1 Introducing Macro Parameters

In Chapter 2, "Defining and Using Macro Variables," macro variables were introduced and defined through the use of the %LET macro statement. Unfortunately, %LET becomes cumbersome and often limiting when it passes the values of macro variables into a macro. Macro parameters allow you to define macro variables without using the %LET statement. Additionally, these values can be passed into a macro when it is called.

Macro parameters are used to pass values or text strings into a macro, where they are assigned to a macro variable. Parameters are given names in the %MACRO statement, and values are passed into the macro when it is called. The following sections describe this process.

There are two types of parameters: *positional* (Section 4.2) and *keyword*, which is also known as *named* (Section 4.3).

4.2 Positional Parameters

Positional parameters derive their name from the fact that they are defined using a specific position on the %MACRO statement. When the macro is executed, the value is passed using that same position in the macro call.

4.2.1   Defining positional parameters

Positional parameters are defined by listing the macro variable names that are to receive the parameter values in the %MACRO statement. When parameters are present, the macro name is followed by a comma-separated list of macro variables that are enclosed in a pair of parentheses.

Two macro variables (&VAR1 and &VAR2) are defined in the macro %DOCHART shown here:

```
%MACRO DOCHART(VAR1,VAR2);
proc chart data=ptstats;
vbar &var1 &var2;
run;
%mend dochart;
```

In Section 3.1.1 the macro %LOOK was created. It had a single macro variable that was defined using %LET. The following version of %LOOK has two positional parameters, and it is more flexible:

```
%MACRO LOOK(dsn,obs);

    PROC CONTENTS DATA=&dsn;
        TITLE "DATA SET &dsn";
    RUN;

    PROC PRINT DATA=&dsn (OBS=&obs);
        TITLE2 "FIRST &obs OBSERVATIONS";
    RUN;

%MEND LOOK;
```

4.2.2   Passing positional parameters

Because the parameters are positional, the first value is assigned to the macro variable that is listed first in the macro statement's parameter list. When you have multiple parameters, use commas to separate their values. If you want to pass a value that contains a comma, you need to use one of the quoting functions that are described in Section 7.1.

The macro call for %DOCHART becomes

```
%DOCHART(AGE,WT)
```

The macro call for %LOOK could be

```
%LOOK(CLINICS,10)
```

You do not have to give all parameters a value. Alternative invocations of the LOOK macro might include

```
%LOOK()
```

```
%LOOK(CLINICS)
```

```
%LOOK(,10)
```

Macro variables that are not assigned a value will resolve to a null string. Thus, the macro call %LOOK(,10) resolves to

```
PROC CONTENTS DATA=;
      TITLE "DATA SET ";
RUN;

PROC PRINT DATA= (OBS=10);
      TITLE2 "FIRST 10 OBSERVATIONS";
RUN;
```

The resolved code contains syntax errors, and it will not run. Be careful to construct code that will resolve to what you expect.

The following macro sorts a data set with one to three BY variables. The macro would not be needed or used if there was not at least one BY variable.

```
%MACRO SORTIT(DSN,BY1,BY2,BY3);

    PROC SORT DATA=&DSN;
          BY &BY1 &BY2 &BY3;
    RUN;

%MEND SORTIT;
```

The macro call `%SORTIT(CLINICS,LNAME,FNAME)` resolves to

```
PROC SORT DATA=CLINICS;
    BY LNAME FNAME;
RUN;
```

Because undefined parameters result in a null string, &BY3 is dropped from the resolved code. This technique enables us to create generalized code that will be syntactically correct at execution time. The macro %SORTIT will work correctly for one, two, or three BY variables.

The previous definition of %SORTIT could be made more flexible by creating a single macro variable to hold all of the BY variables. &BYLIST replaces &BY1, &BY2, and &BY3 in the following example of %SORTIT:

```
%MACRO SORTIT(DSN,BYLIST);

    PROC SORT DATA=&DSN;
          BY &BYLIST;
    RUN;

%MEND SORTIT;
```

Now, a call to %SORTIT could be

```
%SORTIT(CLINICS,CLINNO LNAME FNAME SSN)
```

This call also resolves to

```
PROC SORT DATA=CLINICS;
    BY CLINNO LNAME FNAME SSN;
RUN;
```

Notice that there is **no** comma between names of the BY variables in the macro call. These four variables become a text string that forms the single definition to the macro variable &BYLIST. In this definition of %SORTIT, the user is not limited to three BY variables.

4.3 Keyword Parameters

Parameters may be designated as *keyword* in the %MACRO statement. Unlike positional parameters, keyword parameters may be used in any order and may be assigned default values. Keyword parameters are especially useful if the user who will be calling a macro needs to be reminded of parameter specifications.

4.3.1   Defining keyword parameters

Keyword parameters are designated by following the parameter name with an equal sign (=). Default values, when present, follow the equal sign. You can use keyword parameters to redefine the %LOOK macro from Section 4.2.2 like this:

```
%MACRO LOOK(dsn=CLINICS,obs=);

    PROC CONTENTS DATA=&dsn;
        TITLE "DATA SET &dsn";
    RUN;

    PROC PRINT DATA=&dsn (OBS=&obs);
        TITLE2 "FIRST &obs OBSERVATIONS";
    RUN;

%MEND LOOK;
```

4.3.2   Passing keyword parameters

Macro variables that are not assigned a value resolve to their default value or to a null string when you do not specify a default. In Section 4.2.2 the macro call (using positional parameters) %LOOK(,10) results in syntax errors because the data set is unnamed. When you use the macro %LOOK that is defined with keyword parameters in Section 4.3.1, the macro call %LOOK(OBS=10) resolves to

```
    PROC CONTENTS DATA=CLINICS;
        TITLE "DATA SET CLINICS";
    RUN;

    PROC PRINT DATA=CLINICS (OBS=10);
        TITLE2 "FIRST 10 OBSERVATIONS";
    RUN;
```

Because the macro call %LOOK(obs=10) did not include a definition for &DSN, the default value of CLINICS was used. The resulting code eliminates the syntax errors that were generated in the %LOOK example in Section 4.2.2.

4.4 Using Keyword and Positional Parameters Together

Although you may specify both keyword and positional parameters in the %MACRO statement, the list of positional parameters must precede the list of keyword parameters.

In the following version of the macro %LOOK, there is one positional and one keyword parameter. The keyword parameter, OBS, has the default value of 10.

```
%MACRO LOOK(dsn,obs=10);
    PROC CONTENTS DATA=&dsn;
          TITLE "DATA SET &dsn";
    RUN;

    PROC PRINT DATA=&dsn (OBS=&obs);
          TITLE2 "FIRST &obs OBSERVATIONS";
    RUN;
%MEND LOOK;
```

The macro call %LOOK(CLINICS) would have the same result as %LOOK(CLINICS,OBS=10) and would resolve to

```
PROC CONTENTS DATA=CLINICS;
     TITLE "DATA SET CLINICS";
RUN;

PROC PRINT DATA=CLINICS (OBS=10);
     TITLE2 "FIRST 10 OBSERVATIONS";
RUN;
```

When you develop a series of macros (macros that call macros that call macros...), it can be very tiresome to use comments to edit individual macros so that they turn on (or off) the system options that control the LOG (see Section 3.3.2). A more flexible version of the OPTIONS statement is shown next and is controlled with a keyword parameter.

In the portions of the macros shown, there is at least one keyword parameter (&NO) that is assigned a default value of NO. In the OPTIONS statement ❶ &no.mprint will default to nomprint. If you need to debug %PRECOMP, then call the macro as %PRECOMP(NO=) and &no.mprint will resolve to mprint.

```
%macro precomp(no=no);

options ps=47 pageno=1 ls=80;
options &no.mprint &no.symbolgen &no.mlogic; ❶


... code removed ...

* Load the current date and time;
data _null_;
   call symput('time',left(put(time(),time8.0)));
   call symput('date',left(put(date(),worddate18.0)));
run;

* Create the location data set;
%locate(&subject,no=&no) ❷

... code removed ...

%mend precomp;
```

Notice that %LOCATE ❷ uses the same system, but it also has a positional parameter. If the &NO is blank for %PRECOMP (MPRINT is turned on), then it will be automatically turned on for %LOCATE as well.

4.5 Chapter Summary

You can make macros more flexible by adding the ability to pass parameter values directly into the macro. There are two types of parameters: positional and keyword(named). When you use parameters, be careful to construct code that will resolve to what you expect.

Parameter names are determined in the macro definition. Although keyword parameters may be used in any order and may be assigned default values, the order of positional parameters is fixed.

Macro variables that are not assigned a value resolve to their default value or to a null string when no default has been specified.

4.6 Chapter Exercises

Sample Program:

```
********************************************************;
**** The class data set, CLINICS, contains 80      ****;
**** observations and 20 variables.  The following ****;
**** program will be used to complete the exercises ****;
**** in this chapter.                               ****;
********************************************************;

PROC PLOT DATA=CLASS.CLINICS;
      PLOT EDU * DOB;
      TITLE1 'YEARS OF EDUCATION COMPARED TO BIRTH DATE';
RUN;

PROC CHART DATA=CLASS.CLINICS;
      VBAR WT / SUMVAR=HT TYPE=MEAN;
      TITLE1 'AVERAGE HEIGHT FOR WEIGHT GROUPS';
RUN;
```

1. What are the two types of parameters that are available in macros?

2. (True/False) You can specify keyword parameters in any order.

3. Change the macro that you wrote in Chapter 3 Exercises 1 and 2 to include at least one positional and one keyword (named) macro parameter (do **not** use %LET). Then execute the macro by passing parameters into the macro.

4. How many positional parameters are found in this statement?

    %MACRO TOOL(DSIN,DSOUT,STOP=500);

5. Why must keyword parameters follow positional parameters?

6. What is wrong with the following macro code?

    ```
    MACRO MYCOPY;

        PROC COPY IN=WORK  OUT=MASTER;
            SELECT PATIENTS;
        RUN;

    %MEND COPY;
    ```

Part 2   # Using Macros

Chapter 5 # Program Control through Macros

A great deal of the power of the macro language comes from its ability to utilize conditional logic as well as a substantial number of macro statements and functions. This chapter introduces several of the more commonly used macro programming statements.

Examples are also included in this chapter that will show you how to write programs that use macros as building blocks by having macros execute other macros.

5.1 Macros That Invoke Macros

It is not unusual for macros to call other macros and in the process of doing so to pass values to the macro that is being called. Often values defined in one macro will be used to affect the flow of logic and execution within a different macro. When a macro calls another macro, the call is said to be *nested* within the macro. It is often advantageous to nest macro calls (macro definitions, however, usually are not nested).

5.1.1 Passing parameters between macros

Consider the two macros %LOOK and %SORTIT (Sections 4.2 and 4.3). These macros have one common parameter (&dsn), and it might be nice to have a utility or controlling macro to do both steps at once. Consider the macro %DOBOTH shown here:

```
%MACRO DOBOTH;
    %SORTIT(CLINICS,LNAME,FNAME)
    %LOOK(OBS=10)
%MEND DOBOTH;

%MACRO LOOK(dsn=CLINICS,obs=);
    PROC CONTENTS DATA=&dsn;
        TITLE "DATA SET &dsn";
    RUN;
    PROC PRINT DATA=&dsn (OBS=&obs);
        TITLE2 "FIRST &obs OBSERVATIONS";
    RUN;
%MEND LOOK;
```

```
%MACRO SORTIT(DSN,BY1,BY2,BY3);
    PROC SORT DATA=&DSN;
        BY &BY1 &BY2 &BY3;
    RUN;
%MEND SORTIT;
```

Notice that the macro DOBOTH is defined before the macros that it calls. The order does not matter as long as each macro is defined before it is called. The macro call to %DOBOTH will be resolved as

```
PROC SORT DATA=CLINICS;
    BY LNAME FNAME;
RUN;
PROC CONTENTS DATA=CLINICS;
    TITLE "DATA SET CLINICS";
RUN;
PROC PRINT DATA=CLINICS (OBS=10);
    TITLE2 "FIRST 10 OBSERVATIONS";
RUN;
```

In the example shown above, it is necessary to change or edit the definition of %DOBOTH in order to change what it does. %DOBOTH would be much more flexible if the parameters for the macros %SORTIT and %LOOK could be passed directly through the call to %DOBOTH.

The following example contains a rewritten macro %DOBOTH. This macro is written to receive the parameters that are used by %SORTIT and %LOOK. Notice that the parameters for the calls to %SORTIT and %LOOK are all %DOBOTH macro variables, whose resolved values are passed on to %SORTIT and %LOOK.

```
%MACRO DOBOTH(d,o,b1,b2,b3);
    %SORTIT(&d,&b1,&b2,&b3)
    %LOOK(&d,&o)
%MEND DOBOTH;

%MACRO LOOK(dsn,obs);
    PROC CONTENTS DATA=&dsn;
        TITLE "DATA SET &dsn";
    RUN;
    PROC PRINT DATA=&dsn (OBS=&obs);
        TITLE2 "FIRST &obs OBSERVATIONS";
    RUN;
%MEND LOOK;

%MACRO SORTIT(DSET,BY1,BY2,BY3);
    PROC SORT DATA=&DSET;
        BY &BY1 &BY2 &BY3;
    RUN;
%MEND SORTIT;
```

Notice that the macro variable names in %DOBOTH need not be the same as in %SORTIT and %LOOK. The macro call

```
%DOBOTH(CLINICS,10,LNAME,FNAME)
```

resolves to

```
%SORTIT(CLINICS,LNAME,FNAME,)
%LOOK(CLINICS,10)
```

which, in turn, resolves to

```
PROC SORT DATA=CLINICS;
     BY LNAME FNAME;
RUN;
PROC CONTENTS DATA=CLINICS;
     TITLE "DATA SET CLINICS";
RUN;
PROC PRINT DATA=CLINICS (OBS=10);
     TITLE2 "FIRST 10 OBSERVATIONS";
RUN;
```

The macro variables in %DOBOTH, (for example, &D, &O, and &B1), are resolved before the calls to %SORTIT and %LOOK are made. Consequently, it does not matter that the names of the macro variables in %DOBOTH are different from the ones that are used in the other two macros.

5.1.2 Controlling macro calls

Often it is useful to create a SAS program that consists simply of calls to macros. This enables you to easily control through macro calls the execution of selected portions of the program.

The macro calls shown next execute macros that are either defined earlier in a portion of the program (not shown here) or are stored in a macro library (see Sections 3.3.3 and 3.3.4). Although you do not have the definitions of the macros available to look at here, it is instructive to look at how the macro calls are set up.

%SETUP ❶ ❷ creates a data set, for example, NEW1, based on some criteria in the second and third parameters. %ALL ❸ then combines all of the NEW$_i$ data sets (for example, NEW1, NEW2, NEW3) that were created by the series of calls to %SETUP into the permanent data set FINAL.COMBINE. The two analysis macros (%CORREL ❹ and %ANOVA ❺) then operate on FINAL.COMBINE to do the selected analyses.

```
    ... code not included ...

    ***************************************;
    **** CREATE DATA AS REQUIRED**********;
    %MACRO DOIT;
      ❶   %SETUP(NEW1,15,32)   * GATHER DATA FOR WORK.NEW1;
          %SETUP(NEW2,33,40)   * GATHER DATA FOR WORK.NEW2;
      ❷ * %SETUP(NEW3,41,72)   * GATHER DATA FOR WORK.NEW3;
      ❸   %ALL(FINAL.COMBINE)  * COMBINE DATA FOR ANALYSIS;
    %MEND DOIT;
    %DOIT                      * CREATE THE ANALYSIS DATA SET;

    **** ANALYZE COMBINED DATA  **********;
    ❹%CORREL                *   CORRELATION OF P/C VARS;
    ❺%ANOVA                 *   ANALYSIS OF VARIANCE (P/C);
```

Using this arrangement of statements gives you a lot of flexibility. You can use comments to eliminate calls to macros that are not required (as is the third call to %SETUP ❷) and all control is located within ten lines of code rather than spread throughout an entire program. Section 3.2 contains more information on commenting out macro calls. This type of arrangement of macro calls can also serve as documentation of what was executed and in what order.

A disadvantage of using the asterisk style comment is that the comment is stored as part of the compiled macro. Comments defined with /* ... */ and macro comments (see Section 5.4.1) are excluded from the compiled macro and can result in a savings in compilation time and storage size. Macro %DOIT could be rewritten as

```
%MACRO DOIT;
    %SETUP(NEW1,15,32)   /* GATHER DATA FOR WORK.NEW1*/
    %SETUP(NEW2,33,40)   /* GATHER DATA FOR WORK.NEW2*/
 /*%SETUP(NEW3,41,72)    /* GATHER DATA FOR WORK.NEW3*/
    %ALL(FINAL.COMBINE)  /* COMBINE DATA FOR ANALYSIS*/
%MEND DOIT;
```

The comments in this definition of %DOIT will be stripped off and the macro compiler will only see

```
%MACRO DOIT;
    %SETUP(NEW1,15,32)
    %SETUP(NEW2,33,40)
    %ALL(FINAL.COMBINE)
%MEND DOIT;
```

5.2 Using Conditional Macro Statements

IF-THEN/ELSE processing in the DATA step enables you to write programs that will act conditionally based on values contained in variables in the Program Data Vector (PDV). The macro %IF-%THEN and %ELSE statements are analogous to the DATA step IF-THEN/ELSE statements. However, they are not constrained to the DATA step and do **not** operate on DATA step variables.

Macro %IF-%THEN and %ELSE statements may appear anywhere inside of a macro and are used to conditionally

- assign values to macro variables

- execute other macros

- create SAS code and SAS statements

Syntax

%**IF** *expression* %**THEN** *result-text* ;
%**ELSE** *result-text* ;

Most of the same rules that apply to the DATA step IF-THEN/ELSE statements apply here as well. Three primary differences that you must keep in mind when using %IF-%THEN/%ELSE statements are

- They **do not** operate on the values of DATA step variables. Macro statements and macro references are resolved before **any** data are read. Macro expressions will **never** directly evaluate the value of a variable on the PDV.

- They control program flow and code construction, **not** the flow of the execution of a DATA step. Again it is very important to remember that whatever the macro statements do they will be resolved and executed long before the SAS program is compiled and executed.

- Comparisons are made on literal text strings and quotes are generally not used. For example, X='X' would be false.

SEE ALSO
Virgile (1997) uses the CALL EXECUTE routine to set up conditional macro logic outside of macros.

5.2.1 Executing macro statements

Like the DATA step IF statement's *action*, the *result-text* in the macro %IF takes place when the *expression* is true. The construction of the *expression* is similar to what it would be for the IF statement; however it will **not**, as was hinted at earlier, be testing values of DATA step variables. This has been repeated multiple times because this is a major point of confusion for many first-time users.

In the following example, the %IF tests the value of the macro variable &CITY. Notice that the value ALBANY is not enclosed in quotes as it would be if CITY were a character variable on the PDV. Remember that you can think of all macro variables as character and because macro variable names are always preceded by an &, quotes are not needed. In this example, when the value ALBANY is stored in &CITY, the macro variable &STATE will be set to NEW YORK. For all other values of &CITY the second %LET statement is executed and &STATE will be set to CALIFORNIA.

```
%IF &CITY=ALBANY %THEN %LET STATE=NEW YORK;
%ELSE %LET STATE=CALIFORNIA;
```

The macro %DOBOTH in Section 5.1.1 will fail with a syntax error if no BY variables are passed. It would be nice if the %SORTIT macro was only executed if at least one BY variable is not blank. In the revised %DOBOTH below, it is assumed that if any BY variables are to be listed one will be placed in &B1. An %IF statement is then used to conditionally execute the %SORTIT macro.

```
%MACRO DOBOTH(d,o,b1,b2,b3);
    %IF &B1 ^= %THEN %SORTIT(&d,&b1,&b2,&b3);
    %LOOK(&d,&o)
%MEND DOBOTH;
```

Notice that the expression used in the above example would not work in a DATA step IF statement. Because undefined macro variables contain a null value (this is different from a blank) and because quotes are not needed, this syntax is correctly interpreted. But it does look strange. To make it look less strange, the %IF might be rewritten as

```
%IF "&B1" ^= "" %THEN %SORTIT(&d,&b1,&b2,&b3);
```

In both of these examples the result text is a macro statement or a macro call that is then immediately executed. When the result text does not contain any macro variables or calls, the result text becomes part of the SAS code that will be compiled and executed.

5.2.2 Building SAS code dynamically

You can use the %IF to conditionally insert SAS code into a program. This enables you to create programs that are not fully defined until they are actually executed. In the following example, the data set that is named in the SET statement is not known until the parameter (&STATE), which is passed into %DASTEP, is evaluated.

```
%MACRO DASTEP(STATE);
    DATA SUBHOSP;
    SET
 %IF &STATE=CA %THEN CAHOSP;
 %ELSE AZHOSP;
       ; ❶
       WHERE DATE>'19JUN96'D;
    RUN;
%MEND DASTEP;
```

Semicolon Management   Note the use of semicolons in the statements shown above. Each macro statement ends with a semicolon. At first glance, it seems that these semicolons will end the SET statement or at least confuse the DATA step compiler. This will **not** be a problem because all macro references will be resolved before this DATA step is compiled. Any semicolons that are associated with macro statements will be long gone.

In this example, the semicolon that is used with the SET statement is on its own line ❶ (just after the %ELSE statement). It could also have been on the same line as the %ELSE. It was placed on its own line to make it easier for the programmer to read. SAS does not prefer one location over the other.

For the above macro definition, `%DASTEP(AZ)` resolves to

```
DATA SUBHOSP;
    SET
    AZHOSP
    ; ❶
    WHERE DATE>'19JUN96'D;
RUN;
```

The section of code in the following example is one DATA step in the macro %SENRATE. Macro %IF logic is used to determine how the OUTPUT statement will be structured.   The DATA step will create one of a series of tables that are to be written to the library SENRATE. For Table 5 (&NUM=5), a single OUTPUT statement is generated. For all other values of &NUM a comment, two assignment statements, and two OUTPUT statements are inserted into the code to be executed. The macro %DO statement is discussed in Section 5.3.1.

```
%macro senrate(num);

... code not shown ...

data senrate.rtsen&num;
set ratedata;
* Table 5 has sex already defined.  3 & 7 do not;
* output one obs for each sex;
%if &num=5 %then output senrate.rtsen&num; ❶
%else %do;
    * output the obs for each sex;
    sex='F';output senrate.rtsen&num;
    sex='M';output senrate.rtsen&num ❷
%end;; ❸

... code not shown ...

%mend senrate;
```

❶ The semicolon in the %IF statement ends the %IF statement and not the OUTPUT statement.

❷ This statement does not have a semicolon.

❸ The second semicolon that follows the %END statement will be used to close the OUTPUT statement for either the %IF statement ❶ or the %ELSE statement ❷.

For &NUM=3, the resulting DATA step would be

```
... code not shown ...
data senrate.rtsen3;
set ratedata;
* Table 5 has sex already defined.  3 & 7 do not;
* output one obs for each sex;
   * output the obs for each sex;
   sex='F';output senrate.rtsen3;
   sex='M';output senrate.rtsen3
;❸
```

A portion of the example also could have been written

```
* Table 5 has sex already defined.  3 & 7 do not;
* output one obs for each sex;
%if &num ^= 5 %then %do;
   * output the obs for each sex;
   sex='F';output senrate.rtsen&num;
   sex='M';
%end;
output senrate.rtsen&num;
```

The %DO block also is often used for semicolon management (see Section 5.3.1 for another version of the above example). The discussion of macro %DOBOTH in Section 5.3.1 also includes comments on the management of the semicolon.

SEE ALSO
Leighton (1997) contains several examples of dynamic code building.

5.3 Iterative Execution Using Macro Statements

The %DO block, iterative %DO, %DO %UNTIL, and %DO %WHILE statements in the macro language are very similar to the corresponding statements that are used in the DATA step. Like the %IF, however, these statements are not confined to the DATA step. You can use them anywhere inside of a macro.

All forms of the %DO statement must be matched with an %END.

5.3.1 %DO block

The simplest form of the macro %DO statement is the %DO block, and it is analogous to the DATA step's DO block. The %DO block is most commonly needed when you want the result-text of an %IF-%THEN statement to contain multiple macro calls, multiple macro statements, or even multiple SAS statements.

You also can use the %DO block to help with semicolon management when you dynamically create code. The following example removes the hanging semicolon problem that was shown in Section 5.2.2:

```
%macro senrate(&num);

 ... code not shown ...

data senrate.rtsen&num;
set ratedata;
* Table 5 has sex already defined.  3 & 7 do not;
* output one obs for each sex;
%if &num=5 %then %do;
   output senrate.rtsen&num;
%end;
%else %do;
   * output the obs for each sex;
   sex='F';output senrate.rtsen&num;
   sex='M';output senrate.rtsen&num;
%end;

 ... code not shown ...

%mend senrate;
```

It is easier to follow the logic in this code than was in Section 5.2.2 because the %DO blocks contain complete SAS statements.

Macro %DOBOTH in Section 5.2.1 can be greatly simplified by eliminating the calls to %SORTIT and %LOOK. The new macro becomes

```
%MACRO DOBOTH(dsn,obs,by1,by2,by3);

        %IF &BY1 ^= %THEN %DO; ❶
            PROC SORT DATA=&DSN;
                 BY &BY1 &BY2 &BY3;
            RUN;
        %END;

        PROC CONTENTS DATA=&dsn;
             TITLE "DATA SET &dsn";
        RUN;

        PROC PRINT DATA=&dsn
        %IF &OBS>0 %THEN %DO; ❷
            (OBS=&obs);
            TITLE2 "FIRST &obs OBSERVATIONS"
        %END;
            ; ❸
        RUN;
%MEND DOBOTH;
```

❶ The PROC SORT step will never be included in the final code when the first BY variable is blank.

❷ In the PROC PRINT, &OBS is checked before the OBS= option is included in the PROC statement. This allows the insertion of a special title.

❸ Notice that the semicolon that follows the last %END statement will close either the TITLE or PROC statement, depending on the value in &OBS.

The following program conditionally executes blocks of SAS code. The macro %DOIT is used to create the temporary data set TDATA. The difficulty lies in the fact that there are two styles of input data (&STYLE) that must be handled differently. &STYLE is checked and the appropriate code is inserted into the program.

```
%macro doit;
* macro is required because conditional macro logic statements
* are used;

* test for type of data and set up accordingly.;
%if &style=OLD %then %do;
    *   read the data for a specific test;
    proc sort data=old.&dsn out=tdata;
    by varno age;
    where temp=&temp & age le &maxage;
    run;
%end;
%else %do;
    data tdata (keep=varno canno temp age depvar test package);
    set cps.dest (keep=base no &regvar.1-&regvar.6
                       temp test package);
    array can &regvar.1-&regvar.6;
    length age varno 8;
    where base="&dsn";

    ... program statements deleted ...

    proc sort data=tdata;
    by varno age temp;
    run;
%end;
%mend doit;
%doit
```

The %DOIT macro is required because you can only use %IF statements within a macro.

5.3.2 Iterative %DO loops

Although the form of the iterative %DO is similar to the DO statement, it differs in that

■ the WHILE and UNTIL clauses cannot be added to the increments

■ irregular increments are not allowed.

Syntax

%DO *macro-variable = start* %TO *stop* <%BY *increment*>;
... *text* ...
%END;

The iterative %DO defines and increments a macro variable. In the following example, the macro variable &YEAR is incremented by one starting with &START and ending with &STOP. Although the DATA step also has a variable YEAR, the two will not be confused. The incoming data sets are named YR95, YR96, and so on. These are read one at a time, and they are appended to the all-inclusive data set ALLYEAR.

```
%MACRO ALLYR(START,STOP);
    %DO YEAR = &START %TO &STOP;
        DATA TEMP;
            SET YR&YEAR;
            YEAR = 1900 + &YEAR;
        RUN;
        PROC APPEND BASE=ALLYEAR DATA=TEMP;
        RUN;
    %END;
%MEND ALLYR;
```

The call %ALLYR(95,97) produces the following:

```
DATA TEMP;
    SET YR95;
    YEAR = 1900 + 95;
RUN;
PROC APPEND BASE=ALLYEAR DATA=TEMP;
RUN;

DATA TEMP;
    SET YR96;
    YEAR = 1900 + 96;
RUN;
PROC APPEND BASE=ALLYEAR DATA=TEMP;
RUN;

DATA TEMP;
    SET YR97;
    YEAR = 1900 + 97;
RUN;
PROC APPEND BASE=ALLYEAR DATA=TEMP;
RUN;
```

You can greatly simplify this code by taking better advantage of the %DO loop. Rather than having the macro create separate DATA and APPEND steps for each year, you can build the code dynamically.

```
%MACRO ALLYR(START,STOP);
    DATA ALLYEAR;
        SET
        %DO YEAR = &START %TO &STOP;
                YR&YEAR(IN=IN&YEAR)
        %END;;

        YEAR = 1900
        %DO YEAR = &START %TO &STOP;
            + (IN&YEAR*&YEAR)
        %END;;

        RUN;
%MEND ALLYR;
```

This time the call to %ALLYR(95,97) produces the following:

```
DATA ALLYEAR;
   SET
        YR95(IN=IN95)
        YR96(IN=IN96)
        YR97(IN=IN97)
   ;

   YEAR = 1900
        + (IN95*95)
        + (IN96*96)
        + (IN97*97)
   ;

   RUN;
```

In this code, the value of YEAR is assigned by taking advantage of the IN= data set option. The values of IN95, IN96, and IN97 will be either true or false (1 or 0), and only one of the three will be true at any given time.

As in the previous example, the following macro, %READNEW, reads a series of data sets and builds the SET statement dynamically. In this example, however, the %DO loop is placed in the macro call rather than in the macro itself. In the call to %READNEW, the %DO loop is placed as the value of the &DSIN parameter. This simplifies the code in the macro but makes the macro call more complex.

```
*   SOFT BENTHOS ABUNDANCE SUMMARY TABLES BY SPECIES;

%MACRO READNEW(DSIN=,DSOUT=);
DATA &DSOUT;
SET &DSIN;
 BY SURVEY; RETAIN SDATE;
 KEEP SPCODE DEPTH XLOC PERIOD DATE TCNTAB;

... portions of this program were deleted ...

PROC PRINT; TITLE 'TAXALIST';
%MEND READNEW;

**********************************************************;
%MACRO DOIT;
* Use selected surveys
*;
%READNEW(DSOUT=NEW1,DSIN=%DO I=16 %TO 18; DBBIO.SUR&I %END; )
%READNEW(DSOUT=NEW2,DSIN=%DO I=42 %TO 54; DBBIO.SUR&I %END; )
%READNEW(DSOUT=NEW3,DSIN=%DO I=55 %TO 72; DBBIO.SUR&I %END; )
%ALL
%MEND DOIT;

%DOIT          RUN;
```

Because the parameter &DSIN contains the macro statement %DO, the loop will be executed and resolved before the resulting parameter value is passed to %READNEW. In the first call to %READNEW, the value of &DSIN that is passed will be the same as

```
%READNEW(DSOUT=NEW1,DSIN=DBBIO.SUR16 DBBIO.SUR17 DBBIO.SUR18)
```

Notice that no macro statements were passed. Only their resolved values were passed. If you need to pass values that contain the symbols % and &, you may need to use quoting functions (see Section 7.1).

You must be careful when using statements like this in a macro call because the resolved text must be an appropriate parameter value.

SEE ALSO
Leighton (1997) includes examples of %DO loops that are used to build code dynamically.

5.3.3 %DO %UNTIL loops

Continuous loops or blocks of code can also be executed without the use of incremental variables. The %DO %UNTIL statement executes a block repeatedly until the specified condition is met. Be careful when using %DO %UNTIL loops as it is possible to construct an infinite loop. Because the %DO %UNTIL statement contains a logical macro expression and the loop continues to execute until the expression is true, be sure that the condition can be met.

Syntax

> **%DO %UNTIL**(*expression*);
> ... *text* ...
> **%END**;

The expression in the parentheses is evaluated, and when the expression is false the %DO is executed. The loop continues to execute until the expression is true. Like the DATA step DO UNTIL statement, the expression is evaluated at the end of the loop. (This is sometimes expressed as "evaluation at the bottom of the loop.") This means that the loop always executes at least once and will not execute again if the expression becomes true during the execution of the loop.

The following example rewrites the iterative %DO statement found in the first example in Section 5.3.2. The values of the two macro variables &YEAR and &STOP are compared to determine if the loop should execute again ❶. Even though &YEAR is not defined ❷ until the statement after the %DO %UNTIL statement, this will not cause an error because loop evaluation takes place at the bottom of the loop.

```
%MACRO ALLYR(START,STOP);
    %LET CNT = 0;
    %DO %UNTIL(&YEAR >= &STOP);     ❶
        %LET YEAR = %EVAL(&CNT + &START);     ❷

        DATA TEMP;
            SET YR&YEAR;
            YEAR = 1900 + &YEAR;
        RUN;

        PROC APPEND BASE=ALLYEAR DATA=TEMP;
        RUN;

        %LET CNT = %EVAL(&CNT + 1);
    %END;
%MEND ALLYR;
```

❶ The >= comparison operator prevents an infinite loop if &START is larger than &STOP. Because the comparison is evaluated at the bottom of the loop, the loop will execute at least once.

❷ This example uses the %EVAL macro function, which is discussed in more detail in Section 7.3.1. The %EVAL function is used to perform arithmetic operations within the macro language. A special function is required because there are no numeric macro variables.

SEE ALSO
Tassoni (1997) contains an example of a %DO %UNTIL.

5.3.4 %DO %WHILE loops

Like %DO %UNTIL, the %DO %WHILE statement executes a block repeatedly. Unlike %DO %UNTIL, however, the %DO %WHILE loops are executed as long as or while the specified condition is met.

Syntax

> **%DO %WHILE**(*expression*);
> . . . *text* . . .
> **%END**;

Like the DO WHILE statement in the DATA step, the expression in %DO %WHILE is evaluated (at the top of the loop) before the loop is executed. This means that the loop will not automatically execute at least once as the %DO %UNTIL does.

The example in Section 5.3.3 could be rewritten

```
%MACRO ALLYR(START,STOP);
     %LET CNT = 0;
     %DO %WHILE(&YEAR <= &STOP);
          %LET YEAR = %EVAL(&CNT + &START);

          DATA TEMP;
               SET YR&YEAR;
               YEAR = 1900 + &YEAR;
          RUN;

          PROC APPEND BASE=ALLYEAR DATA=TEMP;
          RUN;

          %LET CNT = %EVAL(&CNT + 1);
     %END;
%MEND ALLYR;
```


SEE ALSO
Roberts (1997) uses the %DO %WHILE statement to decompose a macro variable list.

5.4 Macro Program Statements

The macro language is rich in program statements. Several of these have already been introduced and used in previous examples.

Statement	Section
%LET	2.1
%MACRO	3.1
%MEND	3.1
%IF-%THEN	5.2
%ELSE	5.2
%DO	5.3.1 and 5.3.2
%DO %UNTIL	5.3.3
%DO %WHILE	5.3.4

Additional macro program statements are introduced in the following subsections.

Statement	Section
Macro comments	5.4.1
%GLOBAL	5.4.2
%LOCAL	5.4.2
%GOTO & %*label*	5.4.3
%SYSEXEC	5.4.4

5.4.1 Macro comments

Macro comments behave in much the same way as the usual SAS asterisk-style comment. As a general rule, there is little advantage to using macro comments over standard comments. However you might notice the following differences:

- The LOG will contain asterisk-style comments for the text that is generated by the macro when using the MPRINT system option (see Section 3.3.2). Macro comments and comments denoted by /* ....*/ will not be shown in the LOG.

- Asterisk-style comments are stored as part of the macro text and, therefore, take up additional, albeit not many, resources.

Syntax

%* *comment text* ;

In the following example, the three styles of comments are used to document the macro %DOIT:

```
%macro doit;
%* This macro does nothing of interest;
*  This macro var &VAR remains unresolved;
/* Only the previous comment shows with MPRINT */
%mend doit;
```

When %DOIT is executed with the MPRINT system option turned on, the LOG shows only the asterisk-style comment following the macro call:

```
%doit
MPRINT(DOIT):  *  This macro var &VAR remains unresolved;
```

Macro comments can be useful when you dynamically build SAS code. In Section 5.3.2, a %DO loop is used to build a SET statement. You could use macro-style comments to document the process.

```
DATA ALLYEAR;
   SET
   %* Include the data from the years of interest;
   %* Use years from &start to &stop;
   %DO YEAR = &START %TO &STOP;
        YR&YEAR(IN=IN&YEAR)
   %END;;
   ... code not shown ...
```

An asterisk style comment would not work in this situation, although you could use a comment that is defined by /* ... */.

5.4.2 %GLOBAL and %LOCAL

These statements create macro variables that are either available in all referencing environments (GLOBAL) or in a limited referencing environment (LOCAL). Unless first declared otherwise by these statements, macro variables are automatically determined to be global or local when they are defined.

Without these statements macro variables are

- global when they are defined outside of a macro

- local to a macro when they are defined inside of a macro.

Referencing environments will not be a problem for you if you either define macro variables outside of all macros or pass macro variable values into and out of each macro as parameters.

Unfortunately these approaches often are not practical. For more complicated applications, it may be useful to create in one process a macro variable that you want to have available to other macros without having to physically pass it as a parameter. Understanding the referencing environment becomes important for you at this point.

Syntax
%GLOBAL *macro-variable-list*;
%LOCAL *macro-variable-list*;

The following example does nothing except highlight the availability of macro variable values:

```
%let outside = AAA; ❶

%macro one;
  %global inone; ❷
  %let inone = BBB;
%mend one;

%macro two;
  %let intwo = CCC; ❸
%mend two;

%macro last;
  %one %two
  %put &outside &inone &intwo; ❹
%mend last;

%last
```

❶ &OUTSIDE is created outside of any macro. It is, therefore, a GLOBAL macro variable and is automatically available within any macro.

❷ The macro variable &INONE is globalized before it is defined. So, although it is defined inside of a macro (%ONE), it too is now available within other macros.

❸ &INTWO is created inside of %TWO and is not globalized. Its definition or even knowledge of its existence is limited to the macro %TWO.

❹ The %PUT statement in the macro %LAST demonstrates these availabilities. When %LAST is called, the following is written to the LOG:

```
WARNING: Apparent symbolic reference INTWO not resolved.
AAA BBB &intwo
```

%LOCAL seems to be used less frequently than %GLOBAL is used and almost certainly less often than it should be. Most commonly, it is used as a means to protect the values of global macro variables. In the example in Section 5.3.3, the macro variable &YEAR is created in the macro %ALLYR. If %ALLYR is called within an application that has a globalized macro variable of the same name (&YEAR), %ALLYR will change the value of &YEAR. By adding the %LOCAL statement in the following example, the globalized value of &YEAR will not be changed by the value local to %ALLYR. (As added protection &CNT is also included in the %LOCAL statement.)

```
%MACRO ALLYR(START,STOP);
    %local year cnt;
    %LET CNT = 0;
    %DO %UNTIL(&YEAR = &STOP);
        %LET YEAR = %EVAL(&CNT + &START);

        DATA TEMP;
            SET YR&YEAR;
            YEAR = 1900 + &YEAR;
        RUN;

        PROC APPEND BASE=ALLYEAR DATA=TEMP;
        RUN;
```

```
          %LET CNT = %EVAL(&CNT + 1);
      %END;
%MEND ALLYR;
```

The above example hints that it is possible that a macro variable can have more than one definition at a given time depending on whether it is local or global. This dual (or should we say dueling) definition can be confusing, and you should avoid it when possible.

The following macros write two different values for &AA to the LOG. Resetting &AA in %INSIDE does not change its value in the %OUTSIDE macro.

```
%macro outside;
     %let aa = 5;
     %inside(3)
     %put outside &aa;
%mend outside;

%macro inside(aa);
     %put inside &aa;
%mend inside;


%outside
```

In this example, &AA is local to two different macros at the same time and has two different values. The LOG will contain

```
inside 3
outside 5
```

The following two examples further demonstrate the difference between these two referencing environments and the need to protect GLOBAL macro variables. In the following example, &BB is defined using a %LET statement outside of the macro definition, which by default makes it GLOBAL.

```
%macro inside(var);
     %let bb = &var;
     %put inside &bb;
%mend inside;

%* This LET statement makes &BB global;
%let bb = 5;
%inside(3)
%put outside &bb;
run;
```

&BB is global, so when it is redefined in %INSIDE the value of &BB is changed outside of the macro %INSIDE as well. The LOG will contain

```
inside 3
outside 3
```

Adding a %LOCAL statement to %INSIDE protects the global value of the macro variable:

```
%macro inside(var);
     %local bb;
     %let bb = &var;
     %put inside &bb;
%mend inside;
```

```
%let bb = 5;
%inside(3)
%put outside &bb;
run;
```

In this example, &BB is again a global macro variable. However, because of the %LOCAL statement, its instance in %INSIDE is local to that macro. This means that although the global macro
variable &BB is redefined in %INSIDE, the value is not changed outside of %INSIDE. The LOG
will contain

```
inside 3
outside 5
```

5.4.3 %GOTO and %label

These two statements are included in this book because you might encounter them someday in
someone else's code (warning: subtle author bias may be encountered in this subsection).
These statements, like other directed branching statements, enable you to create code that is
very unstructured. So far (when I have tried hard enough), I have always been able to find better ways of solving a problem (both in coding SAS and in my personal life) than by using GOTO
and %GOTO type statements. My recommendation is to use the alternative logic, thereby avoid-
ing the use of these statements.

Like the DATA step GOTO statement, %GOTO (or %GO TO) causes a logic branch in the processing. The branch destination will be a macro label (%label). Therefore, the argument associated with the %GOTO must resolve to a known %label.

Syntax

%**GOTO** *label;*
or
%**GO TO** *label;*

%label:

The *label* associated with the %GOTO statement must resolve to a macro label that you have
defined somewhere within the macro. The label may be explicitly or implicitly named. In the
following example, the label is named explicitly. The branch will be to %NEXTSTEP.

```
%GOTO NEXTSTEP;

... code omitted ...

%nextstep:

... more code omitted ...
```

In code that uses %GOTO, it is not unusual for %GOTO to include a label that contains a reference to a macro variable that will be resolved before the %GOTO is executed. In the following
statement, &STEP must resolve to a defined macro label, for example, NEXTSTEP:

```
%GOTO &STEP;
```

Because the macro label is preceded by a %, the new user often uses a % with the *label* in the %GOTO statement, as in this statement:

```
%GOTO %STEPTOT;
```

Rather than branching to the specified *%label*, however, a call to execute the macro %STEPTOT will be issued. Generally, this will result in an error, but it can work if the macro %STEPTOT resolves to the name of a macro label.

In the following example, %GOTO is used to determine which of two DATA steps will be executed. The macro labels are explicitly defined in the %GOTO statements.

```
%macro mkwt(dsn);
%* Point directly to the label;
%if &dsn = MALE %then %goto male;
   data wt;
   set female;
   wt = wt*2.2;
   run;
%goto next;
%male:
   data wt;
   set male;
   run;
%next:
%mend mkwt;
```

You can rewrite this example to use implicit labels that reflect the incoming macro variable (&DSN). This makes the use of the %IF unnecessary.

```
%macro make(dsn);
%* Point indirectly to the label;
%goto &dsn;
%female:
   data wt;
   set female;
   wt = wt*2.2;
   run;
%goto next;
%male:
   data wt;
   set male;
   run;
%next:
%mend make;
```

Admittedly, this is a rather simplistic case, but you can easily rewrite the previous examples to avoid the use of the %GOTO altogether:

```
%macro smart(dsn);
%* AVOID GOTO WHEN POSSIBLE;
   data wt;
   set &dsn;
   %if &dsn=FEMALE %then wt = wt*2.2;;
   run;
%mend smart;
```

5.4.4 Using %SYSEXEC

You can issue operating environment commands from within a macro, or in open code if you use the %SYSEXEC macro statement. This statement is analogous to the X statement and replaces the earlier statements of %TSO, %CMS, and so on.

- Specified operating system commands are executed immediately.

- Any return codes are assigned to the automatic macro variable &SYSRC.

Syntax

%**SYSEXEC** *operating system command*;

Enter the operating system command just as you would enter it at your operating system prompt. The command is **not** enclosed in quotes. Everything between the %SYSEXEC and its semicolon is passed directly to the operating system for immediate execution.

In the following MVS statement, the partitioned data set member CLEANUP will be executed. The quotes are needed here because they are expected by the operating system:

```
%SYSEXEC ex 'userid.mytools.sascode(cleanup)';
```

The following %SYSEXEC statement is followed by a query to its return code which is stored in the automatic macro variable &SYSRC:

```
%sysexec dir *.sas;
%if &sysrc = 0 %then %do; ....
```

If you have not used the X command before on your operating system, you should consult the appropriate *SAS Companion* so that you will know what to expect in terms of behavior for %SYSEXEC and what values can be taken on by &SYSRC.

5.5 Chapter Summary

The %IF-%THEN and %ELSE statements are similar to the IF-THEN/ELSE statements used in the DATA step, except that the macro %IF statement is not constrained to a DATA step. You can use the %IF-%THEN statement to conditionally insert SAS code into a program.

The %DO block, iterative %DO, %DO %UNTIL, and %DO %WHILE statements in the macro language are very similar to the corresponding statements used in the DATA step. Like %IF, however, these statements are not confined to the DATA step and you can use them anywhere inside of a macro. You must match each form of the %DO statement with an %END statement.

Continuous loops or blocks of code can also be executed, without the use of incremental variables, **until** or **while** certain conditions hold. The %DO %UNTIL statement executes a block repeatedly until the specified condition is met, and the %DO %WHILE statement executes a block repeatedly while the specified condition is met.

The %GLOBAL and %LOCAL statements specify referencing environments. These enable you to control whether or not the value of a macro variable is currently available.

5.6 Chapter Exercises

1. Using the following macro (%PRINTT), construct the macro call that will invoke the PRINT procedure using a SAS System data set called CLINICS:

```
%MACRO PRINTT(DSIN,PROC=);
     PROC &PROC DATA=&DSIN;
     RUN;
%MEND PRINTT;
```

2. Use the %DO, %DO %UNTIL, or %DO %WHILE statement to construct a macro that will print the message "This is Test *number*" in the LOG ten times, each time displaying the test *number*: 1, 2, 3, 4, and so on.

    Extra Credit: Solve this exercise three times, once for each type of %DO.

3. (True/False) Every macro definition must end with a %MEND statement.

4. (True/False) You can use the %LET statement inside as well as outside of a macro.

5. Which statement(s) below is(are) syntactically incorrect? Why?

    A. %GOTO %PRINT;

    B. %GLOBLE SAVE;

    C. %IF &SEX = M THEN %PUT MALE;

6. Write a macro that will be generic enough to handle the MEANS and UNIVARIATE procedures. Include the following minimum information as macro variables:

    ■ name of the procedure

    ■ title line #1

    ■ VAR statement for selection of numeric variables

7. Convert the following PROC MEANS step to a macro that will either print a standard set of statistics or generate the means as shown, depending on whether or not the user specifies an output data set:

```
proc means data=class.clinics noprint;
var ht wt;
output out=stats mean=;
run;
```

    Extra Credit: Allow the user to specify the variable list and the statistics that will be printed.

8. The following program uses the macro variable names &INDAT and &OUTDAT in the macros %REGTEST and %DOTESTS. When %REGTEST is called from within %DOTESTS are the values of these variables in %DOTEST changed? This question can be restated as: is a %LOCAL statement required?

```
%macro regtest(indat,outdat);
  proc reg data=&indat;
  model count=distance;
  output out=&outdat r=resid;
  run;
%mend regtest;

%macro dotests(indat,outdat);
  data r1;
  set &indat;
  if station=1;
  run;
  %regtest(r1,r1out);

  data r2;
  set &indat;
  if station=2;
  run;
  %regtest(r2,r2out);

  data &outdat;
  set r1out r2out;
  run;
%mend dotests;

%dotests(biodat,bioreg)
```

9.   In the macro %TRY, shown here, which %PUT statements will be executed?

```
%let a = AAA;
%macro try;
%put &a;
%if  &a    =  AAA %then %put no quotes;
%if '&a'   = 'AAA' %then %put single quotes;
%if 'AAA'  = 'AAA' %then %put exact strings;
%if "&a"   = "AAA" %then %put double quotes;
%if "&a"   = 'AAA' %then %put mixed quotes;
%if "&a"   =  AAA  %then %put quotes on one side only;
%mend;
%try
```

Chapter 6   # Interfacing with the DATA Step

Very often in macro language programs and applications you will want the data itself to drive the definitions of the macro variables and parameters. The data used to create the macro variable definitions may be the same data that is to be analyzed, or you may have some kind of control file that can be used to provide directions to your program. In either case, you need the ability to take information that is stored in a SAS data set or in some other format and convert it into values for macro variables. This chapter covers various aspects of this process.

6.1 Using the SYMPUT Routine

Like the %LET statement the SYMPUT routine can be used to assign a value to a macro variable. However, SYMPUT is used as part of a DATA step and enables you to directly assign values of data set variables to macro variables.

The routine has two arguments, either of which may be a variable or a constant (such as a character string) or a combination of the two. The first argument identifies the name of the macro variable, and the second argument identifies the value to be assigned to it. The routine's general form is

```
CALL SYMPUT(varname,value);
```

It is common for first-time users to try to use a macro variable in the same DATA step in which it is created. However, you **cannot** define a macro variable using SYMPUT and then use that macro variable in the same DATA step. This makes sense when you remember that values are assigned to the macro variable through SYMPUT during DATA step execution. However, any macro variable references are resolved before the compilation phase of the DATA step. During resolution the macro facility would be attempting to resolve a macro variable that would not be defined until the DATA step's execution phase. It is generally considered unfair to ask any language to resolve or use variables that have not yet been defined. This means that macro variables cannot be referenced in the same step that they are created.

6.1.1   First argument of SYMPUT

The first argument of SYMPUT is used to name the macro variable that is to be created or assigned a value. The argument may be either a character string, DATA step variable, or a combination of the two. Each of the following three examples assigns a value to the macro variable &DSN1:

Character String

A character string enclosed in quotes creates a macro variable that uses the name enclosed in the quotes:

```
CALL SYMPUT('DSN1',argument2);
```

Character Variable

When the first argument is a DATA step character variable, its value becomes the macro variable name:

```
macvar = 'DSN1';
CALL SYMPUT(macvar,argument2);
```

Character Variable and String used together

A character expression, which can be made up of any combination of character variables and strings, may be used to determine the macro variable name:

```
n=1;
CALL SYMPUT('DSN'||LEFT(PUT(n,2.)),argument2);
```

In this case 'DSN' will have a '1' appended onto it forming 'DSN1'. Notice that the PUT function converts the numeric variable N to a character string that is left-justified and is appended using the concatenation operator (||).

6.1.2   Second argument of SYMPUT

The second argument contains the value that is assigned to the macro variable named in the first argument. As is the case with the first argument, the second argument can be a character string, variable name, or a combination of the two. In each of the following examples, the macro variable &DSN1 is assigned the value of CLINICS:

Character String

The character string becomes the value assigned to the macro variable:

```
CALL SYMPUT('DSN1','CLINICS');
```

Character Variable

The value of the DATA step variable is assigned to the macro variable:

```
dataset='CLINICS';
CALL SYMPUT('DSN1',dataset);
```

Character Variable and String used together
The resolved value of the character expression is assigned to the macro variable:

```
PARTNAME='CLIN';
CALL SYMPUT('DSN1',TRIM(PARTNAME)||'ICS');
```

The TRIM function removes trailing blanks and is needed if PARTNAME has a length that is greater than the number of nonblank characters. If the length of PARTNAME was $6, and you did not use TRIM, the character expression would become `CLIN   ICS`.

6.1.3   SYMPUT example

The TITLE1 statement in the following example contains a macro variable (&SEX) that is defined in the previous DATA step. &SEX will contain the value of the data set variable SEX. Because the SYMPUT routine is executed for each observation that is processed (each pass of the DATA step), this code will reassign the value of &SEX for each observation that meets the WHERE criteria:

```
data regn1;
set clinics;
where reg='1' and sex='M';
call symput('sex',sex);
run;

proc print data=regn1;
title1 "Region 1 data for &sex";
run;
```

In this example, the TITLE1 statement **cannot** be placed within the DATA step.

Each of the examples in Sections 6.2 and 6.3 also use the SYMPUT routine.

SEE ALSO
Landers (1997) has several examples that highlight various behaviors of SYMPUT under different conditions.

6.2 Using a SAS Data Set

Often a number of macro variables need to be defined in order to control a process or series of programs. Rather than pass the values into macros through the use of parameters, the control information can be stored in SAS data sets. These can then be used to control a macro by creating macro variables using the SYMPUT routine.

Control data sets are most often used when the number of macro variables is large or for cases where the programs are highly generalized and you want to control not only the values of the macro variables but their names as well.

6.2.1 Macro variable values

Using a control data set

Very often the only information that needs to be passed is the value of the macro variable. The following rather simplistic example illustrates the steps that are needed to control a macro. Two macro variables, &DSN and &OBS, are to be assigned values. The values are stored in the data set CONTROL.

```
DATA CONTROL;
     DSNAME='CLINICS';
     NOBS='5';
RUN;
%MACRO LOOK;
     DATA _NULL_;
          SET CONTROL;
          CALL SYMPUT('DSN',DSNAME);
          CALL SYMPUT('OBS',NOBS);
     RUN;
     PROC CONTENTS DATA=&DSN;
     RUN;
     PROC PRINT DATA=&DSN (OBS=&OBS);
     RUN;
%MEND LOOK;
```

The SAS System generates the following code when %LOOK is executed:

```
PROC CONTENTS DATA=CLINICS;
RUN;
PROC PRINT DATA=CLINICS (OBS=5);
RUN;
```

In the above example, the control file contains only the value of the macro variables and not the name of the macro variable. Because each variable in the data set has a distinct value, only one observation is needed.

In the previous example NOBS is defined as a character variable of length 1. Instead, it could have been defined as a numeric variable:

```
DATA CONTROL;
     DSNAME='CLINICS';
     NOBS=5;
RUN;
```

The resolved macro code then becomes

```
PROC CONTENTS DATA=CLINICS;
RUN;
PROC PRINT DATA=CLINICS (OBS=        5);
RUN;
```

Notice the large number of spaces that are inserted before 5. The spaces result from the conversion of the numeric value to a character string in the SYMPUT function. The following example demonstrates a better way to handle this conversion.

Using the analysis data to provide control

Control parameters can often be determined directly from the analysis data, thus reducing the need for a control data set. The following example produces a separate plot for each value of the variable REGION and places the region name in the title. A similar series of plots could have been generated by using the BY statement in PROC GPLOT along with the #BYVAL option. This method, however, allows more flexibility in more complex situations:

```
%MACRO PLOTIT;
   PROC SORT DATA=CLINICS;
     BY REGION;
   RUN;

     * Count the unique regions and create
     * a macro variable for each value.;
   DATA _NULL_;
     SET CLINICS;
     BY REGION;
     IF FIRST.REGION THEN DO;
        * Count the regions;
        I+1;
        * Create char var with count (II).  Allow;
        * up to 99 unique regions;
        II=LEFT(PUT(I,2.));
        * Assign value of region to a mac var;
        CALL SYMPUT('REG'||II,REGION);
        CALL SYMPUT('TOTAL',II);
     END;
   RUN;

 * Do a separate PROC PLOT step for;
 * each unique region;
%DO I=1 %TO &TOTAL;
   PROC PLOT DATA=CLINICS;
      PLOT HT * WT;
      WHERE REGION="&&REG&I";
      TITLE1 "Height/Weight for REGION &&REG&I";
   RUN;
%END;
%MEND PLOTIT;
```

This code will execute PROC PLOT once for each unique value of the variable REGION. The macro variable &TOTAL counts the number of REGIONS and is used to set up a macro %DO loop (see Section 5.3.2). &&REG&I acts as a macro vector that contains the various values of the variable REGION (Section 2.5.3 discusses the resolution of double ampersand macro variables).

Note that the SYMPUT function that assigns the value to &TOTAL is executed for each region. However, only the last assignment really matters. This could have been avoided by moving this statement outside of the DO block. Also, DATA _NULL_ reads the entire data set (CLINICS) when you are really only interested in the unique values of REGION. Both of these inefficiencies are corrected in the following example:

```
%MACRO PLOTIT;
   PROC SORT DATA=CLINICS
                OUT=REGCLN(KEEP=REGION)
                NODUPKEY;
     BY REGION;
   RUN;
   DATA _NULL_;
     SET REGCLN END=EOF;
     * Count the regions;
     I+1;
```

```
        * Create char var with count (II);
        II=LEFT(PUT(I,2.));
        CALL SYMPUT('REG'||II,REGION);
        IF EOF THEN CALL SYMPUT('TOTAL',II);
    RUN;
%DO I=1 %TO &TOTAL;
    PROC PLOT DATA=CLINICS;
        PLOT HT * WT;
        WHERE REGION="&&REG&I";
        TITLE1 "Height/Weight for REGION &&REG&I";
    RUN;
%END;
%MEND PLOTIT;
```

The following example creates a separate ASCII file for each combination of the variables STA-TION and DEPTH in the data set A1. STATION takes on the values of TS3, TS6, and so on, while DEPTH is measured in whole meters (0, 1, 2, and so on). The objective for the macro DOIT is to break up the data set into a series of flat files. By using this macro you will not need to know what combinations of STATION and DEPTH will exist in the data prior to running the macro.

```
%macro doit;

* Create the macro variables.
* One set for each STATION X DEPTH;
data _null_;
set a1;
by station depth;
length ii $1 dd $2 fn $14;
if first.depth then do;
    i+1;  ❶
    ii = left(put(i,2.));
    * Create a character value of the numeric depth;
    dd = trim(left(put(depth,3.)));
    * Construct the filename;
    fn = compress(station || dd || '.dat');  ❷
    call symput('i',ii);  ❸
    call symput('d'||ii,dd);  ❹
    call symput('sta'||ii,station);  ❺
    call symput('fn'||ii,fn);  ❻
end;
run;

* There will be &i files;
%do j=1 %to &i;
    filename toascii "&&fn&j";  ❼
   * print the ascii files;
    data _null_;
    set a1;
    where station="&&sta&j" and depth=&&d&j;  ❽
    cnt + 1;
    file toascii;
    if cnt=1 then put '**********  ' "&&fn&j";
    put @1 date mmddyy8. @10 aveday;  ❾
    run;
%end;
%mend doit;

%doit
```

❶ Count the unique combinations of STATION and DEPTH.

❷ Build the string variable that contains the name of the new ASCII file.

❸ &I contains the number of unique combinations.

❹ &&D&i contains the *i*th depth, which was converted from a numeric value.

❺ &&STA&i contains the *i*th station.

❻ &&FN&i contains the *i*th ASCII file name.

❼ Build the FILEREF which depends on &J.

❽ In order to subset the data, use the WHERE statement to select observations based on specified values of STATION and DEPTH.

❾ Write the selected data to the ASCII file.

The DATA step that writes the ASCII files is executed &I times. This means that the data set A1 must also be read &I times. A potentially substantial improvement in efficiency could be achieved by recoding the macro to read A1 only once in the final step. Questions 2 and 3 in this chapter's exercises address this issue.

The following table illustrates how the macro variables will be resolved for the first four combinations of STATION and DEPTH in the data set A1:

STATION	DEPTH	&J	&&STA&J	&&D&J	&&FN&J
TS3	0	1	&STA1	&D1	&FN1
			TS3	0	TS30.DAT
TS3	1	2	&STA2	&D2	&FN2
			TS3	1	TS31.DAT
TS3	2	3	&STA3	&D3	&FN3
			TS3	2	TS32.DAT
TS6	0	4	&STA4	&D4	&FN4
			TS6	0	TS60.DAT

The double-ampersand macro variables form the macro equivalent of an array or vector of values. The macro language does not have an ARRAY statement, but the &&VAR&I combination works in much the same way. In the previous table, the &&FN&I combination can be viewed as a vector, as is shown here:

&J (subscript)	&&FN&J (array element)	element value
1	&FN1	TS30.DAT
2	&FN2	TS31.DAT
3	&FN3	TS32.DAT
4	&FN4	TS60.DAT

This table shows that for &J = 3, the macro variable &&FN&J resolves to &FN3, which further resolves to TS32.DAT.

SEE ALSO

Carpenter (1988) contains two similar macros that you can use to split up data into operational subsets for further processing.

6.2.2   Assigning macro variable names as well as values

The control data set can be used to assign the name of the macro variable as well as its value. In this example, the DATA step variable MVARNAME is the name of the macro variable, and VALUE is its intended value. Each observation in CONTROL (there are two) will be used to define one macro variable. Notice that only one SYMPUT is used, and there is no hard coding of macro variable names in the DATA _NULL_ step.

```
DATA CONTROL;
      MVARNAME='DSN';
      VALUE='CLINICS';
      OUTPUT;
      MVARNAME='OBS';
      VALUE='5';
      OUTPUT;
RUN;
%MACRO LOOK;
      DATA _NULL_;
           SET CONTROL;
           CALL SYMPUT(MVARNAME,VALUE);
      RUN;
      PROC CONTENTS DATA=&DSN;
      RUN;
      PROC PRINT DATA=&DSN (OBS=&OBS);
      RUN;
%MEND LOOK;
```

The SAS System generates the following code when %LOOK is executed:

```
PROC CONTENTS DATA=CLINICS;
RUN;
PROC PRINT DATA=CLINICS (OBS=5);
RUN;
```

Notice that neither argument in the SYMPUT statement is a quoted string. Both are data set variables, and their values provide the appropriate information (macro variable name and macro variable value).

In the next example, the data set RELATION contains information on the members of a family (&FAMCODE). The two variables RELATION and NAME provide information on the relationships and names of the members. This data is then used to construct a filter that uses macros to subset a second data set (REUNION) that only contains names but not the family code.

```
data relation;
family = 'MC24';
relation='mom'; name='Sally'; output;
relation='dad'; name='Fred'; output;
relation='son'; name='Clint'; output;
family = 'MC33';
```

```
relation='mom'; name='Jane'; output;
relation='dad'; name='John'; output;
relation='son'; name='Jack'; output;
run;

%macro listfam(famcode);
data _null_;
set relation;
where family="&famcode";
* Create one macro var for each observation.
* Use RELATION to name the macro var and NAME for its value;
call symput(relation,name);
run;

proc print data=reunion(where=(mother="&mom" &
father="&dad"));
run;
%mend listfam;
%listfam(MC24)
```

The PROC PRINT will print all observations in REUNION where the variable MOTHER ='Sally' and FATHER='Fred'.

6.3 Using a Flat File

You can use a flat file or raw data set to define macro variables in a similar manner to that used with SAS data sets. This means that SAS code can be created dynamically using macros by basing macro variable definitions on a control file that may not yet exist when the macro is first written. The following is a portion of PAGES.TXT, a list of what will be parts of data set names:

```
012_015
016_017
018_
```

The actual data set names are preceded with the letter 'P':

```
p012_015
p016_017
p018_
```

These values (without the preceding 'P') are loaded into a series of macro variables, for example &DSN1, &DSN2, and so on:

```
* Load the names of the
* data sets;
data _null_;
length ii $2;
infile 'pages.txt'
       missover;
input @1 dsn $8.;
I+1;
ii = left(put(i,2.));
call symput('n',ii);
call symput('dsn'||ii,left(dsn));
run;
```

This DATA _NULL_ creates &DSN1, &DSN2, and so on to hold the names of the data sets that are read from the raw data in PAGES.TXT. There will be &N of these data set names, and you can use this list of names in a variety of ways.

The following DATA step will read all of the data sets listed in the control file and append them into a single data set (ALL):

```
%macro doit;
DATA ALL; SET
%DO I = 1 %TO &N;
  DEDATA.P&&DSN&I
%END;
;
%mend doit;
```

Using the data set names from PAGES.TXT, the code resolves to

```
DATA ALL; SET
  DEDATA.P012_015
  DEDATA.P016_017
  DEDATA.P018
  ;
```

This process is known as the *dynamic creation of code* and is discussed more in the next section.

SEE ALSO
Yao (1997) discusses a macro that derives control values from a flat file.

6.4 && Macro Variables and Dynamic Coding

Typically the macro variables created in applications such as in the previous examples will be addressed in the form of &&VAR&I, where VAR is the root portion of the variable name and the index number is an integer counter. This type of macro variable has many uses but is especially useful when you need to create code dynamically. You are creating dynamic code when some of the program statements themselves are not completely defined when you write the program.

The examples in this section build on the list of data sets described in Section 6.3.

SEE ALSO
Fehd (1997a,b,c) and Blood (1992) include macros and discussions on the use of macro arrays in dynamic coding situations.

6.4.1   Defining complete steps dynamically

When you use macro variables of the form &&VAR&I, a macro %DO loop is often used to process each of the macro variables. The following code executes PROC FSEDIT for each data set that is listed in the text file in the previous example (see Section 6.3). Notice that the loop counts from 1 to &N, the total number of entries. This means that if the list changes, all you have to modify is the list itself. Because a %DO statement can only exist inside of a macro, the following section of code must have been taken from within a macro that is not shown:

```
%do q = 1 %to &n;
 PROC FSEDIT DATA=dedata.p&&dsn&q  mod
  SCREEN=GLSCN.descn.p&&dsn&q...SCREEN;
 RUN;
%end;
```

Notice that three periods are required in the SCREEN= option because two passes are needed to resolve the &&DSN&Q. The first pass uses the first period as a delimiter character for the &Q (see Section 2.5.2); the second is used with &DSN2 (when &Q=2). This leaves one, which is needed as part of the SCREEN name. For &Q=2 this code resolves to

```
PROC FSEDIT DATA=dedata.p016_017 mod
 SCREEN=GLSCN.descn.p016_017.SCREEN;
RUN;
```

6.4.2 Dynamically building SAS statements

Often code must be written to be flexible in regard to what data sets or even how many data sets will be used. You can use macro variables can be used to construct code that is independent of this knowledge prior to execution. The example in Section 6.3 constructs a SET statement using macro variables, and the code is independent of the number of data sets that are to be read. This is an example of dynamic coding.

The example in this section uses a list to identify a group of data sets that will be processed sequentially with a BY statement in each DATA step. This is fairly easy, unless the BY variables differ for each data set. Then we need a way to associate the appropriate BY variables with the data set that is being processed.

The macro %KEYFLD creates the globalized macro variable &KEYFLD, which contains the list of key variables for a data set whose name ❶ is passed into %KEYFLD as &PGGRP. The globalized macro variable &KEYFLD ❷ is loaded with the appropriate BY variables by using a %LET statement.

```
%global keyfld;
%macro keyfld(pggrp); ❶
 %if &pggrp = 012_015 %then %let keyfld = subject dgtyp; ❷
 %else %if &pggrp = 016_017 %then %let keyfld = subject sess occl;
 %else %if &pggrp = 018 %then %let keyfld = subject aepga_;
%mend keyfld;
```

The call for this macro will be from within an iterative %DO loop that is written to process each data set (&&DSN&I) in the list:

```
%KEYFLD(&&DSN&I)
```

The macro variable &KEYFLD will then contain the list of key BY variables for the selected data set. You can then use this list or dissect it as needed.

In the following DATA _NULL_ step, the number of variables in &KEYFLD are counted (&KEYCNT) and stored individually in macro variables (&KEY1, &KEY2, and so on). This code assumes that each data set has no more than six key variables:

```
%macro chkdup;
%do i=1 %to &n; ❶
   ... code not shown ...

   *determine the list of key vars;
   %keyfld(&&dsn&i) ❷
   data _null_;
   * count the number of keyvars
   * save each for later;
   str="&keyfld"; ❸
   do i = 1 to 6; ❹
      key = scan(str,i,' ');
      if key ne ' ' then do;
         ii=left(put(i,1.));
         call symput('key'||ii,trim(left(key))); ❺
         call symput('keycnt',ii); ❻
      end;
   end;
   run;
... macro continued ...
```

❶ The %DO loop steps through each of the &N data sets of interest.

❷ %KEYFLD loads the list of BY variables into &KEYFLD.

❸ Create a character variable that contains the list of BY variables.

❹ Step through the list of BY variables. You can use a maximum of six variables in this macro.

❺ Use the *i*th BY variable and place it in &KEY$_i$ using SYMPUT.

❻ Save the number of BY variables in the list.

After the previous section of %CHKDUP executes, the macro variable &KEY2 will contain the name of the second variable in the list of BY variables, and &KEYCNT will store the number of BY variables for this data set. These key fields are used in the following DATA step to check for duplicate observations in the selected data set:

```
... macro continued ...

* Make sure that there are no
* duplicate keys;
%let dupp = 0;
data dupp; set dedata.p&&dsn&i;
by &keyfld;
* determine if this is a dup obs;
if not (first.&&key&keycnt and last.&&key&keycnt);❼
call symput('dupp','1'); ❽
run;

   ... code not shown ...
%end;
%mend chkdup;
```

❼ Of the variables in the BY list, the right-most variable is used in FIRST. and LAST. processing, so it will be identified by using &&KEY&KEYCNT.

❽ The number 1 is assigned to &DUPP if a duplicate observation is found.

The previous code will locate duplicate observations in the key fields using the FIRST. and LAST. options. The programmer who wrote the code had no idea what the variables in the BY statement would be, let alone what the last variable in the list would be. In the previous example for &PGGRP = 016_017, the string FIRST.&&KEY&KEYCNT resolves to FIRST.OCC1. Because there are three variables in the BY statement, &KEYCNT is 3, and &KEY3 is OCC1.

SEE ALSO
The DATA _NULL_ step that is used to work with &KEYFLD in this section is not as efficient as it could be. Roberts (1997) and examples in Sections 7.2.3 and 11.4.1 both use the %SCAN macro function to achieve similar results without using the DATA step.

6.5 Moving Text from Macro to DATA Step Variables

You can use several methods to convert information that is stored in macro variables to values that are stored in DATA step variables. Because you will assign a value to a variable on the Program Data Vector, the easiest and most common way is through the use of the assignment statement. In other situations, you may need to use either the SYMGET or RESOLVE functions.

6.5.1 Assignment statement

You can use the DATA step assignment statement to create a DATA step variable or to assign a value to an existing variable. In the following example, the macro variable &DSN is created and assigned the value clinics. Later in the program, &DSN is used to define the character variable DSET in the data set SUBWT.

```
%let dsn = clinics;

.......

data subwt;
set clinics (keep=fname wt);
dset = "&dsn";
run;
```

Because the macro variable is resolved before the DATA step is compiled, DSET will be a constant (with a value of clinics).

The RETAIN statement could have been used to make this step somewhat more efficient. The previous DATA step becomes

```
data subwt;
set clinics (keep=fname wt);
retain dset "&dsn";
run;
```

The assignment statement is the simplest method and usually will be your primary method for creating and assigning DATA step variables. The next most likely method is covered in the next section.

6.5.2   Using the SYMGET function

The SYMGET function is not a macro function. Like the SYMPUT routine, it is used in the DATA step and converts the current value of a macro variable to a character string so that it can be placed into a DATA step variable. This function is the functional opposite of the SYMPUT routine.

The argument is either a macro variable name, a DATA step variable that takes on a value that is a macro variable name, or a character expression that constructs a macro variable name. The general form is

```
variable = SYMGET(ARGUMENT);
```

When using the SYMGET function remember that

- it is used within a DATA step

- the default length for a returned character string is 200

- the *ARGUMENT* is enclosed in quotes to directly specify a macro variable

- if the *ARGUMENT* is written without quotes, it is assumed to be a DATA step

- if the *ARGUMENT* is written without quotes, it is assumed to be a DATA step variable name or an expression that constructs a macro variable name.

Using an assignment statement as opposed to the SYMGET function will have similar but not necessarily exactly the same results. In the following example, the variables DATASET and DSET will have the same value but not the same LENGTH. DATASET will have a length of 200, while DSET will have a length of 7.

```
%let dsn = clinics;

data subwt;
set &dsn(keep=fname wt);
dataset=symget('dsn');
dset = "&dsn";
run;
```

In most cases you will not need to use the SYMGET function because it is easier simply to assign a value, as was done for DSET in the previous example.

SYMGET is most often used when the macro variable is not to be resolved at compile time. If you are going to compile the DATA step or if you are using Screen Control Language (SCL), then SYMGET becomes more helpful.

In the following example, the data set WEIGHTS has a variable CODE that identifies a correction factor that is to be applied to the variable WT. The variable CODE can take on the values of 1, 2, or 3, and the three correction factors have already been loaded into three corresponding macro variables: &CORR1, &CORR2, and &CORR3. One way to apply the correction factors would be to use a series of IF statements:

```
data corrwt;
set weights;
if code=1 then wt = wt*&corr1;
else if code=2 then wt = wt*&corr2;
else if code=3 then wt = wt*&corr3;
run;
```

You can improve performance by eliminating the IF-THEN/ELSE processing and, instead, do a table look-up. The DATA step becomes

```
data corrwt;
set weights;
wt = wt*symget('corr'||left(put(code,2.)));
run;
```

The SYMGET function always returns a character string. In the previous example, this character string must be converted to numeric before the arithmetic operation of multiplication can be performed. This results in the following message in the LOG:

```
NOTE: Character values have been converted to numeric values at the
places given by:
      (Line):(Column).
      10:9
```

The SYMGET function is especially useful in Screen Control Language programs that are compiled. In compiled programs macro variables are not usually referred to using an ampersand. Chapter 8, "Using Macro References with Screen Control Language (SCL)," discusses various issues associated with macros and macro references in SCL.

6.5.3 Using the RESOLVE function

Your third choice for assigning values is the RESOLVE function. This function was new in Release 6.07 and is very similar to the SYMGET function. Although the RESOLVE function tends to use more resources than SYMGET, it will accept a wider variety of arguments. RESOLVE will attempt to resolve some arguments that SYMGET will not attempt.

The arguments for RESOLVE are **not** interchangeable with those of SYMGET. The three types of arguments that RESOLVE will act on are DATA step variables or quoted strings that contain macro variable references. Quoted strings without macro references are passed through. Data step variables are resolved to the value they hold on the Program Data Vector while macro variables are resolved to their symbolic value. Generally, when using RESOLVE with macro variables, the argument will have an & or a % either directly or indirectly.

The following excerpt from the LOG demonstrates some of the differences for these two functions:

```
159       %let dsn = clinics;
160       %let clinics = Bethesda;
161
162       data demo;
163       dname = 'clinics';
164       a1 = symget(dname);
165       a2 = resolve(dname);
166       put / a1= a2=;
167
168       b1 = symget('dsn');
169       b2 = resolve('dsn');
170       put / b1= b2=;
171
172       c1 = symget('&dsn');
173       c2 = resolve('&dsn');
174       put / c1= c2=;
175
176       d1 = symget("&dsn");
177       d2 = resolve("&dsn");
178       put / d1= d2=;
179
180       e1 = resolve('&&&dsn');
181       put / e1= ;
182       run;


A1=Bethesda A2=clinics

B1=clinics B2=dsn
NOTE: Invalid argument to function SYMGET at line 172
column 9.

C1=  C2=clinics

D1=Bethesda D2=clinics

E1=Bethesda
```

A1/A2   The DATA step variable DNAME is used as the argument. Its value is `clinics`, which happens also to be the name of a macro variable. SYMGET assumes that the unquoted string will be a variable name that will point to a macro variable. Thus, DNAME points to &CLINICS, which resolves to `Bethesda`. When the argument of RESOLVE is a DATA step variable, as in this case, the function will return its value on the Program Data Vector, that is, DNAME is `clinics`.

B1/B2   SYMGET assumes that the quoted string is a macro variable name and resolves its value. That is, 'dsn' points to &DSN, which resolves to `clinics`. RESOLVE does not assume that the quoted string is a macro variable, but it anticipates that a macro reference will include a & or %. Because the string 'dsn' does not contain &, it is not resolved further.

C1/C2   SYMGET does not rescan quoted strings and the & is not resolved. This results in the NOTE, and the variable C1 is set to missing. RESOLVE does rescan the string and &DSN is resolved to `clinics`.

D1/D2 Because double quotes are used, SYMGET sees "&DSN" as the resolved quoted string `"clinics"` (as in B1), which is a valid macro variable that resolves further to `Bethesda`. RESOLVE behaves the same as it did for the single quotes in C2.

E1 RESOLVE will continue to rescan the string as long as ampersands are present. In this case, &&&DSN —> &CLINICS —> `Bethesda`.

SEE ALSO

SAS® Technical Report P-222, *Changes and Enhancements to Base SAS® Software, Release 6.07* provides the earliest written documentation for the RESOLVE function (pp. 313–315).

SAS® Macro Language Reference, First Edition documents RESOLVE (pp. 210–212).

6.6 Chapter Summary

Control of a macro can be achieved by reading a file (external or SAS System data set) that contains the values intended for the macro variables and perhaps even the names of the variables as well.

Through the use of macro variables that are defined in a control file, it is possible to dynamically create SAS code that is based on the data itself.

The **SYMPUT** routine is used to assign a DATA step value to a macro variable. The routine has two arguments, either of which may be a variable, a constant (such as a character string), or a combination of the two. The first argument identifies the variable and the second identifies the value to be assigned.

General form: CALL SYMPUT(*argument1,argument2*);

Values are assigned during DATA step execution. However, macro variables are resolved during the compilation phase of the DATA step. Macro variables cannot be referenced in the same step in which they are created.

You can also create data set variables from macro variables. Usually this is done through an assignment statement, but at times you also may wish to use the SYMGET and RESOLVE functions.

6.7 Chapter Exercises

1. In the example that uses macro %PLOTIT in Section 6.2.1, the variable REGION is a character variable. What changes to macro %PLOTIT would be required if REGION were numeric?

2. The macro %PLOTIT in Section 6.2.1 uses a WHERE statement to subset CLINICS when plotting. Rewrite the macro so that one data set is created for each region and then use PROC PLOT on each individual data set (eliminate the use of the WHERE statement).

    The most efficient program will read CLINICS once, creating ten data sets.

    Hint: Write the program without macros first.

    ```
    data reg1 reg2.....;
    set clinics;
    if region='1' then output reg1;
    else if region='2' then output reg2;
    else if......
    ...
    run;
    ```

3. Modify the code from Question 2 so that the data set names reflect the value of the variable REGION in that data set. Is PROC SORT still needed?

4. EXTRA CREDIT
    The SAS data set CLASS.BIOMASS has both numeric and character variables. Create a macro that will convert all the numeric variables to character. If a variable is associated with a format (for example, DATE7.), use it in the conversion.

    All character variables should be passed through to the new data set and the variable names in the new data set should be the same as in the old data set.

    Create a macro that is general enough to operate on any SAS data set.

    HINT1:   The following code will convert the variable AA from numeric to character.

    ```
    data t2 (drop=__aa);
    length aa $8;
    set t1(rename=(aa=__aa));
    aa = left(put(__aa,best9.));
    run;
    ```

    HINT2:   The following code will create the data set CONT, which contains the names (NAME) and type (TYPE {numeric=1 and character=2}) of the variables in T1.

    ```
    proc contents data=t1 out=cont noprint;
    run;
    ```

Chapter 7 # Using Macro Functions

7.1 Quoting Functions

7.2 Character Functions

7.3 Evaluation Functions

7.4 Using DATA Step Functions and Routines

7.5 Chapter Summary

7.6 Chapter Exercises

Macro functions are similar to DATA step functions except that they operate on text strings and macro variables rather than character strings and data set variables.

Macro functions either change or provide information about the strings that are the arguments. Following are the three general categories of macro functions:

- quoting functions   mask or remove meaning from special characters.

- character functions   return information about text strings.

- evaluation functions   perform arithmetic operations.

The following sections cover these types of macro functions in more detail.

SEE ALSO
Once you become familiar with the macro language, it is fairly easy to write macros that behave like macro functions (Whitaker, 1989), and several of the SAS System autocall macros also behave like macro functions. See Chapter 12, "SAS System Autocall Macros," in this book and *SAS® Macro Language: Reference, First Edition* (p. 159).

7.1 Quoting Functions

Quoting functions enable you to pass macro arguments while you selectively remove the special meaning from characters such as ampersands, percent signs, semicolons, and quotes (& % ; ' "). Most of these functions are **not** commonly used and are even less commonly understood. Although they are powerful and can even be necessary, usually programming solutions are available that do not require the use of quoting functions (see Section 7.1.9).

Quoting functions operate by adding what is essentially invisible characters before and after the string that is to be quoted. Once they are added, these characters remain until they are stripped off by the macro processor (by the %UNQUOTE function or by passing the text to the SAS System for processing).

The two issues that make quoting functions more difficult to understand have to do with functions that

- either do or do not rescan the text for % and & references

- are executed at statement compilation or at statement execution.

Rescan and NoRescan

Of special interest in the text strings to be quoted are those that contain the special macro symbols % and &. Normally, these symbols indicate references to macro calls and macro variables that must be resolved prior to the execution of the function. These references are resolved by rescanning the text as many times as it takes to resolve the usage of the % and &. Sometimes you do not want these references resolved. Instead, you want to pass the macro call or macro variable without resolution. To do this you need a function designated as a NoRescan (NR) function. Many of the quoting functions come in pairs (the name either does or does not start with the letters NR, for example, %STR and %NRSTR. The two functions perform essentially the same operation except that the function that begins with the letters NR will also remove the meaning from the % and &. When you hear that *the meaning is removed*, it means that the macro processor will not *see* the % and & as the special characters that it normally does.

Compilation/Execution

Because macro statements are compiled and then executed, you may need to control when the text string is to be quoted. Some quoting functions remove the meaning during compilation while others remove it during macro execution. When the meaning is removed during compilation (%STR and %NRSTR), the resultant text is passed to the processor but not the function call. The other quoting functions are resolved during the execution of the macro. For these functions, the entire call to the function and its text is passed to the macro processor where it is resolved.

This will rarely be an issue for most programmers. Usually you only need to worry if text that is resolved during execution becomes syntactically incorrect or misinterpreted. Consider the following short example:

```
%let type = or;
%if &type ne xx %then %do;
```

The macro variable &TYPE is resolved during the evaluation of the expression, which results in

```
%if or ne xx %then %do;
```

The OR is seen as the logical mnemonic operator, and an error message is produced. If &TYPE is quoted during execution, the resolved OR will be treated as text, and there will not be a problem with the syntax:

```
%let type = or;
%if %quote(&type) ne xx %then %do;
```

SEE ALSO

You can find other examples that contrast compilation versus execution time quoting functions in Chapter 10, "Macro Quoting," (pp. 229–230) in *SAS® Guide to Macro Processing, Version 6, Second Edition* and in Chapter 7, "Macro Quoting," (pp. 76-78) in *SAS® Macro Language: Reference, First Edition.*

Summary
The following list of quoting functions gives a brief overview of the functions and their behavior:

%BQUOTE

removes meaning from unanticipated special characters (except & and %) during execution.

%NRBQUOTE

removes meaning from unanticipated special characters (including & and %) during execution.

%QUOTE

removes meaning from a string (except % and &) during execution.

%NRQUOTE

removes meaning from %, &, special characters, and mnemonics during execution.

%STR

removes meaning from special characters (except % and &) at compilation.

%NRSTR

removes meaning from special characters (including % and &) at compilation.

%SUPERQ

prevents any resolution of the value of a macro variable.

%UNQUOTE

undoes quoting.

It is not necessary to have a complete understanding of each of these functions but rather a general understanding of what they do. You will use some of these functions much more often than others. It has been this author's experience that the %STR function is the most useful and the others are rarely, if ever, used.

SEE ALSO
Bercov (1993) contains a easy-to-read summary of macro quoting.

Chapter 7, "Macro Quoting," (pp. 75–93) in *SAS® Macro Language: Reference, First Edition* provides detailed explanations of macro quoting.

7.1.1   Simple quoting function examples

This section shows simple examples of the quoting functions. Although several of the functions have similar results for these examples, do not interpret this as an indication that the functions always behave in the same ways.

For the following examples, define the macro variable &DSN as

```
%LET DSN=CLINICS;
```

None

Example: `%LET P=PROC PRINT DATA=&DSN; RUN;`
&P: `PROC PRINT DATA=CLINICS`
Results in a syntax error for the missing semicolon.

%STR

Example: `%LET P=%STR(PROC PRINT DATA=&DSN; RUN;);`
&P: `PROC PRINT DATA=CLINICS; RUN;`
Executes the PROC PRINT correctly.

%NRSTR

Example: `%LET P=%NRSTR(PROC PRINT DATA=&DSN; RUN;);`

&P: `PROC PRINT DATA=&DSN; RUN;`

&DSN is not resolved even when the statement is executed. This results in an unknown data set (DSN) and an improper symbol (&).

%UNQUOTE

Example: `%LET P=%NRSTR(PROC PRINT DATA=&DSN; RUN;);`

%UNQUOTE(&P): `PROC PRINT DATA=CLINICS; RUN;`

The macro variable &DSN is resolved and the PROC PRINT executes correctly.

7.1.2 %STR

This is the most commonly used quoting function. It removes meaning from special characters (except % and &) at compilation and is most commonly used to remove meaning from commas, semicolons, parentheses, and mismatched quotes.

The following macro, %EXIST, is based on a macro of the same name in *SAS® Guide to Macro Processing* (pp. 265–266). It creates the globalized macro variable &EXIST that takes on the values of YES or NO, depending on whether or not the stated data set (&DSN) exists. You can then query &EXIST to determine how subsequent steps should be executed.

❶The DATA _NULL_ step is written so an attempt is made to open &DSN.

❷ The DATA step never tries to read any data because the logical expression in the IF statement will always be false.

❸ If &DSN does not exist, the DATA step terminates in an error that is saved in the automatic system macro variable &SYSERR.

The %STR function is used because multiple statements (with semicolons) are needed in the DATA _NULL_ step.

```
%macro exist(dsn);
%global exist;
%if &dsn ne %then %str(
   data _null_; ❶
   if 0 then set &dsn; ❷
   stop;
   run;
);
%if &syserr=0 %then %let exist=yes; ❸
%else %do;
   %let exist=no;
   %put PREVIOUS ERROR USED TO CHECK FOR PRESENCE ;
   %put OF DATASET & IS NOT A PROBLEM;
%end;
%mend exist;
```

%EXIST is called in the following code, which checks for the existence of the data set VARLISTS in the library &PAC.DATA ❹. If it exists, it is subset with a WHERE ❺ and appended to another data set, VARSAVER ❻.

```
%macro dotask;
... code not shown ...

* Check to see if the varlists data set already exists
* (&exist=yes);
%exist(&pac.data.varlists) ❹
```

```
* Add this list of variables to the overall &PAC list;
* If the VARLISTS data set exists use it, otherwise
* create it from VARSAVER;
data &pac.data.varlists;
set

  %if &exist=yes %then
    &pac.data.varlists(where=(tbl ne "&tbl")❺);
      varsaver; ❻
  run;

... code not shown ...
%mend dotask;
```

In the macro %EXIST, the %IF statement that utilizes the %STR function could have been rewritten using the %DO statement rather than the quoting function:

```
%if &dsn ne %then %do;
    data _null_;
    * No observations are actually read;
    if 0 then set &dsn;
    stop;
    run;
%end;
```

Summary

■ STR stands for *string*.

■ The %STR function removes meaning from special characters during compilation.

■ This function does not remove meaning from the percent sign (%) or the ampersand (&).

7.1.3 %NRSTR

The %NRSTR function behaves in the same way as %STR except that meaning is also removed from the % and the &.

In the following example, the macro variable &CITY is not resolved in the %PUT because the special meaning has been removed from the &:

```
%LET CITY = MIAMI;
%PUT %NRSTR(&CITY) IS ON THE WATER.;
```

The LOG would show

```
&CITY IS ON THE WATER.
```

Summary

■ NRSTR stands for *no rescan string*.

■ The %NRSTR function removes meaning from special characters including the percent sign (%) and ampersand sign (&) during compilation.

7.1.4   %QUOTE

This function is very similar to %STR except that the meaning for special characters is removed during the execution of the macro statement.

The following macro creates a DROP statement that you can then insert into a DATA step. You must use the %QUOTE function in case the user passes a string into the macro that would result in an invalid comparison. This might include multiple items, an item that could be confused with a logical operator (AND, OR), or even a variable list that is seen as an arithmetic operation (X1–X4). Use the %STR function to mask the meaning of the semicolon in the DROP statement:

```
%MACRO DROP(DROPLIST);
     %IF %QUOTE(&DROPLIST) NE %THEN
          %STR(DROP &DROPLIST;);
%MEND DROP;
```

You could write the call to %DROP as

```
%DROP(X1-X3 LASTNAME FRSTNAME SSN)
```

This call would generate the following code:

```
DROP X1-X3 LASTNAME FRSTNAME SSN;
```

Without the %QUOTE in macro %DROP, &DROPLIST would be resolved before the %IF expression was evaluated. If the resulting string contains any of the special symbols, the expression could become invalid. The following %DROP will **not** work correctly because the second element in the list has special meaning in the expression. The resulting %IF expression will not be syntactically correct.

```
%MACRO DROP(DROPLIST);
     %IF &DROPLIST NE %THEN
          %STR(DROP &DROPLIST;);
%MEND DROP;

%DROP(BB OR)
```

The resulting %IF becomes

```
%IF BB OR NE %THEN
```

which contains two adjacent logic operators (OR and NE).

The %NRQUOTE function is like %QUOTE except that it also removes the meaning from the % and & during macro execution.

Summary

- The %QUOTE function removes meaning from these special characters and mnemonic operators in a macro variable value during macro execution:

  ```
  ;  ,  +  -  *  /  **  <  >  |  ^  =  blanks
  LT LE NE GT EQ AND OR
  ```

- %QUOTE does not remove meaning from the percent sign (%) or the ampersand (&).

- An argument can be any text string.

- Mismatched quotes and parentheses **do** need to be marked (see Section 7.1.9).

7.1.5   %BQUOTE

Also called the *blind quote*, this function is generally used to remove meaning from unanticipated characters during macro execution. It is especially useful if the text string was entered by a user through an application, and you may not have been able to trap all possible characters that might cause the macro to fail.

Assume that the macro variable &METHOD has been assigned this value:

THE DOCTOR'S NEW THERAPY

It is very likely that when &METHOD is resolved the SAS System would produce an error because there is an unmatched single quote ('). This is demonstrated in the following %LET statement. When it is executed the mismatched quote will mask the semicolon and will almost certainly create syntax problems.

```
%let method2 = &method;
```

becomes

```
%let method2 = THE DOCTOR'S NEW THERAPY;
```

To get around this problem, you could use %BQUOTE as follows:

```
%let method2=%BQUOTE(&method);
```

The special meaning will be removed from the single quote when it is resolved, and it will, therefore, not cause syntax problems.

The %NRBQUOTE function is similar to %BQUOTE except that the meaning is also removed from % and & after resolution.

Summary
- The %BQUOTE function takes its name from *blind quote*.

- This function removes meaning from special characters during macro execution, including mnemonic operators such as AND or OR.

- mismatched quotes and parentheses do not need to be marked (see Section 7.1.9).

7.1.6   %UNQUOTE

Once a quoting function has been applied, its effects remain associated with the text, even in subsequent usages. If you need to remove or change the effects of any of the other quoting functions, use the %UNQUOTE function.

Three macro variables are defined below:

❶ &OTH is defined using the %NRSTR function.

❷ &UNQ will contain the same value as &OTH. However, the %UNQUOTE is used to counter the effects of the %NRSTR function.

❸ Because of the use of %NRSTR, &CITY cannot be resolved when &OTH is resolved. However, when the %UNQUOTE function is applied to &OTH its value (&CITY) is seen as a macro variable that is also resolved.

```
%let city = miami;
%let oth = %nrstr(&city); ❶
%let unq = %unquote(&oth); ❷

%put &city &oth &unq;
```

The LOG shows

```
miami &city miami ❸
```

Although &OTH looks like any other macro variable in the %PUT statement, it will not be treated as such because it is quoted. This can cause programming problems if the programmer does not know that a macro reference or special character has been quoted.

Summary

■ The %UNQUOTE function undoes (turns off) the effect of the %BQUOTE, %NRBQUOTE, %NRQUOTE, %NRSTR, %QUOTE, and %STR functions.

■ The change affected by this function occurs during macro execution.

■ An argument can be any character string.

SEE ALSO

Carpenter (1998b) includes an example of quoted strings that can become problematic.

7.1.7   %SUPERQ

The %SUPERQ function operates only on the values of macro variables. It masks all items that may require quoting at macro execution. The argument to the function is the name of a macro variable (without the ampersand) or text that resolves to the name of a macro variable.

%SUPERQ provides the ultimate in quoting protection and is often used with macro variables that may contain text that is supplied by the user, such as through the use of %INPUT and &SYS-BUFFER. Several of the examples shown in *SAS® Macro Language: Reference, First Edition* (pp. 85–88) refer to the use of %INPUT and &SYSBUFFR, which are not widely used and are not covered in this book.

In the following example, the macro variable &HASCALL contains a call to the macro %DOIT. When the first %PUT ❶ executes and attempts to write the value of &HASCALL to the LOG, the macro %DOIT will be executed. You can prevent this by using the %SUPERQ function. ❷

```
data _null_;
call symput('hascall','Call macro %doit');
run;

%put &hascall; ❶
%put %superq(hascall); ❷
```

Notice that when you use the %SUPERQ function, the macro variable name is stated without the ampersand.

Summary

- ■ The %SUPERQ function is particularly useful for masking the value of macro variables that may be generated through the use of the %INPUT and %WINDOW statements.

- ■ %SUPERQ removes meaning during macro execution from special characters such as & and %, and from mnemonic operators such as AND or OR.

- ■ The argument is either a macro variable name without the ampersand or text that resolves to a macro variable name.

7.1.8   Quoting function summary

Items that may need quoting can be placed into one of three groups:

- ■ A   symbols such as + - * / < > = ^ ; , | and comparison operators such as AND, OR, NOT, EQ, NE, LE, LT, GE, GT

- ■ B   macro symbols such as & %

- ■ C   unmatched and unmarked symbols normally expected in pairs such as ' " ( ) (See Section 7.1.9 for a discussion of the marking of symbols.)

The quoting functions deal with these groups differently:

Function	Groups Affected	Works at
%STR	A	macro compilation
%NRSTR	A, B	
%QUOTE	A	macro execution
%NRQUOTE	A, B	
%BQUOTE	A, C	macro execution
%NRBQUOTE	A, B, C	
%SUPERQ	A, B, C	macro execution (prevents resolution)

SEE ALSO

Table 10.2 (p. 247) and Table 10.3 (p. 248) in *SAS® Guide to Macro Processing, Version 6, Second Edition* and Table 7.4 (p. 89) in *SAS® Macro Language: Reference, First Edition* contain similar summaries.

7.1.9   Marking and quoting mismatched symbols

A number of symbols are usually expected in pairs. These include the single quote, double quote, opening parenthesis, and closing parenthesis. Errors will usually be created if you specify only one-half of the pair in a string. This can especially be a problem if you want to include one of these mismatched symbols in a macro variable.

Some of the quoting functions expect these symbols to be in pairs, for example, %STR. Others allow them to be unpaired, for example, %BQUOTE. When you need to use a mismatched symbol where it will otherwise cause a problem, you can precede the mismatched symbol with a % to mask its meaning.

Problem	Notation	Example	Quoted value stored
Unmatched single quote	%'	%let x=%str(tr=a%';);	tr=a';
Unmatched double quote	%"	%let t=%str(title %"FIRST);	title "FIRST
unmatched left parenthesis	%(	%let a=%str(log%(12);	log(12
unmatched right parenthesis	%)	%let b=%str(345%));	345)
percent sign next to a valid quote or parenthesis	%%	%let p=%str(title "20%%";);	title "20%";

SEE ALSO
The previous table is based on Table 10.1 (p. 246) in *SAS® Guide to Macro Processing, Version 6, Second Edition,* and Table 7.2 (p. 81) in *SAS® Macro Language: Reference, First Edition.*

7.2 Character Functions

Macro character functions either change or provide information about the text string that is provided as one of their arguments. These functions are analogous to similar functions in the DATA step.

The functions discussed in this section are shown in the following table:

Section	Macro Function(s)	Analogous DATA Step Function	Task
7.2.1	%INDEX	index	Locate first occurrence of a text string
7.2.2	%LENGTH	length	Character count
7.2.3	%SCAN %QSCAN	scan	Search for the *n*th word in a text string
7.2.4	%SUBSTR %QSUBSTR	substr	Select text based on position
7.2.5	%UPCASE	upcase	Convert to upper case

It is important to remember the differences between these macro functions and their DATA step equivalents. DATA step functions always work on character strings and DATA step variables. Macro functions are applied to text strings that **never** contain the values of DATA step variables.

Notice that several of these functions have two forms, such as %SCAN and %QSCAN. Functions whose names start with Q (quoting) remove the meaning from special characters that include the ampersand (&), percent sign (%), and mnemonic operators in returned values.

7.2.1   %INDEX

The %INDEX function searches the first argument (*argument1*) for the first occurrence of the text string in the second argument (*argument2*). If the target string is found, then the position of its first character is returned as the function's response.

Syntax

> %**INDEX**(*argument1*, *argument2*)

Value returned
> Position of the string (0 if not found)

This example stores three words in the macro variable &X. The %INDEX function is then used to search in &X for the string TALL, and the result is then displayed using the %PUT statement.

```
%LET X=LONG TALL SALLEY;
%LET Y=%INDEX(&X,TALL);
%PUT TALL CAN BE FOUND AT POSITION &Y;
```

Notice that when TALL is the second argument, it is not in quotes. The %PUT statement results in the following text being written to the LOG:

```
TALL CAN BE FOUND AT POSITION 6
```

It is also common for both arguments to be macro variables. The example could easily be rewritten as follows, which will have the same result:

```
%LET SRCH = TALL;
%LET X=LONG TALL SALLEY;
%LET Y=%INDEX(&X,&SRCH);
%PUT &SRCH CAN BE FOUND AT POSITION &Y;
```

The macro %CHECK below is a simplified version of a macro that monitors an ongoing process. Periodically, %CHECK is executed and &VALUE is examined:

```
%LET VALUE=WATCH ENGINEERING EMERGENCY;

%MACRO CHECK;
    %IF %INDEX(&VALUE,EMERGENCY) > 0 %THEN
         %PUT *** CRITICAL ***;
    %ELSE %PUT *** FINE ***;
%MEND CHECK;
```

SEE ALSO
Aboutaleb (1997b) uses the %INDEX function in an example that deals with character variable strings.

7.2.2 %LENGTH

The %LENGTH function determines the length (number of characters) of its argument. The number of detected characters is then returned. When the argument is a null string, the value 0 is returned.

Syntax

%LENGTH(*argument*)

Value returned
  Number of characters in *argument*
  0 if *argument* is a null string

In the macro %LOOK from Section 4.2, there is no check for data set names that exceed eight characters. The %IF statement in the following example adds this check:

```
%MACRO LOOK(dsn,obs);
%if %length(&dsn) gt 8 %then
     %put Name is too long - &dsn;
%else %do;

     PROC CONTENTS DATA=&dsn;
          TITLE "DATA SET &dsn";
     RUN;

     PROC PRINT DATA=&dsn (OBS=&obs);
          TITLE2 "FIRST &obs OBSERVATIONS";
     RUN;
%end;
%MEND LOOK;
```

The LOG shows the following for data set names that exceed eight characters:

```
53   %look(demographics, 5)
Name is too long - demographics
```

SEE ALSO
Aboutaleb (1997b) uses the %LENGTH function in an example that deals with character variable strings.

7.2.3 %SCAN and %QSCAN

The %SCAN and %QSCAN functions both search a text string (*argument1*) for the *n*th word (*argument2*) and return its value. If *argument3* is not otherwise specified, the same word delimiters are used as in the DATA step SCAN function. For an ASCII system, these include the following (for EBCDIC, the ¬ is substituted for the ^):

```
blank . < ( + | & ! $ * ) ; ^ - / , % > \
```

%QSCAN removes the significance of all special characters in the returned value.

Syntax

 %SCAN(*argument1*, *argument2* <,*delimiters* >)
 %QSCAN(*argument1*, *argument2* <,*delimiters* >)

Returned Value
 *n*th word, where *n* is *argument2*

The macro variable &X in the following example can be broken up using the %SCAN function:

```
%LET X=XYZ.ABC/XYY;
%LET WORD=%SCAN(&X,3);
%LET PART=%SCAN(&X,1,Z);
%PUT WORD IS &WORD AND PART IS &PART;
```

%PUT returns the following:

```
WORD IS XYY AND PART IS XY
```

Notice that the third argument (delimiters) is not enclosed in quotes as it would be in the DATA step SCAN function.

The %QSCAN function is needed when you want to return a value that contains an ampersand or percent sign. This is demonstrated in the following example:

```
%let dsn = clinics;
%let string = %nrstr(*&stuff*&dsn*&morestuf);

%let wscan = %scan(&string,2,*);
%let wqscan = %qscan(&string,2,*);

%put &wscan &wqscan;
```

The %PUT statement writes

```
clinics &dsn
```

Both functions return the value &DSN, but because the meaning of the & is not masked by %SCAN, &WSCAN is resolved to `clinics`.

The following example counts the number of BY variables that are contained in the macro variable &KEYFLD. In this example, each variable name is saved in a macro variable, such as &VAR2, as is the overall count of variables (&CNT). Section 6.4.2 uses the DATA step SCAN function in a similar example.

```
%Macro cntvar;
    %let I = 1;
    %do %until(%scan(&keyfld,&I,%str( )❶)=%str()❷);
        %let var&I = %scan(&keyfld,&I,%str( )❶);
        %let I = %eval(&I + 1);
    %end;
    %let cnt = %eval(&I-1);
%mend cntvar;
```

❶ The word delimiter in both of these %SCAN function calls is a blank character, and the %STR function is used to reserve the space.

❷ Notice that the second %STR function in the %DO %UNTIL statement does not encompass a blank because it is used to test for a null string.

After running the macro shown, you might need to know the name of the final variable in the list so that it can be used in FIRST. and LAST. processing. You might use the following statement in a subsequent DATA step to select for unique observations:

```
if first.&&var&cnt and last.&&var&cnt;
```

Section 11.4.3 expands on this example.

SEE ALSO
The %SCAN function is used in a similar manner in Roberts (1997).

7.2.4   %SUBSTR and %QSUBSTR

Like the DATA step SUBSTR function, these macro functions return a portion of the string in the first *argument*. The substring starts at the *position* in the second argument and optionally has a *length* of the third argument.

Syntax

> %**SUBSTR**(*argument, position <,length>*)
> %**QSUBSTR**(*argument, position <,length>*)

Returns Value
> Substring of *argument*

As is the case with most other macro functions, each of the three arguments can be a text string, macro variable, expression, or a macro call. If you do not specify a value for *length*, a string that contains the characters from *position* to the end of the argument is produced.

```
%LET CLINIC=BETHESDA;
%IF %SUBSTR(&CLINIC,5,4) = ESDA %THEN
      %PUT *** MATCH ***;
%ELSE %PUT *** NOMATCH ***;
```

The SAS System would print `*** MATCH ***` because &CLINIC has the value ESDA in characters five through eight.

As shown in the following example, the %QSUBSTR function enables you to return unresolved references to macros and macro variables:

```
%let dsn=clinics;
%let string = %nrstr(*&stuff*&dsn*&morestuf);

%let sub = %substr(&string,9,5);
%let qsub = %qsubstr(&string,9,5);

%put &sub &qsub;
```

The %PUT statement will write `clinics* &dsn*` in the LOG.

7.2.5   %UPCASE

The %UPCASE macro function converts all characters in the *argument* to upper case. This function is especially useful when it compares character strings that may have inconsistent case.

Syntax

%UPCASE(*argument*)

Returns

ARGUMENT in all capital letters

The following code allows the user to differentially include a KEEP= option in the PROC PRINT statement. The %UPCASE function controls for variations in text that is supplied by the user in the macro call.

```
%macro printit(dsn);
* use a KEEP for CLINICS;
%if %upcase(&dsn)=CLINICS %then
     %let keep=(keep=lname fname ssn);
%else %let keep=;
proc print data=&dsn &keep;
title "Listing of %upcase(&dsn)";
run;
%mend printit;

%printit(cLinICs)
```

This macro call to %PRINTIT produces the following code:

```
proc print data=cLinICs (keep=lname fname ssn);
title "Listing of CLINICS";
run;
```

7.3 Evaluation Functions

Because there are no numbers or numeric variables in the macro language (there is only text and macro variables that contain text), numeric operations such as arithmetic and logical comparisons become problematic. Evaluation functions are used to bridge the gap between text and numeric operations.

Prior to Release 6.12, only the %EVAL function was available. Because this function has some limitations, which are discussed next, the %SYSEVALF function was added to the SAS System starting with Release 6.12.

The evaluation functions are used

- to evaluate arithmetic and logical expressions.

- inside and outside of macros.

- during logical comparisons to specify TRUE or FALSE. Evaluation functions return a value of 1 for logical expressions if the condition is true, 0 if it is false.

- to perform *integer* and *floating point* arithmetic.

The requests for these functions are either *explicit* (called by the user by name) or *implicit* (used automatically without being directly called during comparison operations).

7.3.1   Explicit use of %EVAL

The %EVAL function **always** performs integer arithmetic. Regardless of the requested operation, the result will always be an integer.

Syntax

> %**EVAL**(*argument*)

In the following example, the %EVAL function is called to perform arithmetic operations. The code uses %EVAL to add the value of 1 to &X, which in this case contains 5.

```
%LET X=5;
%LET Y=&X+1;
%LET Z=%EVAL(&X+1);
%PUT    &X    &Y    &Z;
```

The %PUT statement writes the following to the LOG:

```
5    5+1    6
```

Noninteger arithmetic is not allowed. The following statement:

```
%LET Z=%EVAL(&X+1.8);
```

would result in this message being printed in the LOG:

```
ERROR: A character operand was found in the %EVAL
function or %IF condition where a numeric operand is
required. The condition was: 5+1.8
```

Sections 5.3.3 and 5.3.4 provide other examples of the explicit use of the %EVAL function.

7.3.2   Implicit use of %EVAL

Comparisons in %IF statements use the %EVAL function even when it is not explicitly included in the code.

```
%macro chkwt(wt1, wt2);
   %if &wt1 > &wt2 %then %let note = heavier;
   %else %let note = lighter;
   %put First weight is &note.  &wt1 &wt2;
%mend chkwt;

%chkwt(1,2)
%chkwt(2,1)
%chkwt(2.1,2.2)
%chkwt(10.0,9.9)
```

Notice that the third and fourth calls to %CHKWT have noninteger parameters. %EVAL will not be used in noninteger comparisons, and these numbers will instead be compared alphabetically. Because 1 comes before 9 alphabetically, 10.0 is seen as *smaller* than 9.9 in the fourth comparison.

The LOG shows

```
21   %chkwt(1,2)
First weight is lighter  1 2
22   %chkwt(2,1)
First weight is heavier  2 1
23   %chkwt(2.1,2.2)
First weight is lighter  2.1 2.2
24   %chkwt(10.0,9.9)
First weight is lighter  10.0 9.9
```

Some releases prior to Release 6.11 may return an error in the third and fourth comparisons.

7.3.3 Using %SYSEVALF

The floating point evaluation function, %SYSEVALF, is new with Release 6.12 of the SAS System, although it was available but undocumented in Release 6.11. You can use %SYSEVALF to perform noninteger arithmetic. It will even return a noninteger result from an arithmetic operation.

Syntax

%SYSEVALF(*expression* <,*conversion-type* >)

Expression is any arithmetic or logical expression that is to be evaluated, and it may contain macro references.

The second argument, *conversion-type*, is an optional conversion to apply to the value that is returned by %SYSEVALF. Because this function can return noninteger values, problems could occur in other macro statements that use this function but expect integers.

When you need the result of this function to be an integer, use one of the conversion types. A specification of the *conversion-type* converts a value that is returned by %SYSEVALF to an integer or Boolean value so it can be used in other expressions that require a value of that type. *Conversion-type* can be

- BOOLEAN   0 if the result of the expression is 0 or missing.
  1 if the result is any other value.

- CEIL   round to next largest whole integer.

- FLOOR   round to next smallest whole integer.

- INTEGER   truncate decimal fraction.

The CEIL, FLOOR, and INTEGER conversion types act on the expression in the same way as the DATA step functions of the same (or similar) names, that is, the CEIL, FLOOR, and INT functions.

The following table shows a few resulting values:

Example	Result (%put &x;)
%let x = %sysevalf(7/3)	2.3333333333
%let x = %sysevalf(7/3,boolean)	1
%let x = %sysevalf(7/3,ceil)	3
%let x = %sysevalf(7/3,floor)	2
%let x = %sysevalf(1/3)	0.3333333333
%let x = %sysevalf(1+.)	.
%let x = %sysevalf(1+.,boolean)	0

Although *SAS® Macro Language: Reference, First Edition* (p. 237) states that the results will be written using BEST32. under Windows and Release 6.12, the results appear to be written using the BEST12. format.

The macro %FIGUREIT, shown next, was taken from the SAS online help system for Release 6.12. It demonstrates each type of conversion for values that are returned by the %SYSEVALF function.

```
%macro figureit(a,b);
  %let y=%sysevalf(&a+&b);
  %put The result with SYSEVALF is: &y;
  %put  Type BOOLEAN is: %sysevalf(&a +&b, boolean);
  %put  Type CEIL is: %sysevalf(&a +&b, ceil);
  %put  Type FLOOR is: %sysevalf(&a +&b, floor);
  %put  Type INTEGER is: %sysevalf(&a +&b, int);
%mend figureit;

%figureit(100,1.597)
```

Executing this program writes to the SAS LOG:

```
The result with SYSEVALF is: 101.597
Type BOOLEAN is: 1
Type CEIL is: 102
Type FLOOR is: 101
Type INTEGER is: 101
```

7.4 Using DATA Step Functions and Routines

Two macro functions that were introduced with Release 6.12 enable you to execute virtually all of the functions and routines that are available in the DATA step as part of the macro language. %SYSCALL calls DATA step routines, and %SYSFUNC executes DATA step functions.

7.4.1 Using %SYSCALL

You can use %SYSCALL to execute CALL routines that are ordinarily called only from within the DATA step. Because these routines normally operate on data set variables that are not available, the arguments are instead macro variables.

Syntax

> **%SYSCALL** *call-routine* <(*routine-arguments*)> ;

All CALL routines, either user-written with SAS/TOOLKIT software, or supplied with the SAS System, can be used with %SYSCALL, except for LABEL, VNAME, SYMPUT, and EXECUTE. This leaves the routines for random number generation and system command execution. See Chapter 12, "SAS CALL Routines," (pp. 149–160) in *SAS® Language Reference, Version 6, First Edition* for more information on DATA step CALL routines.

When you use %SYSCALL, the arguments will be macro variables without the ampersand. In the following example, the SYSTEM routine is used to execute the operating system directory command at the DOS level:

```
%let cmd = dir;
%syscall system(cmd);
```

Notice that the argument is a macro variable without the ampersand. Inserting the directory command, DIR, directly instead of the macro variable &CMD would not have worked because DIR does not resolve to the name of a macro variable.

If you need to create a macro variable that contains a random number, you can use any of the numerous random number routines. The following example assigns a random number to the macro variable &RAND, which must be initialized prior to the call:

```
%let seed=9876;
%let rand=0   ;
%put seed is &seed pseudo random number is &rand;
%syscall ranuni(seed,rand);
%put seed is &seed pseudo random number is &rand;
```

After execution the LOG will show:

```
5     %let seed=9876;
6     %let rand=0   ;
7     %put seed is &seed pseudo random number is &rand;
seed is 9876 pseudo random number is 0
8     %syscall ranuni(seed,rand);
9     %put seed is &seed pseudo random number is &rand;
seed is 1482492922 pseudo random number is 0.6903395628
```

Note that the value of both macro variables, &SEED and &RAND, were changed by the call to RANUNI.

SEE ALSO

SAS® Macro Language: Reference, First Edition (pp. 231–232) documents the syntax of %SYSCALL.

7.4.2 Using %SYSFUNC and %QSYSFUNC

These two macro functions greatly increase the list of functions that are available to the macro language by making available almost all DATA step and user-written functions. As a consequence, they can substantially reduce the need for single-observation DATA _NULL_ steps.

Syntax

> %**SYSFUNC**(*function-name* (*function-arguments*)<,format >)
> %**QSYSFUNC**(*function-name*(*function-arguments*)<,format >)

The following example shows three ways to add the current date to a TITLE. Although the automatic macro variable &SYSDATE is easy to use, it cannot be formatted. Consequently, prior to Release 6.12, most users used a DATA _NULL_ step with an assignment statement and a CALL SYMPUT to create a formatted macro variable. The DATA step can now be avoided by using the %SYSFUNC macro function, as is shown in TITLE3 below:

```
data _null_;
today = put(date(),worddate18.);
call symput('dtnull',today);
run;

title1 "Using Automatic Macro Variable SYSDATE &sysdate";
title2 "Date from a DATA _NULL_ &dtnull";
title3 "Using SYSFUNC %sysfunc(date(),worddate18.)";
```

This code produces the following three titles:

```
Using Automatic Macro Variable SYSDATE 26MAR97
   Date from a DATA _NULL_     March 26, 1997
        Using SYSFUNC     March 26, 1997
```

The leading spaces before the date in the second and third titles are caused by the date string being right justified. You can use the LEFT and TRIM functions to remove the space. However, if you are not careful, you may encounter a couple of problems.

The first problem is that function calls cannot be nested within %SYSFUNC. Fortunately, this is rather easily handled because you can nest %SYSFUNC requests.

Secondly, the resolved values of interior calls to %SYSFUNC are used as arguments to the outer calls. When the resolved value contains special characters, especially commas, they can be misinterpreted. The following revised TITLE3 will not work because the interior %SYSFUNC uses a formatted value that contains a comma:

```
title3 "Using SYSFUNC %sysfunc(left(%sysfunc(date(),worddate18.)))";
```

After the inner %SYSFUNC is executed, the result is

```
title3 "Using SYSFUNC %sysfunc(left(March 26, 1997))";
```

Because of the comma, the LEFT function will see two arguments (it is expecting exactly one), and the message "too many arguments" is generated.

You can use the %QSYSFUNC function to mask special characters in the text string that is passed to the next function. Rewriting the title as is shown next eliminates the problem with the comma:

```
title3 "Using SYSFUNC %sysfunc(left(%qsysfunc(date(),worddate18.)))";
```

The title becomes

```
Using SYSFUNC March 26, 1997
```

Starting with Release 6.12, functions that were originally included only in the Screen Control Language (SCL) library became available in the DATA step and are now also available to %SYSFUNC.

The following macro uses the PATHNAME function to retrieve the path that is associated with a LIBREF. This path is then used to build a new LIBREF with a different engine. The LIBNAME statements include an ENGINE option so that the copied data sets will be rewritten using the new engine. If the new engine is one associated with a third-party vendor such as DBMS/Engines, the output data set may even be converted to a format other than SAS.

```
%macro engchng(engine,dsn);
* engine - output engine for this &dsn
* dsn    - name of data set to copy
*;

data _null_;
  * libref for location of new file;
  aa = pathname("sasuser"); ❶
  call symput('outpath',aa); ❷
run;

* Create a libref for the stated Engine;
libname dbmsout clear;
libname dbmsout &engine "&outpath"; ❸

* Copy the SAS data set using the alternate engine;
proc datasets;
copy in=sasuser out=dbmsout; ❹
select &dsn;
run;

%mend engchng;

****************************************************;
%engchng(v604,classwt) ❺   * convert to alt. engine;
```

❶ The PATHNAME function is used to return the PATH, which is associated with an established LIBREF (SASUSER).

❷ This PATH is then stored in the macro variable &OUTPATH.

❸ A new LIBREF is established using the alternate engine (&ENGINE) and the original PATH (&OUTPATH).

❹ PROC DATASETS uses the new engine to copy the selected member (&DSN).

❺ This call to %ENGCHNG specifies that the new engine should be V6.04 when copying SASUSER.CLASSWT.

The previous version of macro %ENGCHNG does not take advantage of the %SYSFUNC function and relies instead on the DATA _NULL_ step. This macro is rewritten using %SYSFUNC:

```
%macro engchng(engine,dsn);
* engine - output engine for this &dsn
* dsn    - name of data set to copy
*;

* Create a libref for the stated Engine;
libname dbmsout clear;
libname dbmsout &engine "%sysfunc(pathname(sasuser))";

* Copy the SAS data set using the alternate engine;
proc datasets;
copy in=sasuser out=dbmsout;
select &dsn;
run;

%mend engchng;

****************************************************;
%engchng(v604,classwt)  * convert to alt. engine;
```

Notice that the LIBREF in the PATHNAME function call is **not** in quotes. Remember that arguments to macro functions are always text, so the quotes are not necessary. As you use DATA step functions with %SYSFUNC, you should expect the behavior of many of the arguments of the DATA step functions to vary slightly in ways such as this.

The view SASHELP.VSLIB will also contain path information, and you can use it instead of the PATHNAME function.

SEE ALSO

You can find a summary description and the syntax for DATA step functions that you can use with %SYSFUNC and %QSYSFUNC in Appendix 3, "Syntax for Selected SAS Functions Used with the %SYSFUNC Function," (pp. 277–280) in *SAS® Macro Language: Reference, First Edition*.

Yindra (1998) includes several examples that use %SYSFUNC.

DBMS/Engines is a product of Conceptual Software, Inc. (800-328-2686) and enables a SAS program to read and write SAS data sets to and from formats other than SAS.

7.5 Chapter Summary

Macro functions create new text strings from existing text strings. There are three main categories of macro functions:

- character functions

- evaluation functions

- quoting functions.

Character functions perform character searches, determine the length of an argument, scan an argument for specific words, create a substring from a text string, and translate lowercase characters to uppercase characters.

Evaluation functions perform an evaluation of arithmetic and logical expressions.

Quoting functions remove the meaning of specific characters either during macro compilation or at macro execution time.

In addition, the %SYSFUNC, %QSYSFUNC, and %SYSCALL functions enable you to access most of the routines and functions that are part of the DATA step.

7.6 Chapter Exercises

1. Check all answers that are TRUE. Macro character functions can be used to

    A. perform character searches

    B. determine the length of an argument

    C. scan an argument for specific words

    D. translate lowercase characters to uppercase characters

    E. none of the above

    F. all of the above.

2. (True/False) Quoting functions remove the meaning of specific characters either during macro compilation or at macro execution.

3. (True/False) The %STR quoting function removes meaning from special characters (except % and &) during macro compilation.

4. The macro %CNTVAR in Section 7.2.3 counts the number of words in a macro string. Modify this so that it

    ■ allows the user to optionally pass the delimiter used to separate words

    ■ uses a %DO %WHILE statement instead of a %DO %UNTIL statement

    ■ correctly handles a string with no words

    ■ removes the meaning of the & and % in returned words.

Chapter 8 # Using Macro References with Screen Control Language (SCL)

8.1 The Problem Is ....

8.2 Using Macro Variables

8.3 Calling Macros from within SCL Programs

8.4 Chapter Summary

The Macro Facility is available to your Screen Control Language (SCL) programs. The syntax and usage of macros, macro statements, and macro variables is essentially the same in SCL programs as in your other SAS programs. The primary difference, and the one that causes the most problems, relates to the fact that SCL programs are compiled. Because the compilation process resolves macro references, you may need to adjust your perception of the order and sequence of macro-related events.

During the compilation of the SCL program, all macro references are resolved to their current values. A macro call, for instance, will be executed during the compilation of the SCL program and **not** when the SCL program is executed.

This is a different way of thinking about macro references, and most of this chapter is designed to help you deal with these differences.

SEE ALSO

Beyond the Obvious with SAS® Screen Control Language (Stanley, 1994) contains a summary of warnings and tips on the use of macros and macro variables in SCL programs (pp. 40–43).

Chapter 10, "Using Macro Variables," in *SAS® Screen Control Language: Reference, Version 6, Second Edition* (pp. 99–101) discusses macro variables, and the substitution of text in SUBMIT blocks is discussed on page 110.

Several examples of macro variables in SCL can be found in *SAS® Screen Control Language: Usage, Version 6, First Edition*. Chapter 27, "Using Macro Variables," (pp. 487–500) contains a number of examples of SCL programs that utilize macro variables. Chapter 28, "Submitting SAS and SQL Statements," (pp. 501–530) covers various combinations of macro and SCL variable substitution in SUBMIT blocks.

Norton (1991) contrasts the use of the macro language with SCL and suggests that SCL be used as an alternative to the macro language in some situations.

Davis (1997) shows how you can use macros to provide consistency among SCL frame entries.

8.1 The Problem Is . . .

SCL programs are compiled and external references such as macro variables and macro calls are resolved during compilation, not during execution. The writer of the following SCL section would like to open the data set named in the macro variable &DSN:

```
init:
   * open the data set &dsn;
   dsnid = open("&dsn",'i');
   if dsnid=0 then put "unable to open &dsn";
return;
```

This code will fail even to compile unless &DSN is currently defined. If &DSN is defined at compile time to be `clinics`, then the code that is compiled will be

```
init:
   * open the data set clinics;
   dsnid = open("clinics",'i');
   if dsnid=0 then put "unable to open clinics";
return;
```

Subsequent changes to the macro variable &DSN will have no effect on what data set will appear in the OPEN function.

A similar problem exists for macro calls inside of SCL programs. The following code is supposed to execute an error-check macro (%ERRCHK) when the file named by the SCL variable DSNAME cannot be opened:

```
init:
  * open the data set &dsn;
  dsnid = open(dsname,'i');
  if dsnid=0 then %errchk(dsname);
return;
```

The macro %ERRCHK is supposed to write the name of the missing data set to the LOG. This macro has previously been defined as

```
%macro errchk(d);
   %put "data set not found &d";
%mend errchk;
```

Regardless of the name of the unknown data set, the MESSAGE window will contain the following:

```
"data set not found dsname"
```

The macro is resolved at compilation. At compile time, DSNAME is seen as text, not as an SCL variable. DSNAME is, therefore, passed unresolved to the macro. Here, &D will take on the value of `dsname`. This example highlights the major disadvantages of using macro calls in SCL programs:

- The macro must be defined before SCL compilation.

- SCL variable values cannot be passed into the macro.

- Changes to the macro will not be reflected in the SCL program until the SCL program is recompiled.

Despite these caveats, there are very definite uses for macro variables and macro calls within SCL programs. The following sections cover these topics in more detail.

8.2 Using Macro Variables

Macro variables are not necessarily part of any particular application or data set, and they are not associated with a particular screen, method, or program. This makes them ideal for passing information through various portions of your program or application. Once defined and globalized, the values of the macro variables are available throughout the SAS System.

Macro variables are especially useful when passing information between entries in your application. Values that are set once and then repeated or held constant across screens or data sets are prime candidates for use with macro variables. Macro variables are often used to hold values for

- the name of a SAS data set to be opened or the file identifier of an open data set

- the external file name to be opened or its file identifier once opened

- constant text such as the current date

- values passed between applications

- values passed between programs within an application.

Because SCL programs are compiled, macro variables must be mentioned obliquely in SCL programs. Outside of the SUBMIT block, it is unlikely that you will use the ampersand much, if at all, in SCL programs.

8.2.1 Defining macro variables

You can assign values to macro variables in an SCL program in much the same way as you would in other SAS programs. However, you will probably depend more on the CALL SYMPUT routine and less on the %LET statement. Like %LET statements in non-SCL programs, the characters on the right of the equal sign are taken to be text. Because %LET is executed when the SCL program is compiled, SCL variables are unresolvable. The following %LET statement creates the macro variable DSN, which will contain the string `dsname`:

```
%let dsn = dsname;
```

Even if DSNAME is an SCL variable (screen or nonscreen), the value of DSN is the **string** `dsname`.

The SYMPUT routine is used to create macro variables with a value that is associated with an SCL variable. This routine is used the same in SCL as it is in a DATA step (see Section 6.1 for more information on the SYMPUT routine and its usage). If DSNAME is a character SCL variable that contains the string `class.clinics`, the following statement assigns the macro variable DSN the value taken on by DSNAME, that is, `class.clinics`:

```
call symput('dsn',dsname);
```

As in the DATA step routine, the second argument of SYMPUT is expected to be a character string or the name of a character variable. Unlike the DATA step, however, SCL has a numeric counterpart, SYMPUTN. This routine is used to create macro variables from numeric SCL variables. In the following example, the numeric SCL variable OBS contains the observation number to read:

```
call symputn('obsnum',obs);
```

Often the macro variables that are created within an application are globalized so that they will be available throughout the application. The SCL SYMPUT and SYMPUTN functions always create globalized macro variables, as does the %LET statement in non-SCL programs when you use it outside of a macro.

8.2.2 Macro variables in SUBMIT blocks

SUBMIT blocks are used in SCL programs to pass statements to the SAS System for execution. Statements that are contained in SUBMIT blocks are not SCL but are standard SAS language statements. However, these statements can contain references to both SCL and macro variables.

Inside of a SUBMIT block, SCL variables are identified by preceding them with an ampersand. In the following section of SCL, a SUBMIT block is used to execute the PRINT procedure:

```
if modified(rpt) then submit;
    proc print data=&dsname(obs=10);
    title 'Data Listing for &dsname';
    run;
endsubmit;
```

A couple of things are worth noting in this code. At execution of the SCL program and before the SUBMIT block is passed for execution, the reference &DSNAME is first checked against the list of SCL variables in the SCL Data Vector (SDV) and resolved if found. If it is not found, then it is passed unresolved for execution, where it will be treated as a macro variable reference. Because of this behavior when passing values into SUBMIT blocks, it is generally not a good idea to use the same name for both macro variables and SCL variables.

You may also have noted in the previous example that the title is enclosed by single quotes. In SCL SUBMIT blocks, single quotes will **not** mask the meaning of the ampersand as they will in base SAS language statements. However, if the &DSNAME is passed unresolved, in single quotes, to base SAS for processing, the macro variable reference will remain quoted. In the previous and following example, if DSNAME is not an SCL variable, it will remain unresolved in the title.

If you do need to specify a macro variable in a SUBMIT block and an SCL variable exists with the same name, you can use a double ampersand to prevent its resolution as an SCL variable. In the following example, the &&VARLST will not resolve to the SCL variable VARLST even if it exists on the SDV:

```
if modified(rpt) then submit;
    proc print data=&dsname(obs=10);
    var &&varlst;
    title 'Data Listing for &dsname';
    run;
endsubmit;
```

8.2.3 Using automatic macro variables

The automatic macro variables that are discussed in Section 2.6 are all available within SCL programs. As was noted in Section 8.2.1, however, you need to be careful how you use them. The following SCL code attempts to open the most recently modified data set:

```
dsname = "&syslast";
dsid = open(dsname);
```

The code will not do what the programmer wants because &SYSLAST will be resolved when the SCL program is compiled. Upon execution the program will always try to open the same data set regardless of the value of &SYSLAST at execution. The problem is solved by using the SYMGET function. In the following revised SCL code, the value of &SYSLAST is not retrieved until the SCL program is executed:

```
dsname = symget('syslast');
dsid = open(dsname);
```

When you create a numeric SCL variable, use the SYMGETN function. SYMGETN returns a numeric value rather than the character value that is returned by SYMGET.

8.2.4 Passing macro values between SCL entries

Passing macro variable values between SCL entries is very straightforward. Macro variables are defined using the SYMPUT and SYMPUTN routines, and these variables are then available throughout the application. A subsequent SCL entry (or even code within a SUBMIT block) can retrieve the values by using SYMGET and SYMGETN.

The following INIT section both retrieves macro variables and creates them for later use:

```
INIT:
    * Specify a macro var used for SCL in edit screens;
    call symput('scrntype','DE'); ❶

    * Create a libref for the log used
    * by this Data Entry userid;
    userid = symget('userid');  ❷
    tst = symget('tst');  ❸
    path = compress('h:\studyx\phase2\'
            ||tst||'datprep\d_entry\'
            ||userid);
    call libname('delog',path);

    control enter;
    cursor subject;
return;
```

❶ The macro variable SCRNTYPE is initialized to DE. The macro variables USERID ❷ and TST ❸ (both of which must have been created earlier in the application) are retrieved and placed in SCL variables of the same name. Remember, using the same name for macro and SCL variables is acceptable and only causes problems when used carelessly in SUBMIT blocks.

Macro variables often may not be the best method for passing values between entries within an application or even between applications. Built into Screen Control Language is the concept of an SCL LIST. Analogous to an ARRAY list, entries can be loaded from files, saved to disc, and passed from one entry to another. Like macro variables, LISTS can be global or local. But because LISTS are designed to be a part of SCL (macro variables coexist with SCL), they work more smoothly and have additional support functions. It is likely that SCL LIST functions will be quicker than SYMGET and SYMPUT.

8.3 Calling Macros from within SCL Programs

The brief example using %ERRCHK in Section 8.1 illustrates the problem with calling macros from within SCL programs. Remember, macros are executed when the SCL is compiled and when the macro changes, programs that use that macro will need to be recompiled. Despite this problem macro calls can have a definite place in SCL programs.

Macros called in SCL programs fall into two classes, and these are determined by when the macro is to be executed. Macros in SCL programs can be executed either when the SCL program is compiled (compile-time) or when it is executed (run-time).

8.3.1   Run-time macros

Run-time macros are macros that execute when the SCL program executes. Unlike macros in the base language, which are all run-time, this concept has very little meaning in SCL programs. The exception is found in SUBMIT blocks. Because SAS does not resolve macro references in SUBMIT blocks until the block itself is executed, you can safely call macros here. Because the block of code is essentially set aside, the called macro does not need to exist until the SUBMIT block is actually executed.

Run-time macros avoid the SCL compilation issues that are noted in the previous section and behave as other base system macros behave.

8.3.2   Compile-time macros

Compile-time macros are most often used to write SCL code. These macros will execute when the SCL program is compiled – long before values for the SCL variables are available. If the macro contains reusable code but is not actually generating SCL, as in the example shown later in this section, consider using a METHOD instead of a macro. There is an informative discussion on the advantages and disadvantages of METHODS and compile-time macros in *Beyond the Obvious with SAS® Screen Control Language* by Don Stanley (1994, pp. 42–43).

The example shown in this section illustrates the use of a macro to generate code. A series of over 20 FSEDIT screens were to have similar (but not quite the same) SCL that was used to initialize protected variables. Rather than develop a series of parallel programs that would be difficult to maintain, the entire SCL program for each screen was placed within a single generalized macro. The source screen for each FSEDIT consisted only of the call to the macro %DATASTMP:

```
%datastmp(subject,ptid)
```

The macro arguments are names of SCL variables that will apply to a specific data set and screen. Remember, the **names** of the variables are being passed to the macro not the variable values, which are not yet available.

```
%macro datastmp(var1,var2,var3,var4);

* determine the number of vars;
%do i = 1 %to 4;
   %if &&var&i ne %then %let varcnt = &i;
%end;

fseinit:
   scrntype=symget('scrntype');
   if scrntype in ('CLN', 'PED') then do;
      control enter;

   ... ordinary SCL not shown ...
return;

init:
   if scrntype='DE' or word(1)='ADD' then do;
   %do i = 1 %to &varcnt;
      unprotect &&var&i;
      &&var&i = symget("&&var&i");
      protect &&var&i;
   %end;
   end;
return;

... ordinary SCL not shown ...

%mend datastmp;
```

When the compile process starts to compile the SCL that contains the macro call, the macro executes. First the macro generates SCL code, and then that code is compiled. The INIT section that follows is generated when the SCL that contains the call to %DATASTMP (as previously shown) is compiled (after the macro executes):

```
init:
   if scrntype='DE' or word(1)='ADD' then do;
      unprotect subject;  ❶
      subject = symget("subject");  ❷
      protect subject;  ❸
      unprotect ptid;
      ptid = symget("ptid");
      protect ptid;
   end;
return;
```

The %DATASTMP macro has been used to generate SCL code that has SCL variables with the same name as the macro variables. When this INIT section executes, the ❶ screen variable SUBJECT will be unprotected, assigned a value ❷ based on the value of the macro variable of the same name, and then ❸ reprotected.

As a general rule, you should have a compelling reason to generate SCL code this way, especially for FSEDIT screens. The problem is that the SCL source code is not integral to the SCREEN. If you lose the uncompiled macro, you will be unable to regenerate the SCL code. From a practical point of view, the process itself can be cumbersome. If you need to change the code you will need to

- make the change in the macro source.

- if running interactively, make sure that the current version of WORK.SASMACR contains the correct version. Either delete the catalog entry or recompile the macro.

- start FSEDIT and use modify.

- compile the SCL. (For compile errors, go back to the start of this list.)

The previous example was taken from a program that used a macro %DO loop to simplify the process that included 20 screens. This loop is shown in Section 6.4.1.

SEE ALSO
Bryher (1997b) uses a macro to build SCL code.

8.4 Chapter Summary

The full power of the macro facility is available in Screen Control Language programs. However, because SCL programs are compiled there are special considerations.

Macro variables are usually referenced using the SYMGET function and the SYMPUT routine. A macro variable will rarely be called using the ampersand.

Globalized macro variables have values that are available throughout an application. This makes an easy way to transfer information from one SCL program to another.

Macros called from within an SCL program are called and executed during the compilation of the SCL program.

Macro variables and macro calls in SUBMIT blocks behave as they do in non-SCL programs.

Part 3   # Advanced Macro Topics, Utilities, and Examples

The macros and programs that are contained in Part III were collected from a number of sources. Although the programs have been checked when possible, they cannot be warranted to be error free, nor should you expect them to do just what you want them to do on your system. You should use these macros as examples of coding possibilities that you can adapt to your own situation.

A number of the macros that follow were written by SAS programmers other than the author. These macros are noted with the name and occasionally (with their approval) additional contact information for the macro's author. Sometimes macros such as these are passed from programmer to programmer and it is hard to identify the original author. In these cases, I have included the name of the most recent contributor. In order to control content and to stress certain points, some of the macros have been slightly altered from their original form.

As you look over these macros please remember that programming, as in many creative endeavors, is very individualistic. Many of the programs included here may not reflect your style, and some are more efficient than others. They all have been included to demonstrate both techniques and style. In each case, the authors should be complimented on their contributions to the SAS community.

Examples of other macros and utilities are very common in the SAS literature. SUGI proceedings are especially rich in these kinds of programs. There are also a number of sites on the Internet that have examples of SAS code. The following are just a few locations to check:

> http://www.sas.com/service/techsup/faq/macro.html

> http://www.netcom.net.uk/~rolandrb/index.html

> http://members.aol.com/xlr82sas/utl.html

> http://www.getnet.com/~kairis/valsug.html

> http://www.getnet.com/~kairis/mcode.html

> http://www.qlx.com

The book *SAS® System for Statistical Graphics, First Edition* by Michael Friendly (1991) has a very nice collection of macros that are useful in both statistical and graphical applications.

Chapter 9   # Writing Dynamic Code

9.1   Logical Branches

9.2   Iterative Step Execution

9.3   Building Statements

A dynamic program is one that is incompletely defined prior to execution. Many, if not most, SAS programs are static and the programmer determines through the use of DATA step and PROC step statements the order and logic of execution. In static programs when the programmer *knows* about data exceptions and special cases, he or she must *hard code* logic to handle them. Dynamic programs, on the other hand, use the data itself to determine the path and logic of execution. Rather than *hard coding*, the programmer who writes dynamic programs has the ability to create generalized programs that will execute correctly on a wider variety of data.

Because dynamic programming techniques are such an integral part of the macro language, many of the examples in other sections of this book also demonstrate the topics that are outlined in the following sections of this chapter. The topic of dynamic programming is first introduced in Section 5.2.2, where several basic issues relating to the topic are covered.

Following are three primary areas that benefit from dynamic techniques:

- logical branches that conditionally execute sections of code

- iterative loops that execute sections of code multiple times

- the construction or writing of SAS statements prior to execution.

In dynamic programming, the control of the program is driven by the data. One of the keys to this process is the use of the SYMPUT routine, which is used to store DATA step values in macro variables. Once stored in macro variables, these values can be used by the macro language in subsequent steps. Section 6.1 defines the use of the SYMPUT routine and Sections 6.2 and 6.3 both have examples that build macro variables based on the values in the data. When a series of macro variables are used, they often take the form of &&VAR&i. The use of this type of macro variable is introduced in Section 6.4.

Data set values may also be assigned to macro variables by using the SQL procedure. Examples of the use of SQL to build macro variables can be found in Sections 2.7, 11.2.1, 11.4.1, 13.1.1, and 13.1.2.

SEE ALSO

Several examples of dynamic programming can be found in Blood (1992) and Carpenter (1988 and 1997).

9.1 Logical Branches

Logical branching based on the value of a macro variable is probably the most common form of dynamic coding. Often the use of the macro %DO block is combined with the %IF-%THEN/%ELSE statements. The examples in Section 5.3.1 demonstrate this type of branch.

In this example, the number of observations has been stored in the macro variable &NOBS. This value is then used to determine if the data is to be summarized or printed.

```
%if &nobs ge 10 %then %do;
   proc means data=statdata mean n stderr;
   var ht wt;
   title "Analysis Data - &nobs Observations";
   run;
%end;
%else %if &nobs gt 0 %then %do;
   proc print data=statdata;
   var subject ht wt;
   title "Data NOT Summarized";
   run;
%end;
%else %put Data Set STATDATA is empty;
```

Branching can also include the use of the %GOTO statement, as is shown in Section 5.4.2.

SEE ALSO
Yindra (1997) has an example of a macro that also branches based on the number of observations in a data set.

9.2 Iterative Step Execution

You can use the iterative %DO loop to pass through PROC and DATA steps multiple times. In the following example, the data set CLINICS has a variable REGION that you want to use to summarize the data. Using the BY statement in the PROC steps will order the output so that the summary for all regions is followed by the plots for all regions. However, you would like to group together all of the output for each value of REGION. This, of course, is not how SAS generates output. In order to regroup the output (without shuffling papers at the end), you need to pass through the two procedures once for each value of the BY statement.

Because you want the output grouped for each BY value across procedures, you need a way to loop through the procedures for each BY value. The resulting output will have the data summary and plot for REGION='1' followed by the summary and plot for REGION='2', and so on.

```
%macro onereg;
    proc sort data=sasclass.clinics out=clinics;
        by region;
        run;
    data _null_;
        set clinics;
        by region;
        if first.region then do;
            i+1;
            ii=left(put(i,2.));
            call symput('reg'||ii,region); ❶
            call symput('total',ii); ❷
        end;
        run;

    %do i=1 %to &total; ❸
        proc means data=clinics mean n stderr;
            where region="&&reg&i"; ❹
          var ht wt;
            title1 "summary for height and weight";
            title2 "region &&reg&i";
            run;
        proc plot data=clinics;
            where region="&&reg&i"; ❹
            plot ht * wt;
            title1 "plot of height and weight";
            title2 "region &&reg&i";
            run;
    %end;
%mend onereg;
```

❶ A macro variable for each unique value of REGION is created in the form of &&REG&i.

❷ The total number of regions is saved in &TOTAL.

❸ A macro %DO loop is set up and includes the procedures of interest.

❹ The WHERE statement is used with the procedures to exclude all regions except the one of interest (&&REG&I).

This example is quite inefficient in that it reads the data set CLINICS several times. The solutions to Questions 2 and 3 in the Chapter 6 Exercises (that is, Questions 6.2 and 6.3) address a similar problem more efficiently. The last example in Section 9.3 is similar to those solutions.

SEE ALSO
Carpenter (1988) also discusses two similar macros, %BREAKUP and %SPLITUP, that you can use to control program flow and output organization. Another example of this programming technique can be found in Wobus (1997).

9.3 Building Statements

You can use the macro language in a number of ways to build individual SAS statements. Macro logic based on the %IF statement is often combined with the various forms of the %DO loop to create full statements or just portions of the statements. Examples in Sections 5.2.2, 5.3.1, and 5.3.2 introduce the techniques, while Section 6.4.2 directly addresses issues that are related to building statements.

In the following example, the SET statement is defined conditionally:

```
data new;
%if &cond=YES %then %str(set cond;);
%else %str(set general;);
run;
```

It is not necessary to create the entire statement within the macro text. In the previous example, the SET statement could also have been written without using the %STR function:

```
data new;
set
   %if &cond=YES %then cond;
   %else general;
;
run;
```

As is shown in Section 6.4.2 and a number of examples in the following chapters, you can also use the %DO loop very effectively to build statements.

The DATA step shown in the following example is part of the solution to Question 6.3. Assume that in a previous step a series of macro variables (&REG1, &REG2, and so on) was created (see the example in Section 9.2) to hold the unique values of the character variable REGION (the values in this case are '1', '2', '3', and so on). This DATA step will be used to create a separate data set for each unique value of REGION. For example, all observations with REGION='1' will be written to the data set R1.

```
data  %do i = 1 %to &total; r&&reg&i %end;;  ❶
   set clinics;
   %* Build the &total output statements;
   %do i = 1 %to &total;  ❷
      %if &i=1 %then if region="&&reg&i" then output r&&reg&i;  ❸
      %else else if region="&&reg&i" then output r&&reg&i;
      ;  ❹
   %end;
   run;
```

❶ The %DO loop builds the DATA statement by naming all of the data sets to be created. The resulting statement will look something like this:

```
data r1 r2 r3;
```

❷ This loop creates the statements used to OUTPUT each observation to the appropriate data set and will be executed once for each unique value of REGION.

❸ For three regions, the resolved statements might be

```
if region="1" then output r1
;
else if region="2" then output r2
;
else if region="3" then output r3
;
```

❹ This is the semicolon that closes each of the OUTPUT statements.

SEE ALSO

You can find an additional example of a dynamically built SET statement in Tassoni (1997).

Smith (1997) includes several examples of dynamic code building. These include the use of %DO loops in PROC FORMATS and in AXIS statements.

Chapter 10 **Controlling Your Environment**

10.1 Operating System Operations

10.2 Working with Listings and Reports

Through the use of macro examples, this chapter introduces several concepts that you can use to control your operating environment. This includes the routing of output, control of report appearance, and working with system files other than SAS system files.

10.1 Operating System Operations

As a general rule, the macros in this section perform operations on files, programs, catalogs, and members of catalogs rather than on lines of code. This means that in each case you need to be able to gather the appropriate information on the operating system (for example, file names) and create macro and data set variables. A recent addition to the SAS System gathers a great deal of the system information into a series of SAS Views that are stored in the SASHELP library. You can use these views to generate lists of data sets, members of catalogs, variables within a data set, and more. The macro in Section 10.1.1 uses one of these views to gather information about the members of a SAS catalog, and in Section 10.2 SASHELP.VOPTION is used to read and store current OPTION settings.

SEE ALSO

Geary (1997) discusses a macro that produces summary information on a series of SAS data sets.

A disk space utilization macro is presented in Mast (1997).

10.1.1   Copy members of a catalog

%CATCOPY

You can use this macro to copy selected members of a catalog in the TEST environment to a production area. You do not need to know the names of the members prior to execution. However, a filter is available to select members that begin with certain types of names.

The SASHELP.VSCATLG view ❶ is used to create a list of the members in the TEST library. A DATA _NULL_ step is used with a subsetting IF ❷ to select the members of interest. The macro variables (&&CNAME&I) that contain the member names ❸ and the number of names (&CATCNT) ❹ are used within PROC DATASETS to build the SELECT statement ❺.

```
* Copy catalogs from the TEST to the PRODUCTION
* areas.;

options nomprint nomlogic nosymbolgen;

%macro catcopy(test,prod);
* test  - libref for the test area
* prod  - libref for the production area
*;

* Determine catalogs in TEST area;
data _null_;
set sashelp.vscatlg(where=(libname="%upcase(&test)"));❶
length ii $2;

* Select only some of the catalog members;
if memname in: ('DE', 'ED', 'PH');❷

i+1;
ii=left(put(i,2.));
call symput('cname'||ii,memname);❸
call symput('catcnt', ii);❹
run;

proc datasets ;
copy in=&test out=&prod memtype=catalog;
select
  %do i = 1 %to &catcnt;❺
      &&cname&i
  %end;
;
quit;
%mend catcopy;

%catcopy(appls,work)
```

SEE ALSO

The Technical Support section of *SAS Communications,* Volume xxii, 4th Qtr. 96 (p. 43) has a similar example that uses the BUILD procedure to build the new catalogs with modifications.

10.1.2   Write the first N lines of a series of flat files

%DUMPIT

Clarence Wm. Jackson
CJAC

The %DUMPIT macro is used to list the first few lines of each of a series of flat files. The following example code dumps some QSAM files, PDS's, and so on, using a list. Notice that this was used on the mainframe, so the FILENAME statement ❹ has a DISP=SHR.

```
%MACRO DUMPIT (CNTOUT);
 %* Create a local counter;
 %LOCAL CWJ;

 %DO CWJ=1 %TO &NUMOBS;

   %* Fileref to identify the file to list;
   FILENAME DUMP&CWJ "&&INVAR&CWJ" ❺ DISP=SHR; ❹

   * Read and write the first &CNTOUT records;
   DATA _NULL_; ❻
     INFILE DUMP&CWJ END=DONE; ❼
     * Read the next record;
     INPUT;
     INCNT+1;
     IF INCNT LE &CNTOUT THEN LIST;
     IF DONE THEN DO;
        FILE PRINT;
        PUT //@10 "TOTAL RECORDS FOR &&INVAR&CWJ IS "
              +2 INCNT COMMA9. ;
     END;
   RUN;

   FILENAME DUMP&CWJ CLEAR;

 %END;
%MEND DUMPIT; * The Macro definition ends;

* Read the control file and establish macro variables;
DATA DUMPIT; ❶
 INFILE CARDS END=DONE;
 INPUT FILENAM $25.;
 CNT+1;
 NEWNAME=TRIM(FILENAM);
 * The macro variable INVARi contains the ith file name;
 CALL SYMPUT ('INVAR'!!TRIM(LEFT(PUT(CNT,3.))),NEWNAME); ❸
 * Store the number of files to read;
 IF DONE THEN CALL SYMPUT('NUMOBS',CNT);
CARDS; ❷
PNB7.QSAM.BANK.RECON
PNB7.QSAM.CHECKS
PNB7.QSAM.CHKNMBR
PNB7.QSAM.CKTOHIST
PNB7.QSAM.DRAIN
PNB7.QSAM.RECON
PNB7.BDAM.BDAMCKNO
PNB7.BDAM.VCHRCKNO
PNB7.QSAM.CS2V3120.CARDIN
PNB7.QSAM.CASVCHCK
PNB7.QSAM.CASVOUCH
PNB7.QSAM.VCHR3120.CARDIN
PNB7.QSAM.VOUCHERS
TAX7.JACKSON
;;;
```

```
TITLE "CITY OF DALLAS - ECI (FINSYS), JOBNAME IS &SYSJOBID";
TITLE2 "LIST OF FILES TO DUMP &CNTOUT RECORDS";
PROC PRINT data=dumpit;
RUN;

* Pass the number of records to dump from each file;
%DUMPIT (25);
```

❶ The DATA step is used to read the names of the files ❷ that are to be dumped. These names are stored in NEWNAME.

❷ The list of files in this example is brought in using the CARDS statement. The list could just as easily have been built using CLIST or using other methods.

❸ Use the SYMPUT routine to load the name of the *i*th dump file into the macro variable INVAR$_i$.

❹ The fileref created in this FILENAME statement is used to identify the name of the file that is to be listed.

❺ The macro variable &&INVAR&CWJ in the FILENAME statement ❹ was created in the DATA step ❶ using a CALL SYMPUT ❸ before the macro %DUMPIT is called.

❻ A DATA _NULL_ step is used to read and list the lines in the flat file.

❼ The INFILE points to the fileref that was established in the preceding FILENAME statement ❹.

Note that although this macro only lists the first &CNTOUT lines of each flat file, the entire file is read in order to establish a line count.

SEE ALSO
Widawski (1997b) collects a list of dBase files that are to be converted to SAS files.

10.1.3   Storing system clock values in macro variables

%UPDATE

Jørn Lodahl

The automatic macro variables &SYSDATE and &SYSTIME reflect the time that the SAS session was invoked, and during long sessions they may not accurately reflect the actual time that a particular step executed. The current date and time can be captured and stored using the macro %UPDATE.

%UPDATE can be used to grab the current date and/or time values, and it refreshes or updates the macro variables &TIMESTR, &TODAYSTR, and &NOWSTR. You can specify any one of the three macro variables, or you can specify ALL to update each of the macro variables. Notice that these three macro variables are globalized, so you may need to be selective about the names before using the macro in your system.

```
/******************************************************
SYNTAX:
  %update(string_var)
EXAMPLES:
  %update(all)
  %update(timestr)
This macro updates some or all of the following date/time
string macro variables:
  &timestr
  &todaystr
  &nowstr
******************************************************/

%macro update(string); ❶
%global timestr todaystr nowstr;
  %if &string=all %then %do;
    %let string=nowstr;
  %end;
  data _null_;
    %if &string=todaystr or &string=nowstr %then %do;
      call symput('todaystr',put(today(),worddate.)); ❷
    %end;
    %if &string=timestr or &string=nowstr %then %do;
      call symput('timestr',put(time(),HHMM.));
    %end;
    %if &string=nowstr %then %do;
      %let nowstr=&timestr&todaystr; ❸
    %end;
  run;
%mend update;
```

❶ The user passes in the name of the macro variable to update.

❷ CALL SYMPUT is used to read the current time and to place its formatted value into the appropriate macro variable.

❸ When %UPDATE is called with the parameter `all`, the macro variable &NOWSTR will contain both the date and time strings.

Under Release 6.11 and later, you can avoid the DATA _NULL_ step in situations like this, where data are not actually read, by using the %SYSFUNC macro function (see Section 7.4.2).

10.1.4 Checking for write access

%CHKCOPY

The following macro copies the data sets in one library (COMBINE) to another (COMBTEMP), and it uses &SYSERR to detect whether another user currently has write access to a data set in the library COMBINE. This macro was written so that if the complete copy does not take place, then the whole process will be aborted.

```
%macro chkcopy;
* Copy the current version of the COMBINE files
* to COMBTEMP;
proc datasets memtype=data; ❶
    copy in=combine out=combtemp;
quit;
%if &syserr ge 5 %then %do; ❷
data _null_;
    put '**************************';
    put '**************************';
    put '**************************';
    put '*** combine copy failure **';
    put 'One of the data sets may be in use.';
    put '**************************';
    put '**************************';
    put '**************************';
    abort abend; ❸
run;
* When aborted (inside this macro do block) nothing else
* should execute in this job including the following
* message;
%put JOB ABORTED!!!!;
%put this message should not ever be written!!;
%end;
%mend chkcopy;
```

❶ Copy all members of the libref COMBINE to COMBTEMP. If another user has a write lock on one or more members those members will not be copied.

❷ &SYSERR contains the success code for PROC DATASETS. Five or larger indicates an unacceptable lack of success.

❸ The ABORT statement causes the current SAS process to terminate.

10.1.5 Appending unknown data sets

%CMBNSUBJ

This macro is taken from an application where a series of separate *information* data sets are created (one for each subject in the study). Generally, this is an inefficient storage technique. However, because SAS/SHARE software was not available, these data sets were also used to control which users could access data for a particular subject at any given time. The data sets each contained a single observation that stored various data entry and edit status indicators.

In order to create a unified subject status report, it was necessary to combine these individual data sets, and the following macro is used to concatenate them into one. The problem, of course, is that the number of subjects and the associated code (used to name the data set) is constantly changing. The following macro determines the list of current subjects from the names of the available files and then places the subjects' numbers into a series of macro variables.

```
%macro cmbnsubj;

* Determine the subjects, make a macro var for each;
* DECNTRL.INxxxxxx data sets have one obs per subject;
data _null_;
set sashelp.vtable(keep=libname memname);  ❶
where libname='DECNTRL' & memname=:'IN';  ❷
length ii $3 subject $6;
i+1;
ii=left(put(i,3.));
subject=substr(memname,3);
call symput('subj'||ii,subject);  ❸
call symput('subjcnt',ii);  ❹
run;

proc datasets library=work;
delete subjstat;

* Combine the subject control files;
%do i = 1 %to &subjcnt;
    append base=subjstat data=decntrl.in&&subj&i;  ❺
%end;
quit;
%mend cmbnsubj;
```

❶ The SASHELP.VTABLE view is used to create a list of all of the data sets in the application.

❷ The WHERE statement subsets the entries to those data sets of interest, for example, data sets that start with the letters IN in the DECNTRL library.

❸ A macro variable of the form &SUBJ1, &SUBJ2, and so on is created for each subject number (which is derived from the data set name, for example, IN133032).

❹ The number of subjects is counted.

❺ The selected data sets are combined using the APPEND statement in PROC DATASETS. This is more efficient than dynamically building a SET statement, as was done in Section 6.3, and requires fewer data sets to be open at any given time.

Because the SASHELP.VTABLE ❶ is a view, it must be created each time it is called. Because it always contains a list of **all** members of **all** established librefs, this can be a time-consuming process. A PROC CONTENTS with the OUT= and NOPRINT options may be a faster alternative to building this list. %CMBNSUBJ is modified here to use PROC CONTENTS:

```
%macro cmbnsubj;

* Determine the subjects, make a macro var for each;
* DECNTRL.INxxxxxx data sets have one obs per subject;

* Create a list of all data sets in the libref DECNTRL;
* ALLCONT will have one observation for each variable in each data set;
proc contents data=decntrl._all_
              out=allcont(keep=memname)
              noprint;
run;
```

```
* Eliminate duplicate observations;
proc sort data=allcont nodupkey;
  by memname;
  run;

data _null_;
set allcont;
where memname=:'IN';
length ii $3 subject $6;
i+1;
ii=left(put(i,3.));
subject=substr(memname,3);
call symput('subj'||ii,subject);
call symput('subjcnt',ii);
run;

proc datasets library=work;
delete subjstat;

* Combine the subject control files;
%do i = 1 %to &subjcnt;
    append base=subjstat data=decntrl.in&&subj&i;
%end;
quit;
%mend cmbnsubj;
```

Many directory-based operating systems have operating-system-level commands that can be used to construct a list of files in a directory. The following version of %CMBNSUBJ replaces the PROC CONTENTS with an X statement that contains the operating system DIR command (Windows based systems).

```
%macro cmbnsubj;

* Determine the subjects, make a macro var for each;
* DECNTRL.INxxxxxx data sets have one obs per subject;

* Create a list of all data sets in the libref DECNTRL;
%let depath = %sysfunc(pathname(decntrl));  ❶

x "dir &depath\in*.sd2 /o:n /b > d:\junk\dirhold.txt";  ❷

data null;
infile 'd:\junk\dirhold.txt' length=len;  ❸
input @;  ❹
input memname $varying12. len;  ❺
length ii $3 subject $6;
i+1;
ii=left(put(i,3.));
subject=substr(memname,3,len-6);  ❻
call symput('subj'||ii,subject);
call symput('subjcnt',ii);
run;
```

```
proc datasets library=work;
delete subjstat;

* Combine the subject control files;
%do i = 1 %to &subjcnt;
   append base=subjstat data=decntrl.in&&subj&i;
%end;
quit;
%mend cmbnsubj;
```

❶ Determine the path of the libref of interest and store it in &DEPATH.

❷ The X statement is used with the system's DIR command to build a list of files in the &DEPATH directory. This list is routed to a text file, where it is stored for later use (D:\JUNK\DIRHOLD.TXT).

❸ The text file is identified using the INFILE statement. Because the lengths of the data set names may not be constant, the LENGTH= option is used to store in the variable LEN the length of each data set's name.

❹ A dummy INPUT statement is used to load the next record into the input buffer. This statement also assigns a value to LEN.

❺ The $VARYING12. format is used to read the name of the data set. The variable LEN is used by the $VARYING format to specify the actual length of each incoming record (data set name).

❻ The subject number is extracted from the data set name by using the SUBSTR function. In this example, each data set name (MEMNAME) will be in the form of IN*xxxxx*.SD2, where *xxxxx* represents the subject number (the number of digits, *x*, varies from 1 to 6). You know that the subject number will start in the third column and will not include the last four columns(.SD2). Because the length of the data set is stored in LEN, the number of digits occupied by the subject number will be LEN-6.

SEE ALSO
Widawski (1997a) also uses the X statement to build a list of files.

10.2 Working with Listings and Reports

Macros are often used to control the appearance and order of reports and listings. The examples in this section represent these types of macros. Section 9.2 contains an example that causes a series of procedures to be executed for each level of the BY variable rather than by cycling through the BY groups for each procedure.

SEE ALSO
Aboutaleb (1997a) discusses a macro that you can use to control output lines when you work with proportional fonts.

10.2.1   Combining titles

%TF

David Shannon

The %TF macro shown in this section enables the user to combine up to three text strings on a single title or footnote. These strings can then be individually justified. You can use the macro to prevent overwriting the page number, and the entire title can be underlined. SASHELP.VOPTION is used to determine the current LINESIZE (width of the current output page) option. This value is then used to determine the position of the various strings.

```
/*_____

                                   TF

                                 _____

    TF macro allows Titles or Footnotes to be specified in any
    combination of LEFT, CENTRED or RIGHT aligned in one line.
    The user can optionally stop the output page number from being
    overwritten.  Specifying SLINE in the LEFT parameter will
    print a solid line the width of the page.
   _____

   | Parameter | Default | Description                              |
   |_____|_____|_____|

   | TF=       | TITLE   | OPTIONAL:  Parameter which defines if texts |
   |           |         | are TITLEs or FOOTNOTEs.                  |

   | N=        | 1       | OPTIONAL:  Title/Footnote number.  SAS   |
   |           |         | currently allows up to 10 titles/footnotes. |

   | Left=     |         | OPTIONAL:  Text to be left aligned.  If you |
   |           |         | specify SLINE then a solid line will be  |
   |           |         | drawn the width of the linesize.         |

   | Centre=   |         | OPTIONAL:  Text to be centred on the page. |

   | Right=    |         | OPTIONAL:  Text to be right aligned.     |

   | PNum=     | NO      | OPTIONAL:  Used when TF is a TITLE, and if |
   |           |         | set to YES it stops right aligned title1 |
   |           |         | from over writing the automatic page number. |
   |           |         | NB: Use OPTIONS NUMBER to start page     |
   |           |         | numbering.                               |
   _____

    Usage      : See documentation in the software library.

    Written by : David Shannon, V1.0, Spring 97, Engine 6.10+
                 david@schweiz.demon.co.uk
                 David Shannon, V1.1, 09SEP1997, Engine 6.12.
                 (Reduced to LS-2 allowing paging macros to work).

    References : SAS Language, Version 6, SAS Institute.
               : SAS Guide to Macro Processing, Version 6, SAS Inst.
   _____ */;
```

```
%Macro TF(TF=T,N=1,Left=,Centre=,Right=,PNum=No);
%Local ERRCOD1 ERRCOD2 GAP3 LWAS;
Options NoMprint NoMlogic NoSymbolgen;

%********************************************************************;
%* Determine if TF is title or footnote (defaults to TITLE)       *;

%If %Upcase(%Substr(&TF,1,1))=F %Then %Do; %Let TF=FOOTNOTE; %End;
%Else %Do; %Let TF=TITLE; %End;

%********************************************************************;
%* Ensure that Title and Number parameters are valid.             *;

Data _null_;
     Length N $2 Pnum $3;
     N=symget('N');
     If N not in('1' '2' '3' '4' '5' '6' '7' '8' '9' '10') then ❶
        Do;
            PUT "ERROR: Valid &TF lines are integers from 1 to 10.";Put;
            Call Symput('ERRCODE','1');
        End;
     PNum=Upcase(Symget('PNum'));
     If substr(PNum,1,1) not in ('N','Y') then ❷
        Do;
            Call Symput('PNUM','NO');
            PUT "WARNING: Invalid NUMBER option specified";
            PUT "Defaulted to NO.";PUT;
        End;
Run;
%If &ERRCOD1=1 %Then %Goto EOM;

%********************************************************************;
%* If pnum is set to no then stop page numbering                  *;

%If (%Upcase(%Substr(&pnum,1,1))=N AND &TF=TITLE) %Then
%Do;
    Options NoNumber;
%End;

%********************************************************************;
%* Determine FROM and TO positions of texts and spaces            *;

Data _null_;
Set  SASHELP.VOPTION(Where=(optname='LINESIZE')); ❸
     Length to1 from2 to2 from3 gap1 gap2 settn 8.;
     settn=(input(setting,??best.)-3);
     If Upcase("&LEFT")="SLINE" Then
     Do;
         %Let lwas=&left;
         Call symput('LEFT',Left(Repeat('Ä',settn)));
     End;
     Left=Trim(Symget(Resolve('Left')));
     Centre=Trim(Symget('Centre'));
     Right=Trim(Symget('Right'));
```

```
If Left^="" Then
Do;
   To1=Length(Trim(left));
End;
Else Do;
   To1=0;
End;

If Centre^="" Then
Do;
   From2=Floor( Floor(settn/2) - Length(Trim(centre))/2);
   To2=(from2 + Length(Trim(centre)))-1;
End;
Else Do;
   From2=Floor(settn/2);
   To2=Floor(settn/2)+1;
  Call Symput('Centre',repeat(byte(32),1));
End;

If Right^="" Then
Do;
   From3=( settn+1 - Length(Trim(right))-1);
   If (%Eval(&N)=1 AND upcase(substr("&Pnum",1,1))='Y') then
        From3=from3-4;
End;
Else Do;
   From3=settn+1;
End;

gap1=( (from2) - (to1) -1 );
gap2=( (from3) - (to2) -1 );

If gap1 gt 0 then Call Symput('Gap1', repeat(byte(32),gap1));
Else %let gap1=;; ❹
If gap2 gt 0 then Call Symput('Gap2', repeat(byte(32),gap2));
Else %let gap2=;; ❹

%If %Upcase(&PNum)=YES %Then Call Symput('Gap3', repeat(byte(32),3));
%Else Call Symput('Gap3',repeat(byte(32),1));;;

If ((to1 ge from2) AND centre ne '') then
Do;
   PUT "ERROR: Centre aligned text will overwrite left aligned text.";
   PUT "ERROR: Either shorten text or increase linesize";
   Call Symput ('ERRCOD2','1');
End;

If ((to2 ge from3) AND right  ne '') then
Do;
   PUT "ERROR: Right aligned text will overwrite centre aligned text.";
   PUT "ERROR: Either shorten text or increase linesize";
   Call Symput ('ERRCOD2','1');
End;
   Run;
```

```
%******************************************************************;
%* Check for error status, if true jump to end of macro          *;

%If &ERRCOD2=1 %then %Goto EOM;

%******************************************************************;
%* Create Title/Footnote                                         *;

%If %Upcase(&LWAS)=SLINE %Then
%Do;
     &TF&N " &LEFT ";
%End;
%Else %Do;
     &TF&N " &LEFT&GAP1&CENTRE&GAP2&RIGHT&GAP3.";
%End;
%EOM:
Options Mprint Mlogic Symbolgen;
%Mend TF;
```

❶ Check for valid title numbers.

❷ Check to see that the page number option is valid.

❸ SASHELP.VOPTION view is used to determine system option settings.

❹ This is an example of code that was written with a style different than has been described elsewhere in this book. The intent of the code is to initialize the macro variables &GAP1 and &GAP2, which takes place. However, because the %LET is executed before the DATA step, the conditional logic does not apply. The %LET statements are <u>always</u> executed <u>before</u> the DATA step is executed. The second of the double semicolons closes what is effectively a null ELSE statement (`Else;`). If it had been necessary to conditionally assign a null value to &GAP1, the ELSE statement would have been followed not with a %LET but rather with the executable CALL SYMPUT:

```
If gap1 gt 0 then Call Symput('Gap1', repeat(byte(32),gap1));
     Else Call Symput('Gap1','');
```

SEE ALSO
Andersen (1997) presents a macro that will split and wrap a long text variable when creating a report using a DATA _NULL_ step.

10.2.2   Renumbering listing pages

%REPORT

Paul Kairis
NIKH Corporation
(Originally published in The Valley of the Sun SAS Users Group, VALSUG, Newsletter, 1996)

Typically when running a series of procedures that produce output listings, the page numbers are consecutive starting with one. You can use the system option PAGENO to reset the page numbers *between* PROC and DATA steps but not *within* a step, such as between BY levels. The following macro creates WHERE strings based on the BY variables. A separate PROC REPORT is then called for each combination of BY variables with the PAGENO reset between calls.

```
%macro report(dsn);
proc summary data =&dsn nway;  ❶
    class tpcorder sysname bldgname grpname;
    output out=calllist;
    run;

data _null_;
    set calllist end=eof;
    numcall+1;  ❷
    * Build macro variable(s) to hold WHERE clause;
    call symput('call'||left(put(numcall,3.)),   ❸
        "tpcorder='"||tpcorder||
        "'and sysname= '"||sysname||
        "'and bldgname='"||bldgname||
        "'and grpname= '"||grpname||"'");
    if eof then call symput('numcalls',left(put(numcall,3.)));  ❹
    run;

%do i = 1 %to &numcalls;  ❺
    options nobyline pageno=1;
    proc report data=&dsn nowindows headline;
        by tpcorder sysname bldgname grpname;
        where &&call&i;  ❻
        run;
%end;
%mend report;
```

❶ PROC SUMMARY is used to create a data set (CALLLIST) that contains the unique combinations of the BY variables.

❷ The number of unique combinations of the BY variables is stored in the variable NUMCALL.

❸ The WHERE clause is built by concatenating the names of the BY variables with their values. In this case, note that all the variables are character.

❹ Store the overall number of BY group combinations in the macro variable &NUMCALLS.

❺ The macro %DO loop executes the PROC REPORT once for each BY group combination.

❻ The WHERE statement uses the clause that is stored in &&CALL&i to subset the data prior to the execution of the PROC REPORT.

The example in Section 9.2 and the solutions to Exercise Questions 6.2 and 6.3 utilize a similar approach by creating data subsets.

Chapter 11 **Working with SAS® Data Sets**

One of the things that SAS does best is to work with all types of data sets. You can use the macro language to form powerful tools that can be applied in a variety of situations that interface with these data sets. This chapter includes examples of a number of common problems that are associated with the maintenance, construction, and use of flat files and SAS data sets.

11.1 Creating Flat Files

A number of tools have been written to convert a SAS data set into a flat file. Most of these use PROC CONTENTS to determine the data structure (variable names and type). If you are using Release 6.12 or later, you can also employ the SCL functions and the VIEW SASHELP.VCOLUMN.

SEE ALSO
Kretzman (1992) includes a macro that dumps a SAS data set to a flat file.

11.1.1 Column specified flat file

%SAS2RAW

You can use PROC CONTENTS to determine the attributes of each of the variables in the data set that is to be converted. This information, including formatting, is used to build the PUT statement that is used to write the flat file. The syntax of the PUT statement is also written to the file as a header record to document the data set variable names and column information. Because formats may be used, variables with associated formats will be written in formatted form.

```
* sas2raw.sas
*
* Convert a SAS data set to a RAW or flat text file.  Include
* SAS statements on the flat file as documentation.
*;

* DSN  LIBREF OF THE DATA BASE (data base name) e.g. BEN;
*       This argument can be used to control the path.
* MEM  NAME OF DATA SET AND RAW FILE (member name)
*      e.g. FULLBEN;
* The raw file will have the same name as the data set.
*;
%MACRO SAS2RAW(dsn, mem);

* The libref for incoming data is &dsn;
libname &dsn    "d:\training\sas\&dsn"; ❶
* New text file written to the fileref ddout;
filename ddout "d:\junk\&mem..raw "; ❶

*   DETERMINE LENGTHS AND FORMATS OF THE VARIABLES;
PROC CONTENTS DATA=&dsn..&mem OUT=A1 NOPRINT;
RUN;

PROC SORT DATA=A1; BY NPOS;
RUN;

* MANY NUMERIC VARIABLES DO NOT HAVE FORMATS AND THE RAW FILE;
* WILL BE TOO WIDE IF WE JUST USE A LENGTH OF 8;
* Count the number of numeric variables;
DATA _NULL_; SET A1 END=EOF;
IF TYPE=1 THEN NNUM + 1;
IF EOF THEN CALL SYMPUT('NNUM',LEFT(PUT(NNUM,3.)));
RUN;


%if &nnum > 0 %then %do; ❷
* DETERMINE HOW MANY DIGITS ARE NEEDED FOR EACH NUMERIC VARIABLE;
* _D STORES THE MAXIMUM NUMBER OF DIGITS NEEDED FOR EACH NUMERIC VARI-
ABLE;
DATA M2; SET &dsn..&mem (KEEP=_NUMERIC_) END=EOF;
ARRAY _D  DIGIT1 - DIGIT&NNUM;
ARRAY _N  _NUMERIC_;
KEEP DIGIT1 - DIGIT&NNUM;
RETAIN DIGIT1 - DIGIT&NNUM;
IF _N_ = 1 THEN  DO OVER _D;  _D=1; END;
DO OVER _D;
     _NUMBER = _N;
     _D1 = LENGTH(LEFT(PUT(_NUMBER,BEST16.)));
     _D2 = _D;
     * NUMBER OF DIGITS NEEDED;
     _D = MAX(_D1, _D2);
END;
IF EOF THEN OUTPUT;
RUN;
%end;
```

```
*** THIS SECTION DOES NOT WRITE DATA ONLY THE PUT STATEMENT;
*MAKE THE PUT STATEMENT AND SET IT ASIDE .;
* It will serve as documentation as well as the PUT;
DATA _NULL_; SET A1 END=EOF;
RETAIN _TOT 0 _COL 1;
FILE DDOUT NOPRINT lrecl=250;
IF _N_ = 1 THEN DO;
     %if &nnum > 0 %then SET M2;;
     _TOT = NPOS;
END;
%if &nnum > 0 %then %do;
ARRAY _D (NNUM) DIGIT1 - DIGIT&NNUM;
* TYPE=1 FOR NUMERIC VARS;
IF TYPE=1 THEN DO;
     NNUM + 1;
     DIGIT = _D;
     * TAKE THE FORMATTED LENGTH INTO CONSIDERATION;
     LENGTH = MAX(FORMATL, FORMATD, DIGIT);
END;
%end;
_TOT = _TOT + LENGTH + 1;
CHAR = '                     ';
* SPECIAL HANDLING IS REQUIRED WHEN FORMATS ARE USED.
* CHAR IS USED TO STORE THE FORMAT;
IF FORMAT ^= ' ' | FORMATL>0 | FORMATD >0 THEN DO;
    * BUILD THE FORMAT FOR THIS VARIABLE;
    CHAR = TRIM(FORMAT);
    IF FORMATL>0 THEN CHAR= TRIM(CHAR)||TRIM(LEFT(PUT(FORMATL,3.)));
    CHAR= TRIM(CHAR)||'.';
    IF FORMATD>0 THEN CHAR= TRIM(CHAR)||TRIM(LEFT(PUT(FORMATD,3.)));
END;
IF TYPE = 2 & FORMAT = ' ' THEN CHAR = '$';
* _COL IS THE STARTING COLUMN;
IF _N_ = 1 THEN _COL = 1;
IF _N_ = 1 THEN PUT '/* *** */ PUT @' _COL NAME CHAR;
ELSE            PUT '/* *** */     @' _COL NAME CHAR;
_COL = _COL + LENGTH + 1;
IF EOF THEN DO;
     PUT '/* *** */ ;' ;
     CALL SYMPUT('LRECL',_TOT);
END;
RUN;

* Write out the flat file using the PUT statement in DDOUT;
DATA _NULL_; SET &dsn..&mem;
FILE DDOUT NOPRINT MOD lrecl=250;   ❸
%INCLUDE DDOUT;   ❹
run;
%MEND sas2raw;

***************************************************;

   %SAS2RAW(sasclass,ca88air)    run;   ❺
```

❶ The path information is system dependent. In Release 6.12, SASHELP.VSLIB can be used to determine path information when it is given a libref.

❷ The macro variable &NNUM contains the number of numeric variables in this data set. Several macro %DO blocks are used to provide special processing for numeric variables.

❸ The DDOUT fileref points to both the location of the PUT statement and the file where the data will be written. This causes the data to be appended to the PUT statement, which then serves as file documentation.

❹ The %INCLUDE statement brings the PUT statement into the DATA step, where it can be used to write the flat file.

❺ The macro call contains the arguments for the libref and the member that is to be converted to a flat file.

A PROC PRINT of the first ten observations of the data set SASCLASS.BIOMASS produces the following table:

```
                     Listing of SASCLASS.BIOMASS

 OBS    STATION        DATE      BMPOLY     BMCRUS     BMMOL     BMOTHR     BMTOTL

  1     DL-25        18JUN85      0.40       0.03      0.17      0.02       0.62
  2     DL-60        17JUN85      0.51       0.09      0.14      0.08       0.82
  3     D1100-25     18JUN85      0.28       0.02      0.01      4.61       4.92
  4     D1100-60     17JUN85      0.36       0.05      0.32      0.47       1.20
  5     D1900-25     18JUN85      0.03       0.02      0.11      1.06       1.22
  6     D1900-60     17JUN85      0.54       0.11      0.03      4.18       4.86
  7     D3200-60     17JUN85      0.52       0.14      0.04      0.05       0.75
  8     D3350-25     18JUN85      0.18       0.02      0.11      0.00       0.31
  9     D6700-25     18JUN85      0.51       0.06      0.03      0.01       0.61
 10     D6700-60     17JUN85      0.32       0.14      0.04      0.22       0.72
```

The macro call %SAS2RAW(sasclass, biomass) produces the text file BIOMASS.RAW, a portion of which is shown below:

```
/* *** */ PUT @1 STATION $
/* *** */     @10 DATE DATE7.
/* *** */     @18 BMPOLY
/* *** */     @23 BMCRUS
/* *** */     @29 BMMOL
/* *** */     @34 BMOTHR
/* *** */     @39 BMTOTL
/* *** */ ;
DL-25      18JUN85 0.4  0.03  0.17 0.02 0.62
DL-60      17JUN85 0.51 0.09  0.14 0.08 0.82
D1100-25   18JUN85 0.28 0.02  0.01 4.61 4.92
D1100-60   17JUN85 0.36 0.05  0.32 0.47 1.2
D1900-25   18JUN85 0.03 0.02  0.11 1.06 1.22
D1900-60   17JUN85 0.54 0.11  0.03 4.18 4.86
D3200-60   17JUN85 0.52 0.14  0.04 0.05 0.75
D3350-25   18JUN85 0.18 0.02  0.11 0    0.31
D6700-25   18JUN85 0.51 0.06  0.03 0.01 0.61
D6700-60   17JUN85 0.32 0.14  0.04 0.22 0.72
```

SEE ALSO
Whitlock (1993) provides a description and code for a macro (%FLATFILE) that operates in a similar manner to %SAS2RAW (except with more options).

11.1.2 Creating comma-delimited files

%DELIM

Susan Haviar

You can use comma-delimited files as import data for a number of applications that include spreadsheets and Microsoft Word tables. The following macro creates a comma-delimited flat file that uses PROC CONTENTS and a DATA _NULL_:

```
%delim(vitals,log)
* delim.sas
*
* Convert a SAS data set to a comma delimited flat file.;
*
* Presented at PharmaSUG April, 1997
* by Susan Haviar
*;

data vitals;
input value $10. target $8. nums err mini maxi;
cards;
Diastolic Baseline 8 64.5 59 74
Diastolic 0.25 hrs 8 66.6 57 72
Diastolic 0.50 hrs 8 62.9 51 70
Diastolic 1 hrs    8 69.5 57 88
Diastolic 2 hrs    8 69.8 53 83
run;
```

```
%macro delim(dsn,oout);

    filename &oout "d:\junk\&dsn..txt";  ❶

    proc contents data=&dsn  ❷
                  out=_temp_ (keep=name npos)
                  noprint;
    run;

    proc sort data=_temp_;  ❸
    by npos;
    run;

    data _null_;
    set _temp_ end=eof;
    call symput('var'||left(put(_n_,5.)),name);  ❹
    if eof then call symput('total',left(put(_n_,8.)));
    run;

    data _null_;
    file &oout noprint;  ❺
    set &dsn;
    put
        %do i=1 %to &total;  ❻
            &&var&i +(-1)','  ❼
        %end;
        +(-1)' ';  ❽
    run;
%mend delim;

%delim(vitals,outfile)
```

❶ Name the flat file that is to be created. In this example, it will be vitals.txt.

❷ Use PROC CONTENTS to create a data set (_TEMP_) that contains the variables and their position in the data set that is named in &DSN.

❸ Sort the variable names according to their position on the PDV.

❹ Create a series of macro variables (&VAR1, &VAR2, and so on) that contain the variable names in the data set &DSN. The total number of variables is stored in &TOTAL.

❺ Name the output file in a FILE statement.

❻ Dynamically create the PUT statement that will contain each variable in the data set.

❼ The +(−1) moves the pointer back one space and prevents a blank from being written between the value and the comma.

❽ Use a blank to cover up the comma that follows the last variable.

SEE ALSO

Hahl (1995) demonstrates a similar example that places quotes around character variables.

11.2 Subsetting a SAS Data Set

It is often of interest to create subsets of a data set based on some predefined criteria. This might include randomly selected observations or a certain percentage of the observations with the largest values of a particular variable. This section discusses some of these selection techniques.

11.2.1   Selection of top percentage using SQL

%TOPPCNT

Diane Goldschmidt

This macro creates a data set that is a subset of an original data set, and the subsetting criterion is based on a percentage of the largest values of a particular variable. You might use this macro if you want to regularly run a report on the top 10% of a data set that is constantly changing size, and you don't want to manually calculate and then edit the number of observations that you want to look at.

SQL is used to count the number of observations with distinct values of the ID variable (&IDVAR) ❶. The requested fraction of this number ❷ is then loaded into a macro variable &IDPCNT ❸. The first &IDPCNT observations are then written to the new data set TOPITEMS ❹ using the OBS= data set option.

```
%macro toppcnt(dsn,idvar,pcnt);
****************************************************************;
* CREATE TABLE PCNT FOR INDICATING &PCNT OF Ids   *;
****************************************************************;

PROC SQL NOPRINT;
      SELECT
             COUNT(DISTINCT &IDVAR) ❶ *&PCNT ❷ INTO :IDPCNT ❸
FROM
      &dsn;        ****<-- Number of obs in &dsn is unknown;


****************************************************************;
*              SORT ON DESCENDING &IDVAR                      *;
****************************************************************;

PROC SORT DATA= &dsn OUT=ITEMS;
BY DESCENDING &IDVAR;
RUN;

****************************************************************;
*    KEEP TOP % USING GLOBAL MACRO VARIABLE                  *;
****************************************************************;

DATA TOPITEMS;
SET ITEMS(OBS=%UNQUOTE(&IDPCNT)); ❹       **<-- Reflects the % ;
RUN;
%mend toppcnt;


%toppcnt(sasclass.biomass,bmtotl,.25);
```

The macro %TOPPCNT counts the distinct values of the variable named by &IDVAR. If each observation does not contain a unique value for that variable, the percentage of observations in TOPITEMS may not be accurate.

11.2.2 Selection of top percentage using the POINT option

%SELPCNT

You can also use the POINT and NOBS options in the SET statement to select data subsets. In the following macro, which uses many of the same naming conventions as the macro in Section 11.2.1, the data are sorted first ❶ and then subsetted in the following DATA step. The NOBS= option ❷ creates a variable on the PDV (NOBS) that is equal to the number of observations in the data set. This enables you to calculate the number of observations to read (IDPCNT) ❸. Unlike the macro %TOPPCNT in Section 11.2.1, the count is based on total observations not total number of distinct values of the ID variable (&IDVAR).

```
%macro selpcnt(dsn,idvar,pcnt);

* Sort the incoming data set in descending order;
proc sort data=&dsn ❶
          out=items;
by descending &idvar;
run;

* Read the first IDPCNT observations from ITEMS;
data topitems;
idpcnt = nobs*&pcnt; ❸
do point = 1 to idpcnt;
    set items point=point nobs=nobs ❷;
    output;
end;
stop;
run;
%mend selpcnt;

%selpcnt(sasclass.biomass,bmtotl,.25);
```

11.2.3 Random selection of observations

A variety of routines have been written to create a data subset that is based on the random selection of observations. The use of the macro language is actually secondary to the process, which is fairly simple.

Random selection routines either select with or without replacement. WITH replacement selection means that a given observation is eligible for selection more than once. Each observation can be selected one time, at most, when using a WITHOUT replacement criteria.

The two macros presented here represent these two selection methods.

Selection without replacement %RAND_WO

In this macro, the user selects the data set that the observations are to be selected from and the fraction of observations to select. This routine will result in an approximate subset. Other routines that are based on conditional probabilities have also been written. These routines result in a more precise number of observations in the subset.

```
%macro rand_wo(dsn,pcnt=0);

* Randomly select an approximate percentage of
* observations from a data set.
*
* Sample WITHOUT replacement;
*         any given observation can be selected only once
*         all observations have equal probability of selection.
*;

* Randomly select observations from &DSN;
data rand_wo;
set &dsn;
if ranuni(0) le &pcnt then output; ❶
run;
%mend rand_wo;
```

The RANUNI function ❶ is used to return a random number between 0 and 1. The observation is only written to the new data set RAND_WO if the returned value is less than the requested fraction (&PCNT). A call to %RAND_WO requesting a 25% subset could be written as

```
%rand_wo(study03,pcnt=.25);
```

Using this method only allows any given observation to be selected once.

Selection with replacement %RAND_W

Sampling with replacement allows more flexibility and a more interesting macro. When sampling with replacement, it is possible for the resulting data set to have more observations than the original. This can be very useful when you use bootstrapping statistical techniques.

The following macro, %RAND_W, allows the user to select either the number of desired observations or a percentage. Both may result in numbers that are larger than the number of original observations. The POINT and NOBS options in the SET statement are used to randomly select the observations that are to be included in the sample.

```
%macro rand_w(dsn,numobs=0,pcnt=0); ❶

* Randomly select either a specified number of
* observations or a percentage from a data set.
*
* Sample WITH replacement;
*         any observation can be selected any number of
*         times.

* When NUMOBS is specified create a subset of exactly
* that many observations (ignore PCNT).
* When PCNT is specified (and NUMOBS is not)
* calculate NUMOBS using PCNT*total number in DSN.
*;

* Randomly select &NUMOBS observations from &DSN;
data rand_w;
retain numobs .;
drop numobs i;
```

```
* Create a variable (NUMOBS) to hold number of obs
* to write to RAND_W;
%if &pcnt ne 0 and &numobs=0 %then %do;
   numobs = round(nobs*&pcnt);  ❷
%end;
%else %do;
   numobs = &numobs;  ❸
%end;

* Loop through the SET statement NUMOBS times;
do i = 1 to numobs;
   * Determine the next observation to read;
   point = ceil(ranuni(0)*nobs);  ❹

   * Read and output the selected observation;
   set &dsn point=point nobs=nobs  ;  ❺
   output;  ❻
end;
stop;
run;
%mend rand_w;
```

❶ The user selects one of two named parameters:

NUMOBS=   is used when a specific number of observations is desired.

PCNT=   specifies a fraction (&PCNT can be greater than 1) of the observations to select.

❷ The variable NUMOBS will be used in a DO loop that controls the number of observations in the output data set. Here, NUMOBS is calculated based on the number of observations in the data set (NOBS) and the desired percent (&PCNT).

❸ When a specific number of observations is requested, that value is transferred to the variable NUMOBS.

❹ POINT will be a random integer that can range from 1 to NOBS. It is important that the CEIL function be used to create the integer. Functions such as INT, FLOOR, or ROUND will assign the incorrect probabilities to the first and last observations.

❺ Read the observation indicated by the POINT variable.

❻ Output the observation to the new data set and continue the loop.

Typical calls to %RAND_W might include

```
%rand_w(study03,numobs=100);

%rand_w(study03,pcnt=.25);
```

11.3 Checking the Existence of SAS Data Sets

At times, you will want to be able to determine if a data set exists before you execute a procedure such as PROC PRINT against it. When creating systems dynamically, some data sets may not exist under certain circumstances, and you need to be able to determine their status at execution time.

The macro %EXIST, described in Section 7.1.2, uses a DATA step to determine if a data set exists. In the following example, the EXIST function is used in conjunction with the %SYSFUNC macro function to eliminate the DATA step and the annoying error message in the LOG when the data set is not found:

```
%macro exist(dsn);
%global exist;
%if %sysfunc(exist(&dsn)) ❶ %then %let exist=YES;
%else %let exist=NO; ❷
%mend exist;
```

❶ The EXIST function returns a value that is equal to 1 when the data set exists. Otherwise, it returns a 0 causing the %IF to be false, which results in &EXIST being set to NO ❷.

SEE ALSO

The EXIST function is combined with the %SYSFUNC macro function in a similar example in *SAS® Macro Language, Reference, First Edition* (p. 242).

Whitlock (1997) uses a data step to determine if a data set contains any observations.

11.4 Working with Lists of Data Set Variables

The use of macros and macro variables is often important when dealing with a list of data set variables. This is especially true when the data sets and variable lists are generated dynamically in such a way that the developer does not know what the program will be operating on at the time of execution. The following examples create or work with macro variables that contain a list of data set variable names.

SEE ALSO

The documentation for %SYSFUNC (*SAS® Macro Language, Reference, First Edition*, p. 242) contains an example that counts the number of both observations and variables in a SAS data set.

Hahl (1996) describes the macro %DROPVAR that can be used to DROP any variable in a data set that only takes on MISSING values.

Whitaker (1989) provides several utilities to work with lists, including

- counting and extracting words
- eliminating duplicate words

- ■ building lists with SYMPUT

- ■ building lists with %INCLUDE.

11.4.1   Create a list of variable names from the PDV

Kim Kubasek
Consultant

Sometimes it becomes necessary to create a macro variable that contains a list of variable names. When you deal with programs that were written dynamically, you may not know what those names will be, especially when the data sets are created by SAS procedures.

One procedure that commonly creates new variables is PROC TRANSPOSE. When you use the ID statement, the names of the new variables will be the values taken on by the ID variable (or some variation of those values). The following example creates a list of variable names and places them in a macro variable.

In this code, the data set WORK.TEMP4 was created by PROC TRANSPOSE ❶, and the new (unknown) variables will be the values of the ID variable GROUP1 ❷. PROC SQL is used to access the SASHELP.VCOLUMN view ❸ that contains the names of the variables (PROC CONTENTS could also be used. See Section 11.1.1). A DATA _NULL_ step ❹ is then used to build a %LET statement ❺ that is then included back into the program ❻.

```
*** create the transposed data set;
proc transpose data=temp3 out=temp4 ; ❶
by group2 year &spvar ;
var mean ;
id group1 ; ❷
run ;

*** what variable names did proc transpose create?
    the table VARLIST will contain just the variable
    names of interest;
proc sql noprint ;
create table varlist as
select name
  from sashelp.vcolumn ❸
    where libname='WORK'
      and memtype='DATA'
      and memname='TEMP4'
      and not(name in ('GROUP2' 'YEAR' "%upcase(&spvar)"
                      '_NAME_' '_LABEL_')) ;
quit ;

*** write short files of code to be included later that will
    create a space-delimited variable list ;
data _null_ ; ❹
set varlist end=e ;
file 'temp2.sas' lrecl=70 ;
if _n_=1 then put '%let varlist= ' @ ; ❺
put name @ ;
if e then put ';' ;
run ;

%include 'temp2.sas' / source ; ❻
```

The resulting file TEMP2.SAS will contain a single %LET statement, which will be executed as soon as the file is included ❻. A sample %LET statement might be

```
%let varlist=station date depth;
```

You can replace the PROC SQL and %INCLUDE portions of the previous example with a single DATA _NULL_ if the VNAME routine is used. The following DATA step is designed to fit into the previous example right after the PROC TRANSPOSE:

```
data _null_;
length name $8 str $80;
set temp4;
array allc {*}_character_;  ❶
array alln {*}_numeric_;  ❶
if dim(allc) then do i=1 to dim(allc);  ❷
   call vname(allc{i},name);  ❸
   * Exclude vars we know we do not want;
   if name not in('_NAME_' '_LABEL_' 'NAME' 'STR'
                  'GROUP2' 'YEAR' "%upcase(&spvar)" ) then
       str = trim(str)||' '||trim(name);  ❹
end;
if dim(alln) then do i=1 to dim(alln);
   call vname(alln{i},name);
   str = trim(str)||' '||trim(name);
end;
call symput('varlist',str);  ❺
stop;  ❻
run;
```

❶ Separate arrays are set up for the numeric and character variables.

❷ A DO loop is used to walk through each of the variables in the respective array.

❸ The CALL VNAME routine returns the name of the variable on the PDV (identified by the array ALLC{i}) and places it in the variable NAME.

❹ Because the value of the variable NAME is the name of the unknown variable in the array, it is then appended to the variable STR, which accumulates all the variable names.

❺ Once all variable names have been collected, the variable STR is written to the macro variable VARLIST using the SYMPUT routine. Notice that in this example the variable STR is assigned an arbitrary length of $80, and this may be limiting if the list becomes long. The first example in this section does not have this limitation.

❻ Because you are interested in only the names of the variables and not in the data, the STOP statement is used to prevent further passes of the data.

Section 2.7.2 uses PROC SQL to build a similar list, as does the example in Section 13.1.2.

11.4.2 Create a list of variable names from an ID variable

Jørn Lodahl

PROC SQL can also be used directly to create a macro variable that contains a list of data set variable values. If your data set already contains a variable whose values are to be loaded into a macro variable list, then you can use the following code (which was suggested by Jørn Lodahl and is used in %INDVAR in Section 13.1.2). The examples in Sections 6.2.1 and 6.3 also use a data set to build macro variables, but the results are placed in individual macro variables rather than into a single list.

```
proc sql noprint;
   select distinct loc ❶
     into :loclist separated by ' '❷
     from samdat ❸
     order by loc; ❹
   quit;
```

All unique values of the variable LOC ❶ are written to the macro variable &LOCLIST ❷, where they are separated by blanks. The variables are read from the data set SAMDAT ❸, and the values are placed in ascending order by using the ORDER clause ❹.

SEE ALSO
Widawski (1997a) creates a list of filenames, which is written to a macro variable.

11.4.3   Create individual macro variables from an existing list

This example assumes that you have created a macro variable that contains a list of data set variables (see Sections 11.4.1 and 11.4.2). In this case, the macro variable (&KEYFLD) contains the variables that form the key fields (variables used in a BY statement). Section 6.4.2 also discusses the use of &KEYFLD.

A sample definition of the macro variable &KEYFLD might be

```
%let keyfld = investid subject treatid;
```

In the program that uses this list, we might expect to see a BY statement such as

```
by &keyfld;
```

In order to use FIRST. and LAST. processing, however, you need to know the name of the last variable in the list. This enables you to write statements such as this:

```
by investid subject treatid;
if last.treatid then do;
```

To do this using &KEYFLD, you need to know its component parts (variable names in the list) and the number of names. The following DATA step can be used to create a series of macro variables (&KEY1, &KEY2, and so on), one for each name in &KEYFLD:

```
*determine the list of key vars;
data _null_;
* count the number of keyvars
* save each for later;
str="&keyfld"; ❶
do I = 1 to 6;
  key = scan(str,i,' '); ❷
  if key ne ' ' then do;
   ii=left(put(i,1.));
   call symput('key'||ii,
        trim(left(key))); ❸
   call symput('keycnt',ii); ❹
  end;
end;
run;
```

❶ An assignment statement creates the variable STR to hold the list. (You also could have used SYMGET.)

❷ This string is then broken into words using the SCAN function.

❸ Macro variables are then created using the SYMPUT routine.

❹ The number of key variables is also counted and assigned to &KEYCNT.

Once the macro variables have been established, statements that require FIRST. or LAST. processing can be rewritten as

```
by &keyfld;
if last.&&key&keycnt then do;
```

Because &KEYCNT is the number of key variables, &&KEY&KEYCNT will resolve to the name of the last variable in the list that is stored in &KEYFLD.

Using the DATA step in the previous example is not very efficient. The same result can be accomplished using only macro statements. In the following example, the %DO %UNTIL loop is used to step through and count the elements in &KEYFLD:

```
%Macro doit;

%let I = 1; ❶
%do %until (%scan(&keyfld,&I,%str( )) = %str()); ❷
   %let key&I = %scan(&keyfld,&I,%str( )); ❸
   %let I = %eval(&I + 1); ❹
%end;
%let keycnt = %eval(&I-1); ❺
%mend doit;
```

❶ Initialize &I, which will be used as the counter in the %DO %UNTIL loop.

❷ Scan &KEYFLD for the *i*th word, using a blank as the separator, and check to see if the function results in a null string. Notice that the first %STR contains a blank space (the word separator), while the second has no space (a null text string).

❸ If the previous line ❷ determined that the *i*th word exists, retrieve it and store it in &KEYi.

❹ Increment the counter by 1 in preparation for the next scan.

❺ The last word has been found, and the counter was incremented one time too many. Reduce the value by 1 and save the count in &KEYCNT.

SEE ALSO
Roberts (1997) presents several macros that work with variable lists. One of his examples is very similar to the above code but uses a %DO %WHILE loop.

11.5 Counting Observations in a Data Set

A variety of methods count the number of observations in a SAS data set. In Sections 2.7.2, 11.2.1, and 13.1.1, PROC SQL is used. The SET statement options (POINT and NOBS) can also be used, as in Sections 11.2.2 and 11.2.3. For users operating under Release 6.11 or later, more efficient tools are available. These use the %SYSFUNC function in conjunction with functions such as ATTRN.

SEE ALSO
Yindra (1997) has an example of a macro that makes a decision branch based on the number of observations in the data set.

11.5.1 Using %SYSFUNC and ATTRN

%OBSCNT

In the following example, the macro %OBSCNT acts like a macro function in that the macro call resolves to a value that is the number of observations in the stated data set:

```
%macro obscnt(dsn);  ❶
%local nobs;
%let nobs=.;

%* Open the data set of interest;
%let dsnid = %sysfunc(open(&dsn));  ❷

%* If the open was successful get the;
%* number of observations and CLOSE &dsn;
%if &dsnid %then %do;  ❸
     %let nobs=%sysfunc(attrn(&dsnid,nlobs));  ❹
     %let rc  =%sysfunc(close(&dsnid));  ❺
%end;
%else %do;  ❻
     %put Unable to open &dsn - %sysfunc(sysmsg());
%end;

%* Return the number of observations;  ❼
&nobs  ❽
%mend obscnt;
```

❶ The user passes the name of the data set into the macro using &DSN.

❷ The selected data set is opened using the %SYSFUNC and OPEN functions. When opened, it is assigned an identification number, which is stored in &DSNID.

❸ If the data set was found and was opened successfully, &DSNID will be greater than 0 and this %IF expression will be true.

❹ The ATTRN function is used to determine the number of observations in the data set. In this case, the NLOBS option returns the number of observations, excluding those marked for deletion. The ATTRN function can be used to make a number of queries on the data set once it is opened. These include password and indexing information, as well as the number of variables and the status of active WHERE clauses.

❺ The data set should be closed after retrieving the desired information.

❻ When the OPEN is unsuccessful, you may want to write a message to the LOG. The SYSMSG( ) function returns the reason the OPEN failed.

❼ This must be a macro comment. An asterisk-style comment would result in the comment itself being written as text along with the number of observations. This would result in syntax errors if the macro is used as in the following code. See Section 5.4.1 for more on macro comments.

❽ Because this is the only text in the macro that is not part of a macro programming statement, the resolved value of &NOBS will be effectively *returned* to the calling program and its value will be a period (.) if the data set was not opened successfully.

The following program creates the data set A and then calls %OBSCNT to write the number of observations to the LOG:

```
data a;
do i = 1 to 10;
  x=i**i;
  output;
end;
run;

%put number of obs is %obscnt(a);
```

The following line is written to the LOG:

```
number of obs is 10
```

The example in the Section 11.5.2 also uses the ATTRN function.

11.5.2   Controlling observations in PRINT listings

%TESTPRT

Jerry Kagan
Kagan Associates, Inc.

In several of the earlier sections of this book, the macro %LOOK is developed to check the contents of a SAS data set. %LOOK is improved in the macro shown in this section.

The macro %TESTPRT is used during program testing and will print out the first *n* observations from the last data set created. The macro is designed to be called immediately after each DATA step so that the first *n* observations will be displayed from the data set that is created or modified in that step. Knowing what is in a data set, of course, helps you to know where things are going wrong.

Additional utility is gained from the macro printing the name of the data set and the number of observations and number of variables in a title line. It is possible to turn the macro on or off by setting a globalized macro variable (&TEST) to 0 or 1. This allows the macro calls to be left in your production code after testing is complete.

```
/*************************************************************************
* Program:   TestPrt.SAS                                                *
* Language:  SAS 6.12/MACRO                                             *
*                                                                       *
* Purpose:   This macro prints samples of the last dataset created for  *
*            program testing                                            *
*                                                                       *
* Protocol:  %let test = 1;    *** Turn macro on;                       *
*            %let obs = 10;    *** Print first 10 obs from dataset;     *
*                                                                       *
*            %testPrt(&obs)    *** First &obs is printed;               *
*                                                                       *
* Author:    Jerry Kagan                                                *
*            Kagan Associates, Inc.                                     *
*                                                                       *
*            jerrykagan@msn.com                                         *
*                                                                       *
* Date:      29Jun1993                                                  *
*                                                                       *
* Revisions:                                                            *
* 21Feb97 JBK Modified to use new sysfunc for simplicity and efficiency *
*************************************************************************/

%macro TestPrt(obs);
   %if &test %then
   %do;
      %let _dsid = %sysfunc(open(&syslast));    ❶
      %if &_dsid %then %do;
         %let _nobs = %sysfunc(attrn(&_dsid,NOBS));    ❷
         %let _nvar = %sysfunc(attrn(&_dsid,NVARS));   ❸
         %let _rc = %sysfunc(close(&_dsid));    ❹
      %end;

      proc print data=&syslast (obs=&obs) uniform;
      %if &obs < &_nobs %then %do;
         title1 "&syslast (Created with &_nobs observation(s) "
                "& &_nvar variable(s), first &obs printed)";
      %end;
      %else %do;
         title1 "&syslast (Created with &_nobs observation(s) "
                "& &_nvar variable(s), all printed)";
      %end;
      run;
   %end;
%mend TestPrt;
```

❶ The most recently modified data set (&SYSLAST) is opened.

❷ The number of observations that are contained in the opened data set (&_DSID) is returned using the ATTRN function with the NOBS option.

❸ The ATTRN function can also be used to return the number of variables in the data set.

❹ The data set is closed using the CLOSE function.

As it stands, %TESTPRT will wipe out any titles that have been set prior to calling the macro. This may or may not be a problem. A potential modification to avoid this situation might be to use TITLE10 and then blank it out after the RUN statement.

SEE ALSO

SAS® Screen Control Language, Reference, Second Edition describes the ATTRN SCL function in detail (pp. 238–239).

%OBSCNT was originally adapted from a similar macro in *SAS® Macro Language, Reference, First Edition* (p. 242). That example uses ATTRN to retrieve both the number of variables as well as the number of observations. The same example was used with slight modification in %TESTPRT.

Kretzman (1992) discusses a similar macro.

Chapter 12 # SAS® System Autocall Macros

12.1   Selected Macros – What They Are

12.2   Selected Macros – How They Work

The AUTOCALL macro facility allows previously written macros to be saved and reused without including their definition in the current program. This facility is introduced in Section 3.3.3. In addition to any macros that you might write and add to your own AUTOCALL library, the SAS System comes supplied with a number of macros in its own autocall library. These can be found in your default SASAUTOS location; under Windows this might be `!sasroot\core\sasmacro`. Depending on your operating environment and what SAS products are leased, additional autocall macros may be available. Consult the *SAS Companion* for your operating environment for more information on the location of the autocall libraries.

Not only are these macros useful in and of themselves, but because the code is available you can modify these macros for your own purposes or use them as patterns for new macros.

SEE ALSO

SAS® Macro Language: Reference, First Edition briefly describes these macros (pp. 158–160) and includes their description with the other macro language elements in Chapter 13, "Macro Language Dictionary" (pp. 161–270).

Chapter 7, "The Autocall Facility," in the *SAS® Guide to Macro Processing, Version 6* lists many of the standard SAS System Autocall macros in one place (pp. 185–187).

12.1 Selected Macros – What They Are

These macros are described fully in Chapter 13, "Macro Language Dictionary," in *SAS® Macro Language: Reference, First Edition*. There they are presented along with functions, options, and other language elements.

Because these macros are available in the autocall library, you can look at the code itself and modify it as needed. Your SASAUTOS system option will tell you where these macros are physically stored. Your operating environment and the modules your site leases from SAS Institute will determine the availability of some autocall macros. The ones listed here should be available to most users.

Several of these macros behave as macro functions, and looking at their code provides insight into writing your own macro functions. Five of these macros are noted briefly here and several are discussed in detail in Section 12.2:

%CMPRES   compresses a text string by removing multiple blanks as well as leading and trailing blanks.

%LEFT   left-justify the text argument by removing leading blanks.

%LOWCASE	convert the text string to lower case (this is the functional opposite of the %UPCASE macro function).
%TRIM	trims trailing blanks from text strings.
%VERIFY	opposite of the %INDEX macro function, the first character not in a string is located.

For the most part, these macros closely mimic DATA step functions in name, syntax, and result. None are difficult to use. Indeed the hardest part about using them is to know of their existence.

Many of these macros also have a 'Q' version (for example, %QLEFT and %QTRIM) for use when the argument contains symbols or characters whose meaning should remain hidden. See Section 7.1 for more on macro quoting and when it may be needed.

Because these are macros (although they sometimes act like functions), the text string or argument cannot contain imbedded commas. When the argument does contain a comma, the macro parser interprets the comma as a parameter delimiter and syntax errors can result. Often when this happens, the argument can be quoted to hide the imbedded comma.

To make matters a bit more complicated, some of these macros (such as %LOWCASE) also call macro functions that use commas to delimit arguments. For these macros, commas in the argument can also cause problems in the interior macro or macro function. Quoting may be of less utility in these cases.

12.2 Selected Macros – How They Work

Four of the SAS System autocall macros that are noted in the previous section are detailed here. They were selected not only for their usefulness but also because it is instructive to look at the macro code itself.

One of the really big advantages of looking at these programs is that you will get to see some macro code that was written by the developers of portions of the SAS System. Often this code includes interesting tricks.

12.2.1 %VERIFY

This macro allows you to search a text string for the first character that is not in the target list. %VERIFY then returns the position of that character. In the following example, the macro variable &YRCODE contains a string that starts with some unknown number of numbers. You want to strip off the numbers and create a new macro variable (&CODE) that starts with the first character that is not a number.

```
%let yrcode = 97CAdwz;
%let code = %substr(&yrcode,%verify(&yrcode,1234567890));

%put &yrcode &code;
```

The first argument is the string to search, and the second contains characters that we want to avoid. The LOG is shown:

```
162   %let yrcode = 97CAdwz;
163
164   %let code = %substr(&yrcode,%verify(&yrcode,1234567890));
165
166   %put &yrcode &code;
97CAdwz CAdwz
```

The %SUBSTR function was used to select the string starting in the position that was occupied by the first non-number.

12.2.2   %LEFT

Like the DATA step function LEFT, this macro has a single argument that it returns without any leading blanks. The example shown here uses %LEFT to left-justify the value of the macro variable &LFIVE:

```
data _null_;
x=5;
call symput('lfive',x);
run;

%put *&lfive*;
%let lfive = %left(&lfive);
%put *&lfive*;
```

This produces the LOG entry

```
171
172   %put *&lfive*;
*          5*
173   %let lfive = %left(&lfive);
174   %put *&lfive*;
*5*
```

The macro %LEFT uses the %VERIFY macro ❶ to check for nonblank characters. When a nonblank character is found, its location is stored in &I, which is used as the column index for the %SUBSTR function ❷.

```
%macro left(text);
%******************************************************************;
%*                                                                *;
%*   MACRO: LEFT                                                   *;
%*                                                                *;
%*   USAGE: 1) %left(argument)                                     *;
%*                                                                *;
%*   DESCRIPTION:                                                  *;
%*     This macro returns the argument passed to it without any    *;
%*     leading blanks in an unquoted form. The syntax for its use  *;
%*     is similar to that of native macro functions.              *;
%*                                                                *;
%*     Eg. %let macvar=%left(&argtext)                            *;
%*                                                                *;
%*   NOTES:                                                        *;
%*     The %VERIFY macro is used to determine the first non-blank  *;
%*     character position.                                         *;
%*                                                                *;
%******************************************************************;
%local i;
%if %length(&text)=0 %then %let text=%str( );
%let i=%verify(&text,%str( ));❶
%if &i❷ %then %substr(&text,&i);❸
%mend;
```

Notice that the %SUBSTR function resolves to the amended text ❸ so that the macro call is replaced with the left-justified string.

12.2.3   %CMPRES

The %CMPRES macro removes multiple blanks from the text string. Effectively, it also calls %LEFT and %TRIM by removing all leading and trailing blanks.

In the examples in Section 6.2.1, a numeric variable is converted to character prior to using the SYMPUT routine. The following example creates the macro variable directly from the numeric variable and then uses %CMPRES to remove the leading blanks. The asterisks are used to help show the position of the blanks.

```
data _null_;
x=5;
call symput('five',x);
run;

%put *&five*;
%let five = *%cmpres(&five)*;
%put &five;
```

The resulting LOG shows

```
138
139   %put *&five*;
*           5*
140   %let five = *%cmpres(&five)*;
141   %put &five;
*5*
```

The code for %CMPRES is shown here:

```
%macro cmpres(text);
%*******************************************************************;
%*                                                                 *;
%*   MACRO: CMPRES                                                 *;
%*                                                                 *;
%*   USAGE: 1) %cmpres(argument)                                   *;
%*                                                                 *;
%*   DESCRIPTION:                                                  *;
%*     This macro returns the argument passed to it in an unquoted *;
%*     form with multiple blanks compressed to single blanks and also *;
%*     with leading and trailing blanks removed.                  *;
%*                                                                 *;
%*     Eg. %let macvar=%cmpres(&argtext)                          *;
%*                                                                 *;
%*   NOTES:                                                        *;
%*     The %LEFT and %TRIM macros in the autocall library are used *;
%*     in this macro.                                              *;
%*                                                                 *;
%*******************************************************************;
%local i;
%let i=%index(&text,%str(  ));  ❶
%do %while(&i^=0);
  %let text=%qsubstr(&text,1,&i)%qleft(%qsubstr(&text,&i+1));❷
  %let i=%index(&text,%str(  ));
%end;
%left(%qtrim(&text))❸
%mend;
```

❶ The %INDEX function is used to find any occurrences of a double blank %STR( ). If found, the starting position is noted in &I.

❷ The %LET is used to rewrite the incoming text string &TEXT. Notice that two macro functions are used in the same statement. The %QSUBSTR function returns the first &I characters in the string (this is where one of the two blanks is left behind). The %QLEFT autocall macro then left-justifies the remainder of the string. Because the function and macro are resolved and executed before the %LET, the two resulting text strings are effectively concatenated into a new string, which is placed in &TEXT. Using %QLEFT eliminates the need to step iteratively through a long string of blanks.

❸ The %LEFT macro will be called last and will resolve to a text string. Effectively, this is the text that is *passed back* from the call to %CMPRES. Actually, nothing is really passed back. Rather, this macro resolves to a potentially modified version of &TEXT, and that string is what is seen as the resolved text in the code that called %CMPRES. Because this is a macro call, a semicolon is not wanted.

You could easily modify this macro to remove any combination of characters, not just double blanks.

12.2.4   %LOWCASE

The %LOWCASE macro can be used to convert all uppercase characters to lowercase characters. The macro accepts a single argument, which is translated using the %INDEX and %SUBSTR functions. This macro is demonstrated in the following example:

```
%let mixed = SAS Macro Language;
%let lower = %lowcase(&mixed);
%put &lower;
```

The resulting LOG shows the macro variable &LOWER to be all lowercase characters:

```
175  %let mixed = SAS Macro Language;
176  %let lower = %lowcase(&mixed);
177  %put &lower;
sas macro language
```

The code for this macro is interesting because of the way it finds uppercase characters and then translates them.

```
%macro lowcase(string);
%********************************************************************;
%*                                                                 *;
%*   MACRO: LOWCASE                                                 *;
%*                                                                 *;
%*   USAGE: 1) %lowcase(argument)                                  *;
%*                                                                 *;
%*   DESCRIPTION:                                                  *;
%*     This macro returns the argument passed to it unchanged       *;
%*     except that all upper-case alphabetic characters are changed *;
%*     to their lower-case equivalents.                            *;
%*                                                                 *;
%*   E.g.:          %let macvar=%lowcase(SAS Institute Inc.);      %*;
%*   The variable macvar gets the value "sas institute inc."       *;
%*                                                                 *;
%*   NOTES:                                                        *;
%*     Although the argument to the %UPCASE macro function may      *;
%*     contain commas, the argument to %LOWCASE may not, unless     *;
%*     they are quoted.  Because %LOWCASE is a macro, not a function, *;
%*     it interprets a comma as the end of a parameter.            *;
%*                                                                 *;
%********************************************************************;
%local i length c index result;
%let length = %length(&string);
%do i = 1 %to &length;
    %let c = %substr(&string,&i,1);❶
    %if &c eq %then %let c = %str( );
    %else %do;
        %let index = %index(ABCDEFGHIJKLMNOPQRSTUVWXYZ,&c);❷
        %if &index gt 0 %then ❸
            %let c = %substr(abcdefghijklmnopqrstuvwxyz,&index,1); ❹
        %end;
    %let result = &result.&c; ❺
    %end;
&result ❻
%mend;
```

When %LOWCASE is called, the value of &MIXED was passed into the macro, where it was assigned to &STRING, for example, &STRING = SAS Macro Language.

❶ The *i*th character in the string of interest (&STRING) is temporarily stored in the macro variable &C. When %LOWCASE is applied to &MIXED, the fifth letter in the string (&I=5) is M (&C=M).

❷ The %INDEX function is used to see if &C contains an uppercase letter. If an uppercase letter is found, its position is stored in &INDEX. For &C=M, the %INDEX function returns a 13 (since M is the thirteenth letter of the alphabet).

❸ If an uppercase letter is found (&INDEX >0), it is converted using the %SUBSTR function.

❹ In the %SUBSTR function, &INDEX becomes the column indicator for the matching lowercase letter. For &INDEX=13, the lowercase m is selected and assigned to &C. The macro variable &C now has been converted to lowercase.

❺ &C is then appended (converted or not) onto &RESULT, which continues to grow until the entire string has been checked.

❻ The macro variable &RESULT contains the converted string, and this will be the final resolved value of the macro call.

Chapter 13 # Miscellaneous Macro Topics

13.1 &&&var – Using Triple Ampersand Macro Variables

13.2 Doubly Subscripted Macro Arrays

13.3 Programming Smarter-Efficiency Issues

This chapter contains several eclectic topics of interest. These include the use of more than two ampersands, which is not terribly common but appears often enough to warrant mention here. Also discussed are a number of efficiency issues that you should be aware of as you begin to write more sophisticated macros, and some of these are also discussed in this chapter.

13.1 &&&var – Using Triple Ampersand Macro Variables

As a general rule, it is usually not necessary to resort to the use of triple ampersand macro variables. There are times, however, when it becomes necessary. The most common use is when you want to store the name of a macro variable in another macro variable. The examples in this section show, with increasing complexity, the use of the triple ampersand.

SEE ALSO
Yindra (1997) has an example that uses a &&& macro variable in a TITLE statement.

The macro presented by Widawski (1997a) to create a list of files is generalized by using &&& macro variables.

SAS® Macro Language: Reference, First Edition gives an efficiency tip that utilizes triple ampersands (pp. 136–137).

13.1.1   Counting observations

%COUNTER

David Shannon

This macro uses a PROC SQL step (see Section 2.7) to count the number of observations in a SAS data set. The macro parameters are the name of the data set and the name of the macro variable that will be created and globalized. In the macro, &INTO resolves to the <u>name</u> of the macro variable that will hold the counter, and &&&INTO will resolve to the number of observations.

Consider the macro call `%counter(mydata,cnt)`. During the execution of %COUNTER, the following occurs:

Macro variable	Resolves to
&INTO	cnt
&&&INTO	<u>&&</u> <u>&INTO</u> —> &CNT
&CNT	{number of observations}

```
/*-------------------------------------------------------------
|                          COUNTER                             |
|                         _____                             |
|                                                              |
| The number of observations contained in the input dataset, after |
| completion of the datastep, is stored in the macro variable. |
|                                                              |
|------------------------------------------------------------- |
| Parameter | Default | Description                            |
|------------------------------------------------------------- |
| DATA      | _Last_  | Optional:  Data source to count number of |
|           |         |            observations.               |
| INTO      | Counter | Optional:  Macro variable to store number of |
|           |         |            observations.               |
|------------------------------------------------------------- |
| Usage      : %COUNTER;                                       |
|            : %COUNTER(NEWDAT,NOOBS);                         |
|                          ^        ^                          |
|                          |        - Macro variable to store count |
|                          - Dataset name                      |
|                                                              |
| Note(s)    : Datasets may be empty, but must have at least one |
|              variable, and therefore must exist.            |
|                                                              |
| Written by : David Shannon, V1, 14/4/97, V6.10+             |
| Bugs to    : David@schweiz.demon.co.uk                      |
| References : Getting Started With the SQL Procedure, S.I., 1994. |
-------------------------------------------------------------*/ ;

%MACRO Counter(data,into);

%*********************************************************************** ;
%* Define local macro variables (those only referred to locally)     * ;

%Local DATA INTO;  ❶

%*********************************************************************** ;
%* Set defaults if not provided in positional macro call.            * ;

%If &DATA EQ %Then %Let DATA=_last_;
%If &INTO EQ %Then %Let INTO=COUNTER;

%*********************************************************************** ;
%* Make output variable global, hence can be referred to outside this * ;
%* macro.                                                             * ;

%Global &INTO;  ❷

%*********************************************************************** ;
%* Count observations and store result in the global macro variable.  * ;

Proc Sql Noprint;
     Select count(*) into:&INTO  ❸
     From &DATA;
Quit;

%PUT Counted &&&INTO. observations, stored in macro variable &&INTO..    ; ❹

%MEND Counter ;
```

The following discussion assumes that this macro call has been made:

```
%counter(mydata,cnt)
```

❶ The macro variables &DATA and &INTO are declared local. In this example, these macro variables will be LOCAL by default, and the statement is not really necessary. However, when you use a macro within an application, it may be wise to get in the habit of using the %LOCAL statement to protect the application. This prevents your macro from inadvertently changing the value of a globalized macro variable of the same name that you might not know about and that has been defined elsewhere in the application.

❷ The macro variable &INTO resolves to CNT, which is then used as the name of a globalized macro variable.

❸ The number of observations is loaded into the macro variable named by &INTO (CNT).

❹ &&&INTO resolves to the number of observations. The macro variable &&INTO. (or &INTO.) resolves to the name of the macro variable that will be available outside of the %COUNTER macro.

If MYDATA has 30 observations, the macro call `%COUNTER(MYDATA,CNT)` will result in the following lines being written to the LOG:

```
137  %counter(mydata,cnt)
NOTE: The PROCEDURE SQL used 0.11 seconds.


Counted       30 observations, stored in macro variable cnt.
```

The macro variable &CNT has now been globalized, is available outside of the macro %COUNTER, and has a value of 30.

13.1.2   Working with a list of class variables

%INDVAR

Jørn Lodahl

Often in statistical analysis, it is desirable to create a matrix of indicator variables where each variable takes on the value of 0 or 1 depending on the value of a classification or variable. This macro creates these variables and assigns each the value of 0 or 1. This is similar to the design matrix created by PROC GLMMOD.

A quick example of this macro uses the following simple data set:

```
data simple;
i=.; output;
i=0; output;
do i= 1 to 3,5;
 output;
end;
run;

%indvar(simple,i,ind,basevar= 2  )
```

```
proc print data=simple;
title 'A Simple data set when basevar is 2';
run;
```

The LOG displays the value taken on by the macro variable &IND:

```
macro indvar created macro variable ind = ind0 ind1 ind3 ind5
```

The PROC PRINT of the modified SIMPLE data set shows the new indicator variables. Notice that although IND2 is not on the list of variables stored in &IND it is in the data set (&BASE-VAR=2).

```
                      A Simple data set when basevar is 2


          OBS     I     IND0     IND1     IND2     IND3     IND5

           1      .      0        0        0        0        0
           2      0      1        0        0        0        0
           3      1      0        1        0        0        0
           4      2      0        0        1        0        0
           5      3      0        0        0        1        0
           6      5      0        0        0        0        1
```

PROC SQL is used to build the list of the names of the new indicator variables. These variables are then constructed with assignment statements in a DATA step. The assignment statements are created dynamically within a %DO %WHILE loop.

```
/****************************************************************
SYNTAX:
%indvar(datasetname,classvar,prefix_for_ind_var,basevar=)

This macro creates a series of indicator variables from a
class-variable and adds them to the dataset. The class-variable
MUST be restricted to positive integers or zero. The prefix_for_ind_var
is used as the prefix for names of the indicator variables.

A macro variable named prefix_for_ind_var is also created as a
string.  This string contains the names of all of the newly
created indicator variables.  The names are separated by a space.
By default (basevar=min), the indicator variable associated with the
minimum value of the class-variable is excluded from this list (the
indicator variable is still included on the data set).  Setting
basevar=none excludes no names from the list.  A specific name can be
excluded by setting basevar=x, where x is a value taken on by the class-
variable.

EXAMPLE:
Consider a data set where the variable class takes values 1, 2 and 4.

   %indvar(&syslast,class,c)

Variables c1 c2 and c4 with values 0 or 1 are added to the data set.
(c3 is always 0 since class is never 3 and therefore c3 is not
created). Moreover the macro variable c equals "c2 c4" (c1 is omitted
since by default basevar=min and 1 is the minimum value of class).
```

```
       If instead %indvar(&syslast,class,c,basevar=2) was called, c2 would be
       omitted from the macro variable. Basevar=none includes all.
       *************************************************************/

       %macro indvar(dataset,byvar,prefix,basevar=min);
       %local item list value min;
       %global &prefix;

         /* generate list */
         PROC SQL NOPRINT;
           SELECT DISTINCT &byvar INTO :list SEPARATED BY ' ' ❶
           FROM &dataset
           ORDER BY &byvar;
           SELECT min(&byvar) INTO :min ❷
           FROM &dataset;
         QUIT;

         /* create variables */
         %LET item=1;
         %LET value = %scan(&list, &item) ; ❸
         /* in other words: element no. &item in &list = &value */
         %LET &prefix= ;   /* turns into a list of "all" ind variables */ ❹

         data &dataset;
           set &dataset;
           %IF &basevar=min %THEN %LET basevar=&min;; ❺
           %do %while( %quote(&value) ^= ) ;
             IF &byvar=&value THEN &prefix&value=1; ELSE &prefix&value=0; ❻
             %IF %quote(&value)^=%quote(&basevar) %THEN ❼
               %LET &prefix=&&&prefix &prefix&value;; ❽
             %LET item = %eval( &item +1) ; ❾
             %let value = %scan( &list, &item );
           %end;
         run;
       %put macro indvar created macro variable &prefix = &&&prefix; ❿
       %mend indvar;
```

❶ The macro variable &LIST contains the unique values that are taken on by the classification variable (&BYVAR). The elements of the list are separated by blanks.

❷ The minimum value taken on by the classification variable is stored in &MIN. This is used if &BASEVAR=min ❺.

❸ The %SCAN macro function is used to return the *i*th (&ITEM) word of the classification variable (&LIST), and this word is temporarily stored in &VALUE. At this point in the program, &ITEM= 1 so the first word is selected.

❹ &PREFIX is used to store the text portion of the name of the indicator variables. This same text (in the previous example IND) is used to name the macro variable that holds the list of indicator variable names. When &PREFIX appears in the %LET statement, IND becomes the name of a macro variable.

❺ When &BASEVAR=min, then substitute the minimum value taken on by the classification variable.

❻ This DATA step IF statement sets up the assignment statements that create and load the indicator variables. A resolved statement might be

```
IF i=2 THEN ind2=1; ELSE ind2=0;
```

❼ Exclude the &BASEVAR value from the list (not the data set).

❽ This %LET statement appends the new variable name (&PREFIX&VALUE) onto the existing list (&&&PREFIX) and stores the result back into &IND, which is pointed to using &PREFIX. Here, &&&PREFIX ⟶ &IND ⟶ IND1 IND2...

❾ Increment the item number to step through the list of values taken on by the classification variable.

❿ This %PUT statement displays the name of the macro variable (&PREFIX) that contains the list of variables and the value of that variable (&&&PREFIX).

13.1.3 Totals based on a list of macro variables

%SUMS

Justina M. Flavin
STATPROBE, Inc.
jflavin@statprobe.com

This macro is used in a program that generates an adverse event incidence table. In many non-crossover studies, the client wants the rightmost column of the table to be a Total column, which contains a simple sum of all of the counts in all of the treatment groups (for a given adverse event or body system). The macro %SUMS calculates these total counts. When %SUMS is called, the parameters TOTAL and NUMTREAT are actually the names of the macro variables that contain the number of treatment or dosing groups.

The data set FREQPREF has variables for the *adverse event name* (preferred term), the body system, and a series of variables (PREF1, PREF2,...,PREFn) that contain the number of unique patients that have that adverse event for that particular treatment or dosing group. That is, PREF1 is the number of patients in dose group 1; PREF2 is the number in dose group2, and so on.

In the same manner, the data set FREQBODY has variables for the body system, and a series of variables (BODY1, BODY2,...,BODYn) that contain the number of unique patients in the body system for that particular treatment or dosing group. (A patient can have multiple adverse events in a body system, but on the body system line in the table, the patient should only be counted once.)

The data set EVENT, contains a series of variables (EVENT1–EVENTn) that contain the number of unique adverse events within a body system. These variables are used to determine the proper sorting order for printing the table.

Because the program is completely data driven, the number of treatment or dosing groups is determined early on and is assigned to the macro variable &NUMTREAT. Another macro variable, &TOTAL, is &NUMTREAT+1.

The following three DATA steps create synthetic data in the same form as might be expected in an actual application of this macro. Each data set has the key variable BODY and a list of variables (that in this case contain random numbers).

```
%let total=4;
%let numtreat=3;

data freqpref;
drop i;
array lst {&numtreat} pref1 - pref&numtreat;
do body = 1 to 5;
  do i = 1 to &numtreat;
     lst{i} = int(ranuni(9999)*10);
  end;
  output;
end;
run;

data freqbody;
drop i;
array lst {&numtreat} body1 - body&numtreat;
do body = 1 to 5;
  do i = 1 to &numtreat;
     lst{i} = int(ranuni(9999)*5);
  end;
  output;
end;
run;

data event;
drop i;
array lst {&numtreat} event1-event&numtreat;
do body = 1 to 5;
  do i = 1 to &numtreat;
     lst{i} = int(ranuni(9999)*3);
  end;
  output;
end;
run;
```

The macro %SUMS is used to dynamically generate a single assignment statement. The following call to %SUMS

```
%let total=4;
%let numtreat=3;
%sums(pref,  total, numtreat)
```

will generate the following assignment statement:

```
pref4=sum(of pref1-pref3);
```

The macro %SUMS expects to be passed the root portion of the name of the variable to be created (&PREFIX), the name of the macro variable that contains the number of the new variable (&SUFFIX), and the name of the macro variable that contains the number of variables in the list (&STOPNUM).

```
%macro sums(prefix, suffix, stopnum);
      &&prefix&&&suffix=sum(of &prefix.1-&&prefix&&&stopnum);
%mend sums;
```

The macro is called from within a DATA step. In the following step, it is called three times, resulting in the creation of three assignment statements:

```
data counts(drop=j);
   merge freqpref freqbody event;
   by body;
   array zeroes{*} _numeric_;
   do j=1 to dim(zeroes);
     if zeroes{j}=. then zeroes{j}=0;
   end;
   %sums(pref,  total, numtreat)
   %sums(body,  total, numtreat)
   %sums(event, total, numtreat)
run;

proc print data=counts;
id body;
title1 'Counts and Totals';
run;
```

The PROC PRINT generates the following output, which contains the totals in PREF4, BODY4, and EVENT4:

					Counts and Totals							
BODY	PREF1	PREF2	PREF3	BODY1	BODY2	BODY3	EVENT1	EVENT2	EVENT3	PREF4	BODY4	EVENT4
1	4	9	8	2	4	4	1	2	2	21	10	5
2	7	1	8	3	0	4	2	0	2	16	7	4
3	2	3	8	1	1	4	0	1	2	13	6	3
4	5	3	1	2	1	0	1	1	0	9	3	2
5	0	7	2	0	3	1	0	2	0	9	4	2

For the macro call %sums(body, total, numtreat), the triple ampersands are resolved as shown here:

Pass Number	String	Resolves to
1	&&prefix&&&suffix	&prefix&total
2	&prefix&total	body4

The version of %SUMS that is presented in this section is very much simplified from the version that was used in the actual application. For this particular version, you can simplify it further and eliminate triple ampersands. %SUMS can be rewritten as

```
%macro sums(prefix, suffix, stopnum);
       &prefix&suffix=sum(of &prefix.1-&prefix&stopnum);
%mend sums;
```

The macro call now must pass the resolved values of the macro variables (&TOTAL and &NUMTREAT) rather than the macro variable names. You can do that in this example because you really only need the value of the two macro variables inside of %SUMS. The macro call becomes

```
%sums(body, &total,&numtreat)
```

If %SUMS also needed the name of the macro variable (perhaps to put it in a title or to be used as a label in a %GOTO), then the original version with the triple ampersands would be required.

13.1.4   Selecting elements from macro arrays

%GETKEYS

Richard O. Smith
Science Explorations

This macro is taken from an application that contains a series of data sets that exist with slight variations in different libraries. The data sets are similar enough so that many of the same processing programs can be used across libraries. Primarily, they differ in the names of the key (BY) variables. Globalized macro variable arrays are created that store the names of the data sets and the associated key variables for each libref. Typical arrays might be

libref	number of data sets	data set names	key variables
live ❶	&livecnt ❸	&livedb1, &livedb2, ...	&keys1, &keys2, ...

Given the data set name (for example, LIVE.AE) you need to be able to retrieve the associated key variables. The macro %GETKEYS uses the libref and data set name to look up the associated key variable list, which is then stored in the macro variable &KEYVARS.

```
%macro getkeys(inlib❶,indsn❷);
* getkeys.sas
* 25Jun97 - ROSmith
* macro to get the key variables for selected library & member.
* assumes that the global macros for the databases & keys are created.
* Outputs a macro variable KEYVARS.
*;

%do k = 1 %to &&&inlib.cnt;  ❸
   %if %upcase(&indsn❷) = %upcase(&&&inlib.db&k❹) %then
        %let KEYVARS = &&KEYS&k;  ❺
%end;

%mend getkeys;
```

❶ The libref (LIVE) is also used in the name of the macro variable that counts the number of data sets in this libref (❸).

❷ &INDSN is used to store the name of the data set.

❸ The list of data set names in this libref is stepped through one at a time. The number of data sets (elements in this pseudo array) is stored in a macro variable whose name is made up in part with the name of the libref. &&&inlib.cnt ==> &livecnt

❹ The list of data set names is stored in macro variables that are formed using the libref and followed by DB and then a number, for example, &LIVEDB3. This array is indirectly referenced by using &&&inlib.db&k.

❺ The key variables for this data set are assigned to the macro variable &KEYVARS.

13.1.5   Checking if a macro variable exists

%SYMCHK

The macro %SYMCHK can be used to determine if a macro variable exists. If the macro variable does not exist, you will receive the following warning in the LOG:

```
WARNING: Apparent symbolic reference TMP not resolved.
```

The macro returns a YES or NO depending on whether or not the passed parameter is a macro variable.

```
%macro symchk(name);

%if %nrquote(&&&name)=%nrstr(&)&name %then ❶
    %let yesno=NO;

%else %let yesno=YES;

&yesno ❷
%mend symchk;

%put 'Does &tmp exist? ' %symchk(tmp); ❸
```

❶ The macro variable &NAME contains the name of the macro variable that needs to be checked. When three ampersands are used, as in &&&NAME, the first two ampersands resolve to &. For %SYMCHK(TMP) this means that &&&NAME resolves to &TMP. If &TMP has been defined, it will be further resolved to its value; otherwise, if &TMP is not defined a warning is issued and &TMP remains unresolved.

%NRSTR(&)&NAME will resolve to &TMP and because of the %NRSTR function it will not be further resolved. When &TMP is not defined, the unresolvable &TMP on the left side of the equal sign will equal the &TMP on the right and the expression will be true. When the expression is true, the macro variable does not exist and &YESNO is set to NO.

❷ The macro will return either a YES or a NO.

❸ The %PUT is used to demonstrate a call to %SYMCHK.

This macro is posted on SAS Institute's home page at

```
http://www.sas.com/service/techsup/faq/macro.html
```

13.2 Doubly Subscripted Macro Arrays

In numerous examples elsewhere in this book, a series of macro variables have been used as a macro array. Because the macro language has no true array, you can fake it by creating macro variables in the form of &&VAR&i (see Sections 6.2.1 and 6.4 for introductory examples). These macro variables create a vector or what is essentially an array with a single subscript.

A *doubly subscripted array* describes a matrix of values or the rows and columns of a SAS data set or table. This enables you to store all of the values that are contained within a table in a single set of macro variables. You can approach the subscripting problem in a couple of ways. Initially, one might try creating a logical extension of &&VAR&i as &&&&VAR&&i&j, where &i and &j indicate the desired row and column. Life, however, is never quite this simple, and there are complications with this approach. Fortunately, there are a couple of solutions (or this section would not have appeared in the book).

Assume that you want the macro variable &VAR34 to resolve to 5.62. That is, the fourth variable (column) in the third observation (row) and has the value of 5.62. Assign the macro variables as follows:

```
%let i=3;
%let j=4;
%let var34 = 5.62;
```

The sequence of resolution is shown here:

Pass Number	String	Resolves to
1	&&&&var&&i&j	&&var&i4
2	&&var&i4	&var&i4

Because &i4 is undefined, a WARNING is issued. In this example, you need to separate the &i from the 4. To do this, you can use the macro variable &&&&var&&i.&j .

Now the sequence of resolution becomes:

Pass Number	String	Resolves to
1	&&&&var&&i.&j	&&var&i.4
2	&&var&i.4	&var34
3	&var34	5.62

In this simple case, it would have been easier to write &&&&var&&i.&j as &&var&i&j, which resolves in only two passes.

This approach works fine as long as the number of rows and columns is fewer than ten. Larger numbers can result in naming conflicts. Does &var345 refer to row 34 and column 5 or row 3 and column 45? For small tables, this is not a problem. However, a more robust method exists.

Rather than combining the row and column indicators into a single number, they can be kept separate. The macro variable &R3C4 completely specifies the location that the value came from without conflict. Further, it can be referenced without using quadruple ampersands, for example, &&R&i.C&j. Notice that the dot (.) is still needed following the &i.

```
%let i=3;
%let j=4;
%let r3c4 = 5.62;
```

The sequence of resolution is shown here:

Pass Number	String	Resolves to
11	&&r&i.c&j	&r3c4
2	&r3c4	5.62

The following example reads a SAS data set (table) and builds a macro variable for each value. The data set is taken directly from the one used in the example in Section 13.1.3. There are four variables that you would like to place into the array (PREF1, PREF2, BODY1, and BODY2) for each observation in the data set.

```
data _null_;
set counts (keep=body  pref1 pref2 body1 body2);
array vlist {4} pref1 pref2 body1 body2; ❶
length name $8 ii jj $2;
i+1;
ii = trim(left(put(i,2.)));
call symput('rowcnt',ii); ❷
if i=1 then call symput('colcnt','4');

* Store values for this row;
rowname = 'r'||ii||'c'; ❸

* Step through the values for this observation;
do j = 1 to 4;
   jj= left(put(j,2.));

   * Save the value for this row and column;
   call symput(trim(compress(rowname))||jj,vlist{j}); ❹

   * Save the variable name;
   call vname(vlist(j),name); ❺
   if i=1 then call symput('vname'||jj,name);
end;
run;
```

❶ The variables of interest are loaded into the array VLIST.

❷ &ROWCNT stores the number of observations, and &colcnt stores the number of columns. These macro variables are often useful when stepping through the array in a %DO loop.

❸ The variable ROWNAME is used to store the first portion of the macro variable name, for example, r3c.

❹ The SYMPUT routine is used to load the value into the appropriate macro variable from within a DO loop that steps through the variables in the VLIST array.

❺ The VNAME routine is used to capture the variable name that is associated with this column. This is not usually needed but may be handy.

In the following statements, a %PUT is used to access one of the values in the table (row 4 and column 3):

```
%let rr = 4;
%let cc = 3;
%put Row &rr and col &cc (%cmpres(&&vname&cc)) is %left(&&r&rr.c&cc);
```

The %PUT causes the following line to be written to the LOG. Notice that the two AUTOCALL macros %CMPRES and %LEFT are used to control spacing (see Chapter 12, "SAS System Autocall Macros," for more on the AUTOCALL macros).

```
Row 4 and col 3 (BODY1) is 2
```

Usually, some type of loop is used to step through the macro array. The macro %DBVAL displays each value in the table.

```
%macro dbval(maxrow,maxcol);
    %put row   col   value;
    %do row = 1 %to &maxrow;
        %do col = 1 %to &maxcol;
            %put &row    &col    %left(&&r&row.c&col);
        %end;
    %end;
%mend dbval;

%dbval(&rowcnt, &colcnt);
```

The macro call passes in the maximum number of rows and columns. These maximums are then used inside of two %DO loops with a %PUT statement. The following are the first few lines that are written to the LOG:

```
row   col   value
1     1     4
1     2     9
1     3     2
1     4     4
2     1     7
2     2     1
2     3     3
```

The DATA _NULL_ used in this example is fairly simple. In an actual application, it is more likely that the number of variables and their names will be unknown and the names will themselves be stored in a macro variable list. This type of processing would be a direct extension of the example in Section 13.1.3.

SEE ALSO
Bryher (1997a) and Geary (1997) both contain more sophisticated examples of doubly subscripted macro arrays of the form &&&VAR&&J&K.

13.3 Programming Smarter – Efficiency Issues

When you use the macro language, it is easy to get carried away and to overuse it. This is especially a problem for SAS users who are new to macros. They tend to use macro language elements at the least excuse and often when they are not at all needed. Some SAS sites have restricted the use of the macro language for this reason. Restrictions should not be necessary if you program smarter and more efficiently. A number of papers have been written about various efficiency issues and programming techniques (Culp 1991, Norton 1991, O'Connor 1992, Tindall 1991, and Westerlund 1991). However, you can find the most recent and comprehensive information in Chapter 11, "Writing Efficient Macros," in *SAS® Macro Language: Reference, First Edition.* This well-written chapter covers all of the major issues regarding macro efficiency and should be consulted for details not covered in the following summary.

Remember during the discussion in this section that there is more than one kind of efficiency. Usually, one thinks of efficient code in terms of its execution by the SAS System, but also consider programmer efficiency (time to code and time to maintain code). Macro code can be very difficult to maintain (especially if you are maintaining someone else's code). A program that is *down* a week for maintenance may completely undo any savings realized by fast execution.

The following are some thoughts and tips on macro efficiency.

Macro Language: to use or not to use
The macro language is very useful and powerful for situations that require

- conditional execution of blocks of code or procedures

- the storage of reusable or generalized code

- a block of constant code to be re-executed multiple times

- code to be written dynamically with parameters that depend on data values

- a series of repetitive tasks.

The use of macros <u>may</u> be inappropriate or inefficient when

- macro code is used just because the language is fun to program.

- macros are used to store constant text (see the macro %COMMENT in Section 3.1.2).

- macros that include the %WINDOW and %DISPLAY macro statements are used to interact with the user (SAS/AF screens are much more flexible and easier to develop).

%MACRO versus %INCLUDE

When macro language features are not required, you can use both the %INCLUDE statement and a macro to store portions of programs. As a general rule, I have not noticed a big difference between the two in terms of efficiency. Because the %INCLUDE statement accesses the code as an external file, this operation can have some additional overhead. Also, if the code is used more than once, the %INCLUDE will need to be re-executed and recompiled.

The use of macros can provide real savings when the code is used in multiple places. By compiling and storing the macro in a catalog, those operations are performed only once.

Nested Macros

A *nested macro* is one that is defined inside of another macro. Although this programming *technique* is not as uncommon as it should be, it is rarely necessary, and it is almost always inefficient. Defining macros this way has two efficiency problems:

- The macro definition may be difficult to find for maintenance.

- The nested macro will be recompiled EVERY time the outside macro is called.

Statement- and Command-Style Macros

Named-style macros always begin with a percent sign (%). This makes it easy for the macro processor (and the programmer) to find the names of the macros to be executed. Statement- and command-style macros (see Section 3.5) do not use the percent sign, and therefore, additional resources are required to locate the macro calls. When they debug programs, few programmers will be looking for statement-style macros, and this can also lead to programmer confusion.

Multiple Ampersands

Programmers who use the macro language quickly become accustomed to seeing and using macro variable references of the form &VAR. Programmers who write dynamic code-building macros will become familiar (although often begrudgingly) with &&VAR&I macro variables. When the code calls for three or more ampersands together, try to rethink your code. Usually, there is a better way to handle the situation.

Macro Quoting

The entire concept of macro quoting is difficult for many macro programmers (I hesitate to say *most*, but believe that *most* may be more accurate). Fortunately, macro quoting is not needed in most programming situations. When it is needed, ask yourself if you can code the task in a different way. If quoting is required, try to use one of the basic quoting functions such as %STR.

Macro System Options

Sections 3.3 and 3.5.1 discuss several system options that are associated with the macro facility. As a general rule, when system options are turned on additional system resources are required. Some of these options are necessary; however, many options are situational. A summary of some of these system options follows:

MACRO

If you are not using any portion of the macro facility, it can be turned off. As a general rule, you should leave it on because some statements that are not thought of as part of the macro language actually need it to be available.

MLOGIC, MPRINT, and SYMBOLGEN

These options are used to display macro text. When a program is placed into production, there may no longer be any need to have these turned on. Because they generate text in the LOG, programs run more efficiently with these options turned off.

Often the MPRINT and NOMPRINT options are paired with the SOURCE and NOSOURCE options. For example, programs that have SOURCE turned on would also have MPRINT turned on.

CMDMAC and IMPLMAC

Used to turn on command- and statement-style macros, these should be off unless you must use one of these styles of macros. These options can cause a large efficiency loss.

MAUTOSOURCE, MRECALL, and SASAUTOS

These options are used when macros are stored in AUTOCALL libraries. These libraries can be very convenient for the programmer, but some overhead is required to search the libraries. Turn off MAUTOSOURCE if you do not want to use the AUTOCALL facility.

MSTORED and SASMSTORE

When macros become permanent and are placed into production, a compiled version can be stored. Because these macros are only compiled once, you can realize a savings through their use. If you are not using stored compiled macros, turn off MSTORED.

Session Compiled and Compiled Stored Macros

Production macros can be compiled and stored in a library as a Compiled Stored Macro. Once stored, these macros will not need to be compiled again. During a session, SAS will automatically store the compiled version (Session Compiled) of any called macro that is not already compiled. If you have macros in production that are not changing, they can be compiled and stored in a library. This is even more efficient than storing them uncompiled in an AUTOCALL library. See Section 3.3.4 for more on Compiled Stored Macros.

Use of the AUTOCALL Facility

Macros that are used by a number of programs but are in a state of flux (or have not yet been certified for production) should be stored in an AUTOCALL library. This prevents the generation of multiple versions of the macro, and it removes the macro definition from the calling program itself. Macros defined in a calling program <u>must</u> be recompiled every time that program is executed, even if it has already been executed during that session. By moving the macro to an AUTOCALL library, it will only have to be compiled once.

SEE ALSO

Levine (1989) discusses issues related to the efficient construction of macro-based systems in terms of standards and maintainability.

Appendix 1 # Exercise Solutions

Several of the chapters in this book contain a section titled "Chapter Exercises." These problems are designed to help you assess your understanding of the material that is contained within that chapter. Some of the questions require the writing of SAS macros or code, and many of the questions have "solutions" that are included in this appendix.

Many of the solutions to exercises, especially those that require programming, should be considered *a* solution and not *the* solution. As the saying goes, "If it can be done one way, in SAS it can be done three ways." Of course, the cynic then adds, "And the fourth way (*my way*) is the best."

Chapter 2

1. Selected portions of text have been replaced with macro variables.

```
LIBNAME CLASS 'd:training\sas\sasclass';

%let dsn = clinics;
%let var1 = edu;
%let var2 = dob;
%let type = mean;

PROC PLOT DATA=CLASS.&dsn;
     PLOT &var1 * &var2;
     TITLE1 'YEARS OF EDUCATION COMPARED TO BIRTH DATE';
RUN;

PROC CHART DATA=CLASS.&dsn;
     VBAR WT / SUMVAR=HT TYPE=&type;
     TITLE1 'AVERAGE HEIGHT FOR WEIGHT GROUPS';
RUN;
```

2. False

3. You can use the following %PUT statements to test your answers:

```
%let dsn=clinic;
%let lib=sasuser;
%let i=3;
%let dsn3 = studydrg;
%let b=dsn;

%put '&lib&dsn ' &lib&dsn;
%put '&lib.&dsn ' &lib.&dsn;
%put '&lib..&dsn ' &lib..&dsn;

%put '&dsn&i ' &dsn&i;
%put '&&dsn&i ' &&dsn&i;
%put '&dsn.&i ' &dsn.&i;
```

```
%put '&&bb ' &&bb;
%put '&&&b ' &&&b;

* Extra credit;
%put '&dsn..&&dsn&i ' &dsn..&&dsn&i;
```

These produce the following LOG entry:

```
66    %let dsn=clinic;
67    %let lib=sasuser;
68    %let i=3;
69    %let dsn3 = studydrg;
70    %let b=dsn;
71
72    %put '&lib&dsn ' &lib&dsn;
'&lib&dsn ' sasuserclinic
73    %put '&lib.&dsn ' &lib.&dsn;
'&lib.&dsn ' sasuserclinic
74    %put '&lib..&dsn ' &lib..&dsn;
'&lib..&dsn ' sasuser.clinic
75
76    %put '&dsn&i ' &dsn&i;
'&dsn&i ' clinic3
77    %put '&&dsn&i ' &&dsn&i;
'&&dsn&i ' studydrg
78    %put '&dsn.&i ' &dsn.&i;
'&dsn.&i ' clinic3
79
80    %put '&&bb ' &&bb;
WARNING: Apparent symbolic reference BB not resolved.
'&&bb ' &bb
81    %put '&&&b ' &&&b;
'&&&b ' clinic
82
83    * Extra credit;
84    %put '&dsn..&&dsn&i ' &dsn..&&dsn&i;
'&dsn..&&dsn&i ' clinic.studydrg
```

Notice the Warning. &&bb resolves to &bb, not `dsnb`.

The triple ampersand (line 81 in the LOG) resolves in two passes. On the first pass, && goes to & and &B goes to `dsn` leaving &DSN, which is resolved to `clinic` on the second pass.

4. Automatic macro variables are like any other macro variable except that they are initialized and defined by the SAS System.

5. &SYSPARM is a macro variable that allows the user to pass information into a job at execution time from outside of SAS.

Chapter 3

1. & 2. The macro %PLOTIT executes the desired code.

```
LIBNAME CLASS 'd:training\sas\sasclass';

options mlogic mprint symbolgen;
%macro plotit;
PROC PLOT DATA=CLASS.CLINICS;
     PLOT EDU * DOB;
     TITLE1 'YEARS OF EDUCATION COMPARED TO BIRTH DATE';
RUN;

PROC CHART DATA=CLASS.CLINICS;
     VBAR WT / SUMVAR=HT TYPE=MEAN;
     TITLE1 'AVERAGE HEIGHT FOR WEIGHT GROUPS';
RUN;
%mend plotit;
%plotit
```

3. True – unless you are using statement-style or command-style macros.

Chapter 4

1. POSITIONAL and KEYWORD (also called NAMED).

2. True – they can be specified in any order but must follow ALL positional parameters.

3. The following macro passes the data set name and two plot variables:

```
LIBNAME CLASS 'd:training\sas\sasclass';

options mlogic mprint symbolgen;
%macro plotit(var1, var2, dsn=);
PROC PLOT DATA=CLASS.&dsn;
     PLOT &var1 * &var2;
     TITLE1 'YEARS OF EDUCATION COMPARED TO BIRTH DATE';
RUN;

PROC CHART DATA=CLASS.&dsn;
     VBAR WT / SUMVAR=HT TYPE=MEAN;
     TITLE1 'AVERAGE HEIGHT FOR WEIGHT GROUPS';
RUN;
%mend plotit;
%plotit(edu,dob,dsn=clinics)
```

4. Two positional parameters and one keyword parameter.

5. The order and placement of position determines the values to be passed. It is not possible to determine this placement when positional parameters are mixed with keyword parameters.

6. There are two syntax corrections required:

❶ `%MACRO MYCOPY;`

```
    PROC COPY IN=WORK  OUT=MASTER;
         SELECT PATIENTS;
    RUN;
```

`%MEND MYCOPY;` ❷

❶ % is a required part of the %MACRO statement.

❷ The macro name must be consistent on both the %MACRO and %MEND statements.

Chapter 5

1. `%printt(class.clinics,proc=print)`

2.
```
%macro loop1;
  %do cnt = 1 %to 10;
     %put This is Test &cnt;
  %end;
%mend loop1;

%macro loop2;
  %let cnt=1;
  %do %while(&cnt <= 10);
     %put This is Test &cnt;
     %let cnt = %eval(&cnt + 1);
  %end;
%mend loop2;

%macro loop3;
  %let cnt=1;
  %do %until(&cnt > 10);
     %put This is Test &cnt;
     %let cnt = %eval(&cnt + 1);
  %end;
%mend loop3;

%put loop1; %loop1
%put loop2; %loop2
%put loop3; %loop3
```

3. True

4. True

5. Only A is correct, and it is correct only if the first characters in the macro %PRINT resolve to a valid macro label. B. %GLOBAL is misspelled. C. In a macro %IF statement, the %THEN requires a %.

6. Macro %GENPROC passes in the name of the data set as well as the name of the procedure.

```
%macro genproc(proc,dsn,varlst);
   proc &proc data=&dsn;
      var &varlst;
      title1 "&proc Procedure for &varlst";
   run;
%mend genproc;

%genproc(means,class.clinics, edu ht wt)
%genproc(univariate,class.clinics, edu ht wt)
```

The commas are used to separate positional parameters so that a list of variables (separated by spaces) can be passed in a single macro variable &VARLST.

7. The following macro contains a PROC MEANS that can produce printed output or an output data set:

```
%macro mymeans(dsn, varlst, statlst,
               outdsn, print=noprint);
proc means data=&dsn &statlst  ❶
  %if &outdsn = %then print;  ❷
  %else &print;;  ❸

var &varlst;
%if &outdsn ne %then  ❹
  output out=&outdsn mean=&varlst;;  ❺
run;
%mend mymeans;

* print selected stats (no output data set);
%mymeans(class.clinics, ht wt, mean stderr)  ❻

* no printed stats (output data set only);
%mymeans(class.clinics, ht wt,,outstat)  ❼
proc print data=outstat;
run;

* printed stats & an output data set ;
%mymeans(class.clinics, ht wt,sum  ❽
max,outstat,print=print)
```

❶ &STATLIST will contain the list of statistics to be printed.

❷ When an output data set is not named in &OUTDSN, printed statistics are requested using the PRINT option.

❸ Printed statistics can be requested even if an output data set is requested by passing PRINT into &PRINT.

❹ An OUTPUT statement is generated if an output data set is named in &OUTDSN.

❺ The list of means will have the same variable names as the analysis variables. The first semicolon closes the %IF, and the second semicolon closes the OUTPUT statement.

❻ This call to %MYMEANS will result in only printed output because the fourth argument (&OUTDSN) is blank.

❼ This call to %MYMEANS produces an output data set (OUTSTAT) and no printed output.

❽ This call to %MYMEANS produces both an output data set (OUTSTAT) and printed statistics (SUM and MAX).

8. Macro variables that are passed into a macro are local to that macro. The macro will operate correctly. It would not be a bad idea, however, to add the %LOCAL statement to %REGTEST.

9. The LOG shows:

```
128   %let a = AAA;
129   %macro try;
130   %put &a;
131   %if   &a   =   AAA %then %put no quotes;
132   %if '&a'   = 'AAA' %then %put single quotes;
133   %if 'AAA'  = 'AAA' %then %put exact strings;
134   %if "&a"   = "AAA" %then %put double quotes;
135   %if "&a"   = 'AAA' %then %put mixed quotes;
136   %if "&a"   =   AAA %then %put quotes on one side only;
137   %mend;
138   %try
AAA
no quotes
exact strings
double quotes
```

Chapter 6

1. Convert the numeric region variable to character before assigning it to the macro variable:

```
CALL SYMPUT('REG'||II,left(put(REGION,3.)));
```

The WHERE statement would also need to reflect the change, for example, quotes would not be needed.

```
WHERE REGION=&&REG&I;
```

2. In the CLINICS data set, there are ten regions that are numbered from '1' to '10'. The following solution would not work if the region values were not consecutive, starting at one. Notice that although REGION='10' sorts between '1' and '2' it is plotted in its more logical order (not its sorted order).

```
libname class 'd:\training\sas\sasclass';

%MACRO PLOTIT;
   PROC SORT DATA=CLASS.CLINICS OUT=CLINICS;
      BY REGION;
      RUN;
   DATA _NULL_;
      SET CLINICS;
      BY REGION;
      IF FIRST.REGION THEN DO;
         I+1;
         II=LEFT(PUT(I,2.));
         CALL SYMPUT('REG'||II,REGION);  ❶
         CALL SYMPUT('TOTAL',II);  ❷
      END;
      RUN;

   data
      %* Build the names of the new data sets;
      %do i = 1 %to &total;  ❸
         reg&i
      %end;
      ;
      set clinics;
      %do i = 1 %to &total;
         %* Build the output statements;
         %if &i=1 %then if region='1' then output reg1;
         %else else if region="&i" then output reg&i;  ❹
         ;
      %end;

   * Plot the &total regions one at a time;
   %DO I=1 %TO &TOTAL;  ❺
      PROC PLOT DATA=reg&i;
         PLOT HT * WT;
         TITLE1 "Height/Weight for REGION &I";
      RUN;
   %END;
%MEND PLOTIT;

%plotit
```

❶ The value of the *i*th region is stored in &REG$_i$.

❷ The total number of regions is stored in &TOTAL.

❸ The DATA statement is built dynamically using the %DO loop.

❹ The IF-THEN/ELSE statements are built dynamically for each region. These statements depend on the values of the variable REGION. This is a limitation of this solution, which is removed in Q6.3.

❺ This loop does a separate PROC PLOT step for each region.

The limitations of this approach are removed in the solution for Question 3.

3. The sort is still needed but only so that the FIRST.REGION can be used to get the regional values in the DATA _NULL_ step. This solution does not require that the values of REGION take on any particular sequence. Indeed, you may notice that the output now has regions back in sorted order, that is, '1', '10', '2', and so on.

```
libname class 'd:\training\sas\sasclass';

%MACRO PLOTIT;
    PROC SORT DATA=CLASS.CLINICS OUT=CLINICS;
        BY REGION;
        RUN;
    DATA _NULL_;
        SET CLINICS;
        BY REGION;
        IF FIRST.REGION THEN DO;
            I+1;
            II=LEFT(PUT(I,2.));
            CALL SYMPUT('REG'||II,REGION);
            CALL SYMPUT('TOTAL',II);
        END;
        RUN;

    data %do i = 1 %to &total; r&&reg&i %end;;   ❶
        set clinics;
        %* Build the &total output statements;
        %do i = 1 %to &total;
          %if &i=1 %then if region="&&reg&i" then output r&&reg&i;  ❷
          %else else if region="&&reg&i" then output r&&reg&i;
          ;
        %end;
        run;

    %DO I=1 %TO &TOTAL;
        PROC PLOT DATA=r&&reg&i;
            PLOT HT * WT;
            TITLE1 "Height/Weight for REGION &&REG&I";
            RUN;
    %END;
%MEND PLOTIT;

%plotit
```

❶ The data sets created will be named R*xx*, where *xx* is the region number.

❷ &&REG&I contains the region number for the &Ith region.

Suppose the variable REGION took on the values '1', '23', and '42'.

I	REGION	R&&REG&I
1	1	R1
2	23	R23
3	42	R42

Some discussion of this macro can be found in Section 9.3.

4. The macro %ALLCHAR converts all numeric variables to character, including the use of any available formats.

```
libname class 'd:\training\sas\sasclass';

%macro allchar(dsn);
* Determine the numeric vars in &dsn;
proc contents data=&dsn out=cont noprint;
run;

* Create the macro variables for each numeric var;
data _null_;
set cont(keep=name type format formatl formatd label);
length fmt $15;
where  type=1; ❶

* Count the numeric vars and save the total number;
i+1;
ii=left(put(i,3.));
call symput('n',ii); ❷

* create a format string;
fmt = 'best.';
if format ne ' ' then fmt = trim(format)
     ||trim(left(put(formatl,3.)))
     ||'.'||left(put(formatd,3.));
fmt = compress(fmt);
call symput('fmt'||ii,fmt); ❸

* Save the variable name;
call symput('name'||ii,name); ❹

* Save the label for this variable;
if label = ' ' then label = name;
call symput('label'||ii,label); ❺
run;

* Establish a data set with only character variables;
* &n        number of numeric variables in &dsn;
* __aa&i    temporary var to hold numeric values;
* &&name&i  name of the variable to convert from numeric;
*
* The numeric value of &name1 is stored in __aa1
* by renaming the variable in the SET statement.  __aa1
* is then converted to character and stored in the
* 'new' variable &name1 in the data set CHARONLY.
* ;
data charonly (drop=
   %* Drop the temp. vars used to hold numeric values;
   %do i=1 %to &n;
      __aa&i ❻
   %end;
    );
```

```
length
   %* Establish the vars as character;
   %do i=1 %to &n;
      &&name&i
   %end;
    $8;

set &dsn (rename=(
   %* Rename the incoming numeric var to a temp name;
   %* This allows the reuse of the variables name;
   %do i=1 %to &n;
      &&name&i=__aa&i  ❼
   %end;
   ));

   * Convert the numeric values to character;
   %do i=1 %to &n;
      &&name&i = left(put(__aa&i,&&fmt&i));  ❽
      label &&name&i = "&&label&i";
   %end;
run;

proc contents data=charonly;
proc print data=charonly;
run;
%mend allchar;

%allchar(class.biomass)
```

❶ Numeric variables have TYPE=1;

❷ Save the number of numeric variables.

❸ Save the format for this numeric variable.

❹ Save the name of the variable.

❺ Save the label of the variable.

❻ Incoming numeric variables will be temporarily renamed using the RENAME= data set option ❼.

❼ The RENAME= option is built dynamically inside of the %DO loop.

❽ Use the PUT function to convert the numeric variable that is temporarily stored in &&__AA&I to character using the appropriate format (&&FMT&I).

SEE ALSO
Roberts (1997) uses an analogous approach to converting all character variables to uppercase.

Chapter 7

1. A, B, C, and D. Give yourself half credit if you selected F. (Technically F (All of the above) includes E, which is clearly false).

2. True

3. Mostly true. It does not mask some special characters, such as quotes or parentheses.

4. The following macro can be used to count the number of words in a macro string. The global macro variable &COUNT is assigned the number of words in the string that is passed in through the first parameter (&STRING). An optional second parameter (&PARM) can be used as a word delimiter.

```
* Count the number of words in a string
* see p256 in SAS Guide to Macro Processing;

%macro count(string,parm);
    %local word;  ❶
    %if &parm= %then %let parm = %str( );  ❷
    %let count=1;
    %let word = %qscan(&string,&count,&parm);  ❸
    %do %while(&word ne);
        %let count = %eval(&count+1);
        %let word = %qscan(&string,&count,&parm);❸
    %end;
    %put word count for |&string| is %eval(&count-1);❹
%mend count;

%count(this is a short string)  ❺
%count(%nrstr(this*&is*a*string),%str(*))❻
```

❶ &WORD will be local.

❷ When no parameter is passed in, use a blank to separate words.

❸ Retrieve the word designated by &COUNT. &PARM holds the word separator.

❹ &COUNT was incremented one too many times.

❺ The word count will be 5 using the default word separator (blank).

❻ Four words will be counted. The &IS is quoted and will not be resolved.

Appendix 2 **Utilities Locator**

This appendix is designed to assist you with locating examples of certain types of macro utilities in this book. Obviously, this static list is a brief and incomplete compilation of the many fine utilities developed by various users of the SAS Macro Language. For sources other than those in this book, consult the References section.

Utility Topic or Task	Source
Appending Unknown Data Sets	10.1.5
Converting Numeric Variables to Character	Q6.4
Copying Libraries	2.6.3, 7.4.2, 10.1.4
Counting Observations	2.7.1, 11.2.1, 11.5, 13.1.1, 13.1.2
Counting Words in a String	6.4.2, 7.2.3, 11.4.3, Q7.4
Creating Flat Files	6.2.1, 11.1.1, 11.1.2
Data Subsetting	6.2.1, 9.2, 9.3, 11.2.1, 11.2.2, 11.2.3, Q6.2, Q6.3
Data Set Contents	5.3.1, 11.1.1, 11.1.2
Debugging	2.3, 3.2, 3.3.2, 4.4
Dumping or Listing Flat Files	10.1.2
Existence of a Data Set, Checking for	7.1.2, 11.3
Loading Dates and Times into Macro Variables	4.4, 7.4.2, 10.1.3
Output Control	10.2.1, 10.2.2, 11.5.2
Random Number Generation	7.4.1, 11.2.3
Variable List (Building)	2.7.2, 11.4.1, 11.4.2, 13.1.2
Variable List (Using)	4.2.2, 6.4.2, 7.1.4, 7.2.3, 11.4.3
Write Access, Checking for	10.1.4

Appendix 3 # Example Locator

This appendix is designed to assist you with locating examples of certain topics or statements. This table shows an alphabetical listing of topics/statements, the sections in this book where they are introduced or discussed, and a list of additional sections that contain examples that pertain to that topic or utilize that statement.

Topic / Statement	Primary Discussion	Also Used in Examples
%* (macro comment) and comments within macros	5.4.1	2.3, 3.1.2, 5.1.2, 6.7.4, 7.1.2, 11.5.1
%BQUOTE %NRBQUOTE	7.1.5	7.1.8, 7.1.9
%CMPRES	12.2.3	13.2
%DO	5.3.1	2.6.3, 5.2.2, 6.7.2, 7.1.2, 7.2.2, 9.3, 10.1.3, 11.2.3, 12.2.4
%DO (iterative)	5.3.2	5.4.1, 5.6.2, 6.4.1, 6.7.3, 6.7.4, 8.3.2, 9.3, 10.1.2, 10.1.5, Q6.2, Q6.3
%DO %UNTIL	5.3.3	5.4.2, 7.2.3, 11.4.3
%DO %WHILE	5.3.4	7.6.2, 12.2.3, 13.1.2, Q7.4
%EVAL	7.3.1	5.3.4, 5.6.2, 7.2.3, 7.6.4, 11.4.3, 13.1.2, Q7.4
%GLOBAL and %LOCAL	5.4.2	6.4.2, 10.1.2
%GOTO and %label	5.4.3	
%IF - %THEN / %ELSE	5.2	5.2.1, 5.2.2, 5.3.1, 5.6.7, 6.4.2, 7.1.2, 7.1.4, 7.1.6, 7.2.2, 7.2.5, 7.3.1, 7.3.2, 7.6.4, 8.3.2, 9.3, 10.1.3, 11.2.3, 13.1.2
%INDEX	7.2.1	12.2.3, 12.2.4
%LEFT	12.2.2	12.2.3, 13.2
%LENGTH	7.2.2	12.2.4

Topic / Statement	Primary Discussion	Also Used in Examples
%LET	2.2	2.3, 2.5, 2.9.1, 2.9.2, 5.3.4, 5.4.2, 7.1.5, 7.1.6, 7.2.1
%LOWCASE	12.2.4	
%MACRO and %MEND	3.1	3.1.1, 3.1.2, 3.7.1, 4.2.1, 4.3.1, 4.4, 4.6.3, 5.1.2, and so on
%PUT	2.4	2.6.5, 2.6.6, 2.7, 3.1.1, 5.4.2
%QUOTE %NRQUOTE	7.1.4	7.1, 7.1.1, 7.1.8, 13.1.2
%SCAN %QSCAN	7.2.3	7.6.4, 11.4.3, 13.1.2, Q7.4
%STR %NRSTR	7.1.2, 7.1.3	7.1, 7.1.1, 7.1.6, 7.1.8, 7.1.9, 7.2.3, 7.2.4, 7.2.5, 7.6.4, 12.2.3, 12.2.4
%SUBSTR %QSUBSTR	7.2.4	12.2.1, 12.2.2, 12.2.3, 12.2.4
%SUPERQ	7.1.7	7.1.8
%SYSCALL	7.4.1	
%SYSEVALF	7.3.3	
%SYSEXEC	5.4.4	
%SYSFUNC %QSYSFUNC	7.4.2	10.1, 11.3, 11.5.1, 11.5.2
%TRIM	12.1	12.2.3
%UNQUOTE	7.1.6	
%UPCASE %QUPCASE	7.2.5	13.1.4
%VERIFY	12.1.1	12.2.2
&&var&i	2.5.3, 6.2.1, 6.4	2.9.3, 6.3, 6.4.1, 6.4.2, 6.7.3, 6.7.4, 7.2.3, 8.3.2, 13.1.4, 13.2
Dynamic Programming	5.2.2, 6.4, 9.0	5.3.2, 5.3.3, 5.3.4, 6.3, 8.3.2, 10.1.1, 11.1.2, Q6.2, Q6.3

Topic / Statement	Primary Discussion	Also Used in Examples
PROC SQL	2.7	11.2.1, 11.4.1, 11.4.2, 13.1.1, 13.1.2
RESOLVE	6.5.3	
SASHELP Views		10.1.5, 10.2.1
SYMGET	6.5.2	
SYMPUT	6.1	4.4, 6.1.1, 6.1.2, 6.1.3, 6.2.1, 6.2.2, 6.3, 6.4.2, 6.7.1, 6.7.2, 6.7.3, 7.4.2, 7.4.3, 8.2.1, 10.1.3, 10.2.2, 11.1.2, 11.4.3, 13.2
SYMPUTN	8.2.1	

Appendix 4 **Example Data Sets**

The programs included in this Appendix will generate the data sets that are used in several of the examples and exercises in this book.

You can obtain the example programs included throughout the text, as well as the code needed to generate the databases in electronic form, from the SAS Online Samples. See the inside front cover of this book for more information.

BIOMASS.SAS

Biomass (wet weight in grams) estimates were made for several types of soft-bottom benthic organisms (critters that live in the mud) over a period of several years along the southern California coast. The BIOMASS data set contains data that were taken from selected stations and depths during the summer of 1985. The August 5, 1985 *outlier* is a valid datum that represents a core that caught a large single organism.

```
****************************************************;
* biomass.sas;
*
* Create the benthos biomass data set.
****************************************************;

data sasclass.biomass;
input   @1 STATION $
        @12 DATE DATE7.
        @20 BMPOLY
        @25 BMCRUS
        @31 BMMOL
        @36 BMOTHR
        @41 BMTOTL ;

format date date7.;

label BMCRUS    = 'CRUSTACEAN BIOMASS (GM WET WEIGHT)'
      BMMOL     = 'MOLLUSC BIOMASS (GM WET WEIGHT)   '
      BMOTHR    = 'OTHER BIOMASS (GM WET WEIGHT)     '
      BMPOLY    = 'POLYCHAETE BIOMASS (GM WET WEIGHT)'
      BMTOTL    = 'TOTAL BIOMASS (GM WET WEIGHT)     '
      DATE      = 'DATE                              '
      STATION   = 'STATION ID                        ';

cards;
DL-25       18JUN85 0.4  0.03  0.17 0.02 0.62
DL-60       17JUN85 0.51 0.09  0.14 0.08 0.82
D1100-25    18JUN85 0.28 0.02  0.01 4.61 4.92
D1100-60    17JUN85 0.36 0.05  0.32 0.47 1.2
D1900-25    18JUN85 0.03 0.02  0.11 1.06 1.22
D1900-60    17JUN85 0.54 0.11  0.03 4.18 4.86
D3200-60    17JUN85 0.52 0.14  0.04 0.05 0.75
D3350-25    18JUN85 0.18 0.02  0.11 0    0.31
D6700-25    18JUN85 0.51 0.06  0.03 0.01 0.61
D6700-60    17JUN85 0.32 0.14  0.04 0.22 0.72
D700-25     18JUN85 0.23 0.03  0.02 0.07 0.35
D700-60     17JUN85 1.11 0.32  0.07 0.02 1.52
DL-25       10JUL85 0.92 0.09  0.1  0.03 1.14
DL-60       09JUL85 0.29 0.14  0.03 0.06 0.52
D1100-25    10JUL85 0.14 0.05  0.05 4.79 5.03
D1100-60    09JUL85 0.88 0.07  0.01 0.01 0.97
D1900-25    10JUL85 0.35 0.05  0.05 1.82 2.27
D1900-60    09JUL85 0.87 0.08  0.42 3.35 4.72
D3200-60    09JUL85 0.22 0.1   0.08 0.01 0.41
D3350-25    10JUL85 0.36 0.06  0.01 0.02 0.45
D6700-25    10JUL85 1.84 0.02  0.11 0.05 2.02
D6700-60    09JUL85 0.47 0.19  0.06 0.06 0.78
D700-25     10JUL85 1.46 0.19  0.12 0.38 2.15
D700-60     09JUL85 0.48 0.18  0.02 0.11 0.79
```

```
DL-25       05AUG85 0.92 0.08  0.09 0.02 1.11
DL-60       02AUG85 0.4  0.1   0.59 0.5  1.59
D1100-25    05AUG85 0.18 0.02  0.36 2.33 2.89
D1100-60    02AUG85 0.39 0.12  0.03 0.01 0.55
D1900-25    05AUG85 1.23 0.06  0.04 2.15 3.48
D1900-60    02AUG85 0.56 0.07  0.02 0.11 0.76
D3200-60    02AUG85 0.39 0.11  0.05 0.02 0.57
D3350-25    05AUG85 0.45 44.82 0.02 0.16 45.45
D6700-25    05AUG85 1.13 0.01  0.11 0.04 1.29
D6700-60    02AUG85 0.43 0.15  1.1  0.01 1.69
D700-25     05AUG85 0.31 0.02  0.26 0.03 0.62
D700-60     02AUG85 0.38 0.07  0.12 1.87 2.44
DL-25       26AUG85 0.57 0.01  0.14 0.04 0.76
DL-60       27AUG85 0.46 0.05  0.5  0.18 1.19
D1100-25    26AUG85 0.63 0.02  0.04 0.03 0.72
D1100-60    27AUG85 0.57 0.04  0.09 0.31 1.01
D1900-25    26AUG85 0.26 0.03  0.01 3.89 4.19
D1900-60    27AUG85 0.73 0.07  0.06 0.09 0.95
D3200-60    27AUG85 0.46 0.07  0.02 0.01 0.56
D3350-25    26AUG85 0.57 0.02  0.05 0.05 0.69
D6700-25    26AUG85 0.87 0.01  0.03 0.02 0.93
D6700-60    27AUG85 0.69 0.07  0.03 0.01 0.8
D700-25     26AUG85 0.48 0.19  0.53 0.62 1.82
D700-60     27AUG85 0.25 0.09  0.07 0.01 0.42
run;
```

CLINICS.SAS

Patient medical data were collected from 80 patients at various clinics and hospitals nationwide.

```
*********************************************;
* clinics.sas;
*
* Create the clinics data set.
*********************************************;

data sasclass.clinics;
infile cards missover;
input clinnum  $ 1-6
      clinname $ 7-33
      region   $ 34-35
      lname    $ 36-45
      fname    $ 46-51
      ssn      $ 52-60
      sex      $ 61
      dob        mmddyy8.
      death      mmddyy8.
      race     $ 78
      edu        79-80
      wt         81-83
      ht         84-85
      exam       mmddyy8.
      symp     $ 94-95
      dt_diag    mmddyy8.
      diag     $ 104
      admit      mmddyy8.
      proced   $ 113
      disch      mmddyy8.;

format dob death exam dt_diag admit disch date7.;

label clinnum  = 'clinic number'
      clinname = 'clinic name'
      region   = 'region'
      lname    = 'last name'
      fname    = 'first name'
      ssn      = 'social security number'
      sex      = 'patient sex'
      dob      = 'date of birth'
      death    = 'date of death'
```

```
race     = 'race'
edu      = 'years of education'
wt       = 'weight in pounds'
ht       = 'height in inches'
exam     = 'examination date'
symp     = 'symptom code'
dt_diag  = 'date of diagnosis'
diag     = 'diagnosis code'
admit    = 'admit date'
proced   = 'procedure code'
disch    = 'discharge date'
;

cards;
031234Bethesda Pioneer Hospital    3Smith     Mike   123456789M03/18/52    1161627102/13/870102/14/87302/15/87
03632Naval Memorial Hospital       3Jones     Sarah  043667543F07/02/46    3141056407/01/830607/03/83207/05/83307/10/83
02447New York General Hospital     2Maxwell   Linda  135798642F05/20/53    3141056407/01/830607/03/83207/05/83307/10/83
065742Kansas Metropolitan         7Marshall  Robert489012567M03/11/53     1121556711/02/8702
108531Seattle Medical Complex     10James     Debra  563457897F06/19/4208/03/85117163630422/830505/03/83607/27/85208/03/85
014321Vermont Treatment Center     1Lawless   Henry  075312468M09/17/60    1101957411/02/860411/05/86311/19/86
09527San Francisco Bay General     9Chu       David  784567256M06/18/51    5161476810/10/830410/10/833
04320Miami Bay Medical Center      4Halfner   John   589012773M03/02/47    2171556709/14/850209/14/852
05134Battle Creek Hospital         5Cranberry David  153675389M11/21/3104/13/86113215681028/851010/29/85510/29/85204/13/86
063901Dallas Memorial Hospital     6Simpson   Donna  373167532F04/18/3305/21/87115187630512/870405/12/87305/12/87205/21/87
09378Sacramento Medical Complex    9Wright    Sarah  674892109F10/21/48    2121776509/10/8306
02447New York General Hospital     2Little    Sandra376245789F08/01/50     1121096307/01/830607/03/83207/05/83307/07/83
04320Miami Bay Medical Center      4Johnson   Randal537890152M08/29/56     11820173
057312Indiana Help Center          5Henderson Robert932456132M02/25/57     2161587208/15/831008/15/832      3
08228Denver Security Hospital      8Adamson   Joan   011553218F            2161587208/15/831008/15/832      3
033476Mississippi Health Center    4Rodgers   Carl   327654213M11/15/48    1131797212/20/84
06678Austin Medical Hospital       6Alexander Mark   743567875M01/15/30    1121757009/15/88
026789Geneva Memorial Hospital     2Long      Margot531895634F02/28/49     414115640815/860108/21/86708/21/86308/21/86
05436Michigan Medical Center       5Cranston  Rhonda287463500F01/03/3704/13/88112160620328/881003/28/88503/28/88204/13/88
094789San Diego Memorial Hospital  9Dandy     Martin578901234M05/21/37     11218570
08489Montana Municipal Hospital    8Wills     Norma  425617894F05/10/51    1121626802/20/840302/20/841
033476Mississippi Health Center    4Cordoba   Juan   327654213M06/06/67    3151336805/07/840905/09/84
108531Seattle Medical Complex     10Robertson Adam   743787764M04/07/4208/03/871121776904/29/850505/03/85603/29/87208/03/87
063742Houston General              6King      Doug   467901234M08/15/34    2122406811/12/881011/12/885
038362Philadelphia Hospital        3Marksman  Joan   634792254F09/28/63    41411265
031234Bethesda Pioneer Hospital    3Candle    Sid    468729812M10/15/17    1101957411/02/860411/05/86311/19/86
046789Tampa Treatment Complex      4Baron     Roger  189456372M01/29/37    1101607006/15/8510
011234Boston National Medical      1Nabers    David  345751123M11/03/21    1101957411/02/860411/05/86311/19/86
023910New York Metro Medical Ctr   2Harbor    Samuel1091550932M01/14/50    3141056405/27/830605/28/832
063742Houston General              6Davidson  Mitch  524189532M02/26/39    2162016905/12/8705      2
059372Ohio Medical Hospital        5Karson    Shawn  297854321F03/05/60    217 9862      04
023910New York Metro Medical Ctr   2Harbor    Samuel1091550932M01/14/50    3141056407/01/830607/03/83207/05/83307/10/83
049060Atlanta General Hospital     4Adams     Mary   079932455F08/12/51    2171556709/14/850209/14/852
```

Hospital ID / Name	Code	Name / Data	Numbers
10721Portland General	10Holmes	Donald315674321M06/21/40	1121776904/29/850505/03/85603/29/87208/03/87
063901Dallas Memorial Hospital	6Simpson	Donna 373167532F04/18/3305/21/87	11151876305/12/870405/12/87305/12/87205/21/87
095277San Francisco Bay General	9Marks	Gerald638956732M03/03/47	1102156709/02/82
065742Kansas Metropolitan	7Chang	Joseph539873164M08/20/58	5181476501/18/860302/03/86102/03/86102/07/86
036321Naval Memorial Hospital	3Masters	Martha029874182F08/20/58	2171556709/14/850209/14/852
095277San Francisco Bay General	9Marks	Gerald638956732M03/03/47	1102156709/02/821009/03/82509/05/82309/08/82
049060Atlanta General Hospital	4Rymes	Carol 680162534F10/05/57	1151316604/01/850204/01/852
031234Bethesda Pioneer Hospital	3Henry	Louis 467189564M04/19/53	1161627102/13/870102/14/87202/14/87302/15/87
036321Naval Memorial Hospital	3Stubs	Mark 319085547M06/11/47	3141056407/01/830607/03/83207/05/83307/10/83
024477New York General Hospital	2Haddock	Linda 219075362F04/04/51	3141056407/01/830607/03/83207/05/83307/10/83
065742Kansas Metropolitan	7Uno	Robert389036754M03/21/44	1221556711/02/8702
108531Seattle Medical Complex	10Manley	Debra 366781237F01/19/4208/03/85	1171636304/22/830505/03/83607/27/85208/03/85
014321Vermont Treatment Center	1Mercy	Ronald190473627M09/27/60	1101957411/02/860411/05/86311/05/86311/19/86
095277San Francisco Bay General	9Chang	Tim 19835256M02/18/51	5164768 10/10/830410/10/833
043320Miami Bay Medical Center	4Most	Mat 10927433M03/02/47	2171556709/14/850209/14/852
051345Battle Creek Hospital	5Rose	Mary 29981743F11/01/3104/13/86	1132156810/28/851010/29/85510/29/85204/13/86
063901Dallas Memorial Hospital	6Nolan	Terrie298456241F10/18/3307/21/87	11151876305/12/870405/12/87305/12/87207/21/87
093785Sacramento Medical Complex	9Tanner	Heidi 456178349F08/08/45	212177650910/8306
024477New York General Hospital	2Saunders	Liz 46045789F03/01/49	1121096307/01/830607/03/83207/05/83307/07/83
043320Miami Bay Medical Center	4Jackson	Ted 33998467M12/29/56	11820173
057312Indiana Help Center	5Pope	Robert83245632M02/05/57	216587208/15/831008/15/832 3
082287Denver Security Hospital	8Olsen	June 743873218F	216587208/15/831008/15/832 3
033476Mississippi Health Center	4Maxim	Kurt 468721213M10/15/40	1131797212/20/84
066789Austin Medical Hospital	6Banner	John 368267875M01/25/32	1121757009/15/88
026789Geneva Memorial Hospital	2Ingram	Marcia367895634F02/13/48	414115608/15/860108/21/86708/21/86308/21/86
054367Michigan Medical Center	5Moon	Rachel37536350F01/23/3706/13/88	11812160 6203/28/881003/28/88505/28/88206/13/88
094789San Diego Memorial Hospital	9Thomas	Daniel486301234M05/23/38	11218570
084890Montana Municipal Hospital	8East	Jody 086317894F10/10/51	1121626802/20/840302/20/841 2
033476Mississippi Health Center	4Perez	Mathew578254213M07/06/57	3151336805/07/840905/09/84
108531Seattle Medical Complex	10Reilly	Arthur476587764M05/17/4209/03/87	1121776904/29/850505/03/85608/29/87209/03/87
063742Houston General	6Antler	Peter 489745234M01/15/34	2122406811/12/881011/12/885
038362Philadelphia Hospital	3Upston	Betty 784793254F09/13/63	41411265
031234Bethesda Pioneer Hospital	3Panda	Merv 387549812M10/11/19	1101957411/02/860411/05/86311/19/86
046789Tampa Treatment Complex	4East	Clint 842576372M01/26/37	1101607006/15/8510
011234Boston National Medical	1Taber	Lee 479451123M11/05/24	1101957411/02/860411/05/86311/19/86
023910New York Metro Medical Ctr	2Leader	Zac 075345932M01/15/50	3141056405/27/830605/28/832
063742Houston General	6Ronson	Gerald474223532M02/27/49	2162016905/12/8705 2
059372Ohio Medical Hospital	5Carlile	Patsy 578854321F03/15/55	217 9862 04
023910New York Metro Medical Ctr	2Atwood	Teddy 066425632M02/14/50	3141056407/01/830607/03/83207/05/83307/10/83
049060Atlanta General Hospital	4Batell	Mary 310967555F01/12/37	2171556709/14/850209/14/852
107211Portland General	10Hermit	Oliver471094671M06/23/38	1121776904/29/850505/03/85603/29/87208/03/87
063901Dallas Memorial Hospital	6Temple	Linda 691487532F04/18/4305/21/87	11151876305/12/870405/12/87305/21/87
095277San Francisco Bay General	9Block	Will 54901453 2M03/12/51	1102156709/02/82
065742Kansas Metropolitan	7Chou	John 310986734M05/15/58	5181476501/18/860302/03/86102/03/86102/07/86

```
036321Naval Memorial Hospital      3Herbal  Tammy 041090882F08/23/46  2171556709/14/850209/14/852
095277San Francisco Bay General    9Mann    Steven48995673 2M03/27/43 1102156709/02/821009/03/82509/05/82309/08/82
049060Atlanta General Hospital     4Rumor   Stacy 409825614F12/05/52  1151316604/01/850204/01/852
run;
```

References

Most of the following references were cited within the text of this book. All, even those not directly cited, contain information that may be of interest to you.

SAS Institute Documentation

SAS® Guide to Macro Processing, Version 6, Second Edition, Cary, NC, SAS Institute Inc., 1990. 319 pp.

SAS® Macro Language: Reference, First Edition, Cary, NC, SAS Institute Inc., 1997. 304 pp.

SAS® Screen Control Language: Reference, Version 6, Second Edition, SAS Institute Inc., Cary, NC, 1994. Chapter 10, "Using Macro Variables," (pp. 99–101) discusses macro variables, and the substitution of text in SUBMIT blocks is discussed on p. 110.

SAS® Screen Control Language: Usage, Version 6, First Edition, SAS Institute Inc., Cary, NC, 1991. Chapter 27, "Using Macro Variables," (pp. 487–500) contains a number of examples of SCL programs that utilize macro variables. Chapter 28, "Submitting SAS and SQL Statements," covers various combinations of macro and SCL variable substitution in SUBMIT blocks.

SAS® Software: Changes and Enhancements, Release 6.10, Cary, NC, SAS Institute Inc., 1994. 160 pp.

SAS® Technical Report P-222, *Changes and Enhancements to Base SAS Software, Release 6.07*, Cary, NC, SAS Institute Inc., 1991. 344 pp.

Articles, Papers, and Books

Aboutaleb, Hany, 1997a, "Printing with SAS 6.10 and 6.11," *Proceedings of the Pharmaceutical Industry SAS® Users Group, PhaRmaSUG 97, Conference*, Cary, NC: SAS Institute Inc., pp. 279–282.

———, 1997b, "More About Missing Character Data," *Proceedings of the Pharmaceutical Industry SAS® Users Group, PhaRmaSUG 97, Conference*, Cary, NC: SAS Institute Inc., pp. 283–284.

Andresen, Robert, 1997, "Macro and Sample Source Code To Wrap Character Variable Text Conditionally on Two Lines Within DATA _NULL_-generated Report Column(s)," *Proceedings of the Twenty-Second Annual SAS® Users Group International Conference*, Cary, NC: SAS Institute Inc., pp. 453–455.

Anonymous, 1996, "Technical Support," *SAS Communications®*, Vol. 6 #1 - Fourth quarter, Cary, NC: SAS Institute Inc., p. 43.

_____, 1997, "Questions and Answers," *SAS Communications*®, Vol. 6 #2 - First quarter, Cary, NC: SAS Institute Inc., p. 48.

Bercov, Mark, 1993, "SAS Macros - What's Really Happening?" *Proceedings of the Eighteenth Annual SAS*® *Users Group International Conference*, Cary, NC: SAS Institute Inc., pp. 440–444; and republished in *SAS*® *Macro Facility Tips and Techniques, Version 6, First Edition*, Cary, NC: SAS Institute Inc. 1994, pp. 17–21.

Blood, Nancy C., 1992, "Using SAS Macros to Generate Code (So Your Program Can Figure Out What To Do for Itself," *Proceedings of the Seventeenth Annual SAS*® *Users Group International Conference*, Cary, NC: SAS Institute Inc., pp. 24-28; and republished in *SAS*® *Macro Facility Tips and Techniques, Version 6, First Edition*, Cary, NC: SAS Institute Inc. 1994, pp. 138–142.

Bryant, Connie, 1997, "Automated Generation of a SAS Macro Cross-Reference Table," *Proceedings of the Twenty-Second Annual SAS*® *Users Group International Conference*, Cary, NC: SAS Institute Inc., pp. 928–933.

Bryher, Monique, 1997a, "How Symbolic Variables Can Reduce Code in a Graphic Environment," *Proceedings of the Twenty-Second Annual SAS*® *Users Group International Conference*, Cary, NC: SAS Institute Inc., pp. 37–42.

_____, 1997b, "Building a Simple SAS Macro to Generate SAQL Instructions in Frequently Used DB2 Tables," *Proceedings of the Twenty-Second Annual SAS*® *Users Group International Conference*, Cary, NC: SAS Institute Inc., pp. 43–47.

Carpenter, Arthur L. and Janice D. Callahan, 1988, "Subsetting Data into Groups for Complete Processing Within Each Group," *Proceedings of the Thirteenth Annual SAS*® *Users Group International Conference*, Cary, NC: SAS Institute Inc., pp. 825–829.

Carpenter, Arthur L., 1994, "Playing with Macros: Take the Work out of Learning to Do Macros," *Proceedings of the Nineteenth Annual SAS*® *Users Group International Conference*, Cary, NC: SAS Institute Inc., pp. 368–372.

_____, 1996, "Programming For Job Security: Tips and Techniques to Maximize Your Indispensability," *Proceedings of the Twenty-First Annual SAS*® *Users Group International Conference*, Cary, NC: SAS Institute Inc., pp. 1637–1640.

_____, 1997, "Resolving and Using &&var&I Macro Variables," *Proceedings of the Twenty-Second Annual SAS*® *Users Group International Conference*, Cary, NC: SAS Institute Inc., pp. 437–440.

_____, 1998a, "Advanced Macro Topics: Utilities and Examples," *Proceedings of the Twenty-Third Annual SAS*® *Users Group International Conference*, Cary, NC: SAS Institute Inc., pp. 287–292.

_____, 1998b, "Programming For Job Security Revisited: Even More Tips and Techniques to Maximize Your Indispensability," *Proceedings of the Twenty-Third Annual SAS*® *Users Group International Conference*, Cary, NC: SAS Institute Inc., pp. 1547–1556.

Carey, Helen and Ginger Carey, 1996, *SAS*® *Today! A Year of Terrific Tips*, Cary, NC: SAS Institute Inc., 395 pp.

Davis, Neil, 1997, "Rapid Applications Development Using the SAS System," *Proceedings of the Twenty-Second Annual SAS*® *Users Group International Conference*, Cary, NC: SAS Institute Inc., pp. 18–24.

Frankel, David S. and Mark A. Kochanski, 1991, "A Debugging Facility for SAS Macro Systems," *Proceedings of the Sixteenth Annual SAS® Users Group International Conference*, Cary, NC: SAS Institute Inc., pp. 209-214; and republished in *SAS® Macro Facility Tips and Techniques, Version 6, First Edition*, Cary, NC: SAS Institute Inc. 1994, pp. 53–58.

Fehd, Ronald, 1997a, "%ARRAY: construction and usage of arrays of macro variables," *Proceedings of the Twenty-Second Annual SAS® Users Group International Conference*, Cary, NC: SAS Institute Inc., pp. 447–450.

_____, 1997b, "%SHOWCOMB: a macro to produce a data set with frequency of combinations of responses from multiple-response data," *Proceedings of the Twenty-Second Annual SAS® Users Group International Conference*, Cary, NC: SAS Institute Inc., pp. 939–943.

_____, 1997c, "%CHECKALL: a macro to produce a frequency of response data set from multiple-response data," *Proceedings of the Twenty-Second Annual SAS® Users Group International Conference*, Cary, NC: SAS Institute Inc., pp. 1084–1088.

Friendly, Michael, 1991, *SAS® System for Statistical Graphics, First Edition*, Cary, NC: SAS Institute Inc., 697 pp.

Geary, Hugh, 1997, "A Macro Tool for Quickly Producing a Handy Documented Listing of SAS Data Sets for Use as a Reference While Writing Programs to Analyze the Same," *Proceedings of the Twenty-Second Annual SAS® Users Group International Conference*, Cary, NC: SAS Institute Inc., pp. 949–960.

Gilmore, Jodie and Linda Helwig, 1990, "Debugging Your SAS Macro Application Under VMS: A Practical Approach," *Proceedings of the Fifteenth Annual SAS® Users Group International Conference*, Cary, NC: SAS Institute Inc., pp. 825–831; and republished in *SAS® Macro Facility Tips and Techniques, Version 6, First Edition*, Cary, NC: SAS Institute Inc. 1994, pp. 66–72.

Grant, Paul, 1994, "The 'SKIP' Statement," *Proceedings of the Second Annual Conference of the Western Users of SAS® Software*, Cary, NC: SAS Institute Inc., pp. 87–88.

Hahl, Thomas J. and Philip R. Shelton, 1995, "Input/Output," *Observations®*, Vol. 4 #2 - First quarter, SAS Institute Inc., Cary, NC, pp. 76–78.

_____, 1996, "Dropping Variables That Have Only Missing Values," *Observations®*, Vol. 5 #4 -Third quarter, SAS Institute Inc., Cary, NC, pp. 18–22.

Hubbell, Katie, 1990, "Conquering the Dreaded Macro Error," *Proceedings of the Fifteenth Annual SAS® Users Group International Conference*, Cary, NC: SAS Institute Inc., pp. 1–7; and republished in *SAS® Macro Facility Tips and Techniques, Version 6, First Edition*, Cary, NC: SAS Institute Inc. 1994, pp. 17–21.

Johnson, Martha and Michael Gilman, 1993, "Submitting Macro Language Code in Window Commands," *Observations®*, Vol. 2 #4 - Third quarter, SAS Institute Inc., Cary, NC, pp. 50–54.

Kretzman, Peter, 1992, "Ifs, Ands, and Buts: A Case Study in Advanced Macro Implementation," *Proceedings of the Seventeenth Annual SAS® Users Group International Conference*, Cary, NC: SAS Institute Inc., pp. 176–182; and republished in *SAS® Macro Facility Tips and Techniques, Version 6, First Edition*, Cary, NC: SAS Institute Inc. 1994, pp. 143–149.

Landers, K. Larry and Monique Bryher, 1997, "Taking the Mystery out of SAS MACRO When Using CALL SYMPUT," *Proceedings of the 5ᵗʰ Annual Western Users of SAS® Software Regional Users Group Conference*, Cary, NC: SAS Institute Inc., pp. 29–34.

Leighton, Ralph W., 1997, "SAS Macros - A Gentle Introduction for the Fearful," *Proceedings of the Twenty-Second Annual SAS® Users Group International Conference*, Cary, NC: SAS Institute Inc., pp. 25–30.

Levine, Howard, 1989, "Building Macro-Based Systems," *Proceedings of the Fourteenth Annual SAS® Users Group International Conference*, Cary, NC: SAS Institute Inc., pp. 96–102; and republished in *SAS® Macro Facility Tips and Techniques, Version 6, First Edition*, Cary, NC: SAS Institute Inc. 1994, pp. 37–43.

Mast, Greg, 1997, "Managing Disk Space With SAS," *Proceedings of the Twenty-Second Annual SAS® Users Group International Conference*, Cary, NC: SAS Institute Inc., pp. 1536–1541.

Norton, Andrew A., 1991, "Screen Control Language versus Macros in Batch Environment," *Proceedings of the Sixteenth Annual SAS® Users Group International Conference*, Cary, NC: SAS Institute Inc., pp. 1325–1330; and republished in *SAS® Macro Facility Tips and Techniques, Version 6, First Edition*, Cary, NC: SAS Institute Inc. 1994, pp. 106–111.

O'Connor, Susan M., 1991, "A Roadmap to Macro Facility Error Messages and Debugging," *Proceedings of the Sixteenth Annual SAS® Users Group International Conference*, Cary, NC: SAS Institute Inc., pp. 215–222; and republished in *SAS® Macro Facility Tips and Techniques, Version 6, First Edition*, Cary, NC: SAS Institute Inc. 1994, pp. 73–80.

_____, 1992, "Macros Invocation Hierarchy: Session Compiled, Autocall, and Compiled Stored Macros," *Proceedings of the Seventeenth Annual SAS® Users Group International Conference*, Cary, NC: SAS Institute Inc., pp. 19– 23; and republished in *SAS® Macro Facility Tips and Techniques, Version 6, First Edition*, Cary, NC: SAS Institute Inc. 1994, pp. 101–105.

Palmer, Lynn, 1997, "Methods of Finding a Small Group of Records in Two Million without Using Merge," *Proceedings of the 5ᵗʰ Annual Western Users of SAS® Software Regional Users Group Conference*, Cary, NC: SAS Institute Inc., pp. 381–386.

Phillips, Jeff, Veronica Walgamotte, and Derek Drummond, 1993, "Warning: Apparent Macro Invocation Not Resolved... Techniques for Debugging Macro Code," *Proceedings of the Eighteenth Annual SAS® Users Group International Conference*, Cary, NC: SAS Institute Inc., pp. 424–429; and republished in *SAS® Macro Facility Tips and Techniques, Version 6, First Edition*, Cary, NC: SAS Institute Inc. 1994, pp. 47–52.

Roberts, Clark, 1997, "Building and Using Macro Variable Lists," *Proceedings of the Twenty-Second Annual SAS® Users Group International Conference*, Cary, NC: SAS Institute Inc., pp. 441–443.

Smith, Robert W., 1997, "Visual Hypothesis Testing with Confidence Intervals," *Proceedings of the Twenty-Second Annual SAS® Users Group International Conference*, Cary, NC: SAS Institute Inc., pp. 1252–1257.

Stanley, Don, 1994, *Beyond the Obvious with SAS® Screen Control Language*, SAS Institute Inc., Cary, NC, 347 pp.

Stuelpner, Janet, E., 1997, "Skipping the Easy Way," *Proceedings of the Twenty-Second Annual SAS® Users Group International Conference*, Cary, NC: SAS Institute Inc., pp. 451–452.

Tassoni, Charles John, Baibai Chen, and Clara Chu, 1997, "One-to-one Matching of Case/Controls Using SAS Software," *Proceedings of the Twenty-Second Annual SAS® Users Group International Conference*, Cary, NC: SAS Institute Inc., pp. 1189–1190.

Tindall, Bruce M. and Susan M. O'Connor, 1991, "Macro Tricks to Astound the Folks on Thursday Morning: Ten Immediately Useful Macro Techniques," *Proceedings of the Sixteenth Annual SAS® Users Group International Conference*, Cary, NC: SAS Institute Inc., pp. 189–195; and republished in *SAS® Macro Facility Tips and Techniques, Version 6, First Edition*, Cary, NC: SAS Institute Inc. 1994, pp. 117–123.

Virgile, Robert, 1997, "MAGIC WITH CALL EXECUTE," *Proceedings of the Twenty-Second Annual SAS® Users Group International Conference*, Cary, NC: SAS Institute Inc., pp. 465–467.

Westerlund, Earl R., 1991, "SAS Macro Language Features for Application Development," *Proceedings of the Sixteenth Annual SAS® Users Group International Conference*, Cary, NC: SAS Institute Inc., pp. 245–248; and republished in *SAS® Macro Facility Tips and Techniques, Version 6, First Edition*, Cary, NC: SAS Institute Inc. 1994, pp. 89–92.

Whitaker, Ken, 1989, "Using Macro Variable Lists," *Proceedings of the Fourteenth Annual SAS® Users Group International Conference*, Cary, NC: SAS Institute Inc., pp. 1531–1536; and republished in *SAS® Macro Facility Tips and Techniques, Version 6, First Edition*, Cary, NC: SAS Institute Inc. 1994, pp. 154–159.

Whitlock, H. Ian, 1993, "A Macro to Make External Flat Files," *Proceedings of the Eighteenth Annual SAS® Users Group International Conference*, Cary, NC: SAS Institute Inc., pp. 258–263; and republished in *SAS® Macro Facility Tips and Techniques, Version 6, First Edition*, Cary, NC: SAS Institute Inc. 1994, pp. 225–230.

——————, 1997, "CALL EXECUTE: How and Why," *Proceedings of the Twenty-Second Annual SAS® Users Group International Conference*, Cary, NC: SAS Institute Inc., pp. 410–414.

Widawski, Mel, 1997a, "A General Purpose Macro to Obtain a List of Files," *Proceedings of the 5th Annual Western Users of SAS® Software Regional Users Group Conference*, Cary, NC: SAS Institute Inc., pp. 94–99.

——————, 1997b, "A General System for Custom Conversion of dBase Data into SAS," *Proceedings of the 5ᵗʰ Annual Western Users of SAS® Software Regional Users Group Conference*, Cary, NC: SAS Institute Inc., pp. 255–260.

Wobus, Diana Zhang and John Charles Gober, 1997, "A Step-By-Step Illustration of Building a Data Analysis Tool with Macros," *Proceedings of the Twenty-Second Annual SAS® Users Group International Conference*, Cary, NC: SAS Institute Inc., pp. 226–232.

Yao, Arthur K., 1997, "SAS Code Generator Based on Table-Drive Methodology in a Batch Environment," *Proceedings of the Twenty-Second Annual SAS® Users Group International Conference*, Cary, NC: SAS Institute Inc., pp. 31–36.

Yindra, Chris, 1997, "&&&, ;;, and Other Hieroglyphics Advanced Macro Topics," *Proceedings of the Twenty-Second Annual SAS® Users Group International Conference*, Cary, NC: SAS Institute Inc., pp. 242–250.

——————, 1998, "%SYSFUNC - The Brave New Macro World," *Proceedings of the Twenty-Third Annual SAS® Users Group International Conference*, Cary, NC: SAS Institute Inc., pp. *unavailable at press time*.

Glossary

Automatic Macro Variables

Special-purpose macro variables. These are automatically defined and provided by the SAS System. These variable names should be considered to be reserved (Section 2.6).

Dynamic Coding

SAS code generated during program execution by macro statements that are often dependent on either the data being processed or on a control file (Section 6.4).

Global

A referencing environment or scope that spans all of the macros in the current session or program. This means that a global macro variable will have a single value (unless changed) that is available to all macros within the program. Macro variables that are defined outside of any macro will be global (Section 1.4). See also Local.

Local

A referencing environment or scope defined for a macro. Local macro variables have values that are available only within the macro in which they are defined. The symbol table may contain multiple local definitions of a macro variable at one time (Section 1.4). See also Global.

Macro

Stored text that contains SAS statements and macro language statements (Section 3.1).

Macro Expression

One or more macro variable names, text, and/or macro functions that are combined together by one or more operators and/or parentheses. Macro expressions are very analogous to the expressions used in standard SAS programming (Section 3.1).

Macro Function

Predefined routines for processing text in macros and macro variables. Many macro functions are similar to functions that are used in the DATA step (Section 3.1).

Macro Language

The elements and tools that provide us with the means to communicate with the macro processor (Section 1.1).

Macro Processor

Software within the macro facility that translates macro code into statements and text that can be used by the SAS System (Section 1.1).

Macro Program Statement

Controls what actions take place during the macro execution. They are always preceded by a percent sign (%) and are often syntactically similar to statements used in the DATA step (Section 3.1).

Macro References

Text that results in a call to a macro language element is said to contain a macro language reference. These calls will contain one or both of the special symbols: ampersand (&) and percent sign (%) (Section 1.3).

Macro System Options
System options that directly deal with the way the SAS System deals with macro code and how the results of macro processing is displayed (Section 3.3).

Macro Variables
Macro, or symbolic, variables are often used to store text. The value of a macro variable is stored in the symbol table, and when used, the names of macro variables are almost always preceded by an ampersand (&) (Sections 2.1 and 3.1).

Open Code
SAS program statements that exist outside of any macro definition.

Operators
Symbols that are used for comparisons, logical operation, or arithmetic calculations. The operators are the same ones used in the DATA step (Section 5.2).

Referencing Environment
Each macro variable's definition in the symbol table is also associated with a referencing environment or scope that is determined by where and how the macro variable is defined. Two environments exist for macro variables: global and local (Section 1.4).

Resolving Macro References
During the resolution process, elements of the macro language (or references) are replaced with text (Section 2.5).

SAS Macro Facility
The tool within base SAS software that contains the essential elements that enable you to use macros (Section 1.1).

Scope
See Referencing Environment.

Statement-Style Macro
Macros that allow the use of macro names that do not start with the % sign (Section 3.5).

Symbol Table
Storage location in memory that is used to store current values of macro, or symbolic, variables (Section 1.4).

Symbolic Variables
See Macro Variables.

Text
A collection of characters and symbols that can contain variable names, data set names, SAS statement fragments, complete SAS statements, or even complete DATA and PROC steps (Section 3.1).

Index

Call your local SAS office to order these books
from Books by Users Press

www.sas.com/pubs

Tuning SAS® Applications in the MVS Environment
by **Michael A. Raithel** ....Order No. A55231

Univariate and Multivariate General Linear Models:
Theory and Applications Using SAS® Software
by **Neil H. Timm**
and **Tammy A. Mieczkowski** ....Order No. A55809

Using SAS® in Financial Research
by **Ekkehart Boehmer, John Paul Broussard,**
and **Juha-Pekka Kallunki** ....Order No. A57601

Using the SAS® Windowing Environment: A Quick Tutorial
by **Larry Hatcher**......................................Order No. A57201

Visualizing Categorical Data
by **Michael Friendly** ....Order No. A56571

Working with the SAS® System
by **Erik W. Tilanus** ....Order No. A55190

Your Guide to Survey Research Using the SAS® System
by **Archer Gravely** ....Order No. A55688

JMP® Books

Basic Business Statistics: A Casebook
by **Dean P. Foster, Robert A. Stine,**
and **Richard P. Waterman**........................Order No. A56813

Business Analysis Using Regression: A Casebook
by **Dean P. Foster, Robert A. Stine,**
and **Richard P. Waterman**........................Order No. A56818

JMP® Start Statistics, Second Edition
by **John Sall, Ann Lehman,**
and **Lee Creighton** ....Order No. A58166

www.sas.com/pubs